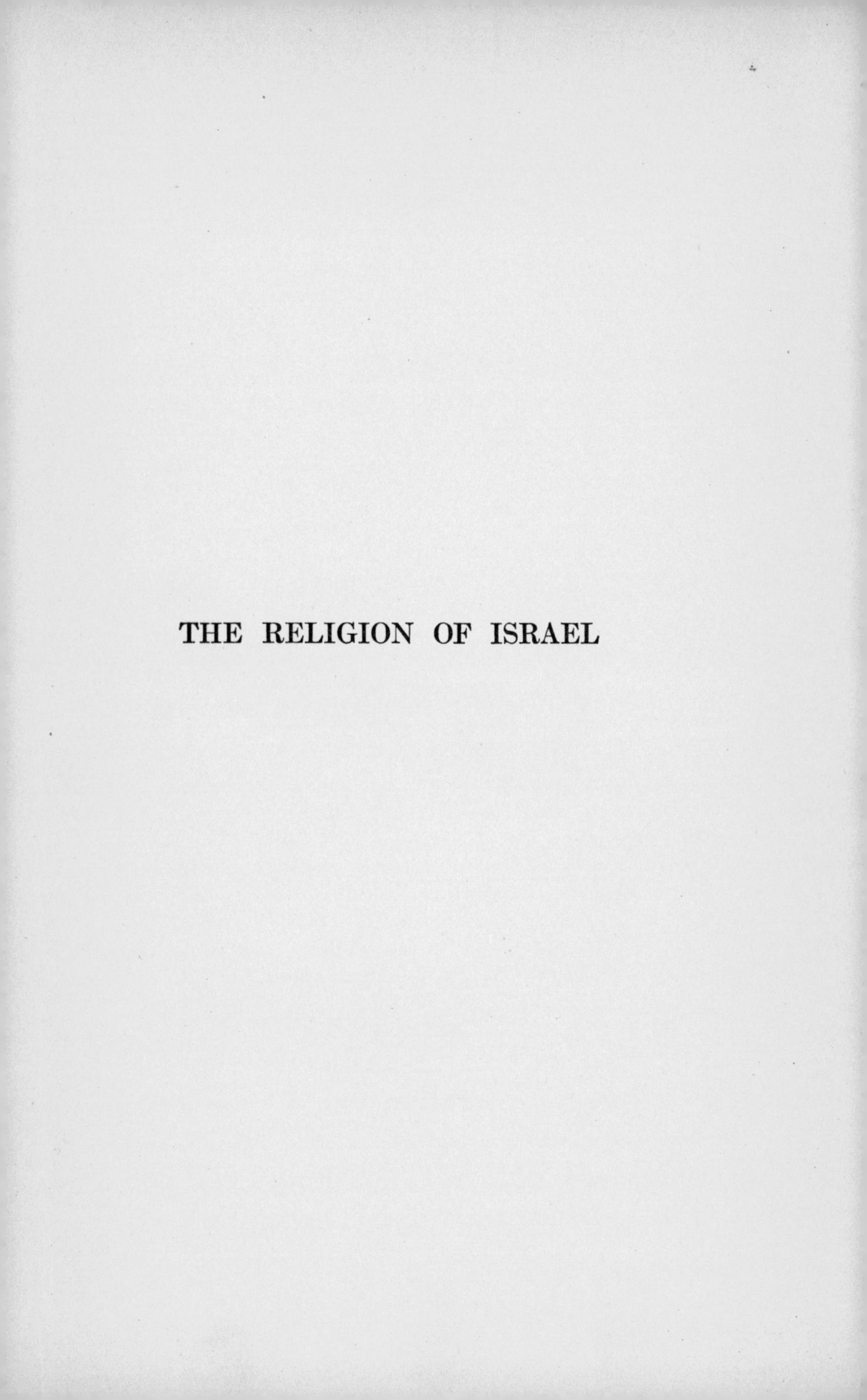

THE RELIGION OF ISRAEL

THE RELIGION OF ISRAEL

AN HISTORICAL STUDY

BY

HENRY PRESERVED SMITH

NEW YORK
CHARLES SCRIBNER'S SONS
1914

Published February, 1914

To

THE MEMORY OF

CHARLES AUGUSTUS BRIGGS, D.D., D.LITT.

WARM-HEARTED FRIEND

ACCOMPLISHED SCHOLAR

DEVOTED DISCIPLE OF THE MASTER

VALIANT DEFENDER OF THE FAITH

PREFACE

The purpose of this book is sufficiently indicated by the title and is set forth more at large in the opening chapter. It is an endeavour to give an intelligible account of the rise and progress of Israel's religion from its beginnings in the nomadic period down to the tragic event which put an end to the Jewish state. The reader who is even superficially acquainted with the progress of biblical study during the last forty years will not be surprised to find that the book proceeds upon the supposition that the results of the so-called higher criticism are fairly certain. All that the book claims for itself is that it represents our present knowledge; what the future has in store for us we cannot forecast. I have avoided controversy and have endeavoured to state my opinion frankly and in positive terms. I have not thought it necessary to make frequent reference to the literature of the subject. Old Testament scholars will discover where I am indebted to my predecessors. The reader who is not a specialist may safely assume that I have not taken any position without examining the arguments for and against.

The frequent references to the biblical writers will be their own justification. And since (according to my observation) few readers have the patience to look up chapter and verse in their Bibles, I have often introduced the words of the authors into my text. In the few cases in which the notation of chapter and verse in the English is not the same as in the Hebrew, I have followed the latter. Where my translation differs from that of the current version it will, I think, command the approval of good authorities.

In preparing this book I thought with pleasure of dedicating it to my friend Dr. Briggs, to whom biblical and theological scholarship owes so much. Before the copy could be put into the hands of the printer he was called from the scene of his earthly labours. There remains to me only the melancholy pleasure of consecrating it to his memory, a belated testimony of my affection, but none the less an evidence of the debt of gratitude I owe him. I count him among them that are wise, who shine as the brightness of the firmament.

NEW YORK,
December 1, 1913.

CONTENTS

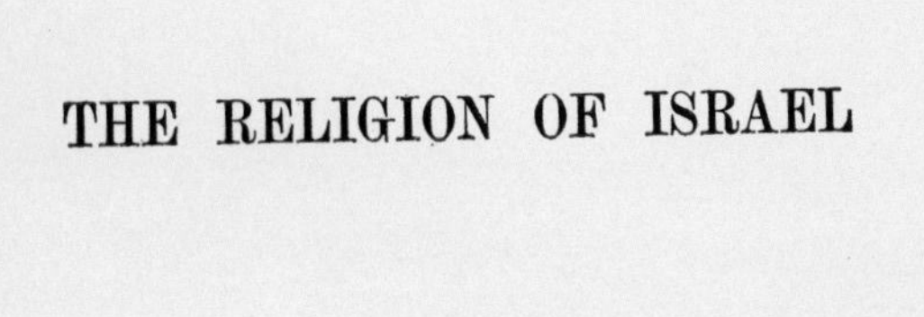

THE RELIGION OF ISRAEL

THE RELIGION OF ISRAEL

CHAPTER I

AIM AND METHOD

OUR purpose is to trace the history of Israel's religion from the earliest discoverable stages down to the Christian era. The subject has been frequently treated in recent years under the name of "Biblical Theology of the Old Testament." The adjective "Biblical" in this title is intended to differentiate this science from dogmatic or systematic theology. Dogmatic theology, which aims to present the philosophy held in any particular religious communion, uses the contents of the Bible to confirm or establish the doctrines of the Church as defined in the creeds. Its purpose may be said to be the discovery of the meaning of the Bible for us and in our philosophical system. With the rise of modern historical science men began to realise that what the biblical writers thought of God and divine things might not always be normative for us. The student of history does not understand a thing unless he can trace the process of growth by which it has come to be what it is. From this point of view it is no longer enough for us to set forth the religious ideas of the Bible in some philosophical arrangement. The principle of arrangement must be organic, according to the stages of growth discoverable in the documents upon which our knowledge depends. Biblical theology, therefore, is correctly defined as the science which sets forth "the theology of the Bible in its historical formation."[1] The same thing is meant by Oehler

[1] Briggs, *General Introduction to the Study of Holy Scripture*, p. 569. Dr. Briggs adds the phrase "within the canonical books." Whether this conception of the canon belongs here we may be able to determine later.

when he speaks of the "historico-genetic presentation of the religion contained in the Scriptures of the Old Testament."[1] The phrase *historico-genetic* means simply that we are to trace the genesis and growth of the Old Testament religion. Since this is a purely historical inquiry, it seems best to state it in the title, and speak of the history of Israel's religion.

The source of our knowledge is, of course, the literature of the Hebrews. For dogmatic theology the same is true. For dogmatic theology the definition of the canon is important; for the historical inquiry this is not so. The canon is the group of books accepted in the Church as authoritative. Historical science knows no authoritative documents; it asks only whether the documents with which it deals contain material bearing on a certain historic development, in this case bearing on the religion of Israel. This consideration shows that the attempt to limit biblical theology to the canonical books of the Old Testament is a mistake. No clear line of demarcation can be drawn between the religion of the canonical books and the religion of those excluded from the canon. The religion of Israel did not stop growing when the latest of the Hebrew books took shape. In fact, as we now know, some of the so-called apocrypha and pseudepigrapha are earlier in date than some portions of the Old Testament.

The advantage of defining our subject as the history of religion instead of a theology is seen when we reflect that while the documents with which we have to deal are full of religion, it is doubtful whether they can be said to contain a theology. The endeavour to make them teach a theology is instructive with reference to this point. The early Church was challenged as to its theology, that is to say, as to its beliefs concerning God and the world, sin and salvation, on two sides. The Jews denied that the beliefs of the Christians were authenticated by the Scriptures; the gentiles called upon them to justify their rejection of the an-

[1] *Old Testament Theology*, § 2.

cestral gods. Against both antagonists Christian thinkers appealed to their sacred book. But the stress to which they were driven is made clear by their method of interpretation. It was a boon to them that the allegorical exposition had been so thoroughly adopted by Philo. Origen, the greatest scholar of the Church, appropriated this method and frankly confessed that many passages of the Old Testament, taken literally, did not teach any important theological truth. The literal sense, he held, is only the *body* of Scripture; we must search for the *soul,* which is the deeper mystical meaning.

It must be evident that this theory and the later assertion of a threefold, fourfold, or even sevenfold sense of Scripture must block the way to a really historical understanding both of the documents themselves and of the religion which underlies them. Protestantism, indeed, rejected the allegorical interpretation and laid stress on the literal interpretation. Luther, although his religious experience gave him a better understanding of the real religious appeal made by the biblical writers than was found among the theologians who preceded him, was not able to free himself from the scholastic philosophy in which he had been brought up, and this is more distinctly true of Melanchthon and Calvin. In one sense the interpretation of Scripture was less open to discussion in the Protestant Churches than in the Church of Rome. In the latter the defects of Scripture could be made good by tradition, and the allegorical method could find a suitable sense almost anywhere. But the Protestants had made their whole system depend on the Bible, and they had rejected the allegories. They must find all that they needed in the text literally interpreted. What actually happened was that a new tradition took the place of the old. What could be used to strengthen the received doctrinal system was taken in the form of proof-texts, and the rest was left out of view. The theory of a fourfold sense now gave way to the doctrine of the analogy of faith, according to which all Scripture, since it proceeded from God as author, must be harmonious. And in place of the allegorical interpretation came a set of types according to which everything in the Old Testament was made to foreshadow Christ.

The endeavour to emphasise the doctrinal parts of Scripture had one curious result. It became the fashion for teachers of theology to collect proof-texts out of the whole Bible and publish them with comments for the use of students. Sebastian Schmidt, of Strassburg, one of the ablest scholars of the seventeenth century, gave a course of lectures on the *dicta probantia,* and afterward published them under the title *Collegium Biblicum.* The example was followed by others, and may have given rise to the idea that there was, after all, a difference between dogmatic and biblical theology. The rise of rationalism, however, was probably more potent in turning thought to the real nature of the biblical books. The clear formulation of the distinction between biblical and dogmatic theology seems to be due to Gabler, whose essay on this subject was published in 1787.[1] Gabler rightly made biblical theology an historic rather than a philosophical study. A considerable part of the theological work of the nineteenth century, especially in Germany, was devoted to the development of this thought; namely, that biblical theology belongs among the historical sciences.

The apprehension of the literature of the Hebrews as an historic source is what distinguishes our age from all that have preceded it. To the Jews the Bible was primarily a code of laws. The earnestness with which they have applied this code to their daily conduct is writ large on their whole later history. This point of view was to a certain extent overcome by the early Church under the leadership of the Apostle Paul. The Church, however, looked upon the documents of the Old Testament as so many predictions

[1] *De justo discrimine theologiæ biblicæ et dogmaticæ, regundisque recte utriusque finibus.* I have not seen this essay, but it is cited by most of the writers on this subject.

of the salvation which was brought by Jesus Christ. This also was a one-sided view. Later, when stress was laid upon a correct philosophy of the universe, the Bible became the divinely inspired treatise on doctrine. The unnatural interpretations forced on the text by both these theories are well known. It is now clear that both theories did violence to the real nature of the Bible. What we now emphasise in describing this book is its character as religious literature; the Bible is the expression of the religious life of the Hebrew people. It is, therefore, a source of religious edification to the reader. This, to be sure, has always been known to devout souls. It was the merit of Pietism that it called men's attention afresh to this truth.

But the view of Pietism may easily lead to extravagancies. If these are to be guarded against they must be accompanied by an historical apprehension. As the Bible is something more than a collection of proof-texts for the dogmatician, so it is more than a series of comforting assurances for the believer. When by a correct exegesis we have discovered the meaning of the sentences which make up the book, we are still far from understanding the book. These sentences are somehow related to each other. They have an organic unity, or rather they express a single continuous life. We must therefore have some principle by which we can bring the isolated fragments into unity. This means that we must seek to discover the organic evolution of which they are the expression.

It follows logically that our science demands as a prerequisite what is known as the higher criticism. Criticism is simply examination of documents to determine their historical value. All our knowledge of antiquity comes to us in fragments. We have a bit of flint as evidence of what the oldest man was doing; we have a half-defaced inscription from which to discover the ideas which were current three thousand years ago; we have a pile of broken clay tablets from which to piece together the cosmology of the dwellers in the Euphrates Valley somewhere near the dawn of history. Even the literature which has come down to us is only a fragment, and the Bible itself is a collection of such fragments. To understand them we must first get an idea of ancient literary methods. This means that we must rid ourself of the idea that authorship implies literary property. In our own time it is unwarrantable to take sections of a book and intersperse them with paragraphs from another source and thus make another book. But in ancient times there was no scruple in doing just this. When a man of Israel had in his possession a book that seemed to him defective in its point of view, he saw no reason why he should not correct it by insertion of what he thought more adequate. This process was almost inevitable in the case of a sacred book, for religious ideas change, and what is edifying to one generation may not be so to another. We have seen how the allegorical interpretation was made to give the old Bible new meanings. Before the text had become fixed the same end was attained by interpolation and redactional changes. If we are rightly to appreciate the historical process which has embodied itself in these documents we must first apply the critical process and separate earlier elements from those which are later.

It would be a mistake to suppose that what, for want of a better name, we call interpolations are of less value to us than the older strata with which they are interspersed. These later additions reveal most clearly, and often most touchingly, the state of mind of religious men who felt the defects of the documents which had come down from antiquity. All that we need to guard against is the temptation to take the later portions as evidence of what went on at an earlier time. This temptation naturally beset the first generation of critics, and it took a long time to establish the real historical order of the documents. The difficulty was caused by the strength of the tradition embodied in the Hebrew documents themselves. This tradition made the Law of Moses the starting-point of Israel's history. At the present day it is generally conceded that this is a mistake. With such a presupposition the history of Israel is unintelligible, whereas on the modern theory we get a well-ordered development culminating in the priestly legislation instead of starting from it.

In saying that our method must be critical we mean that we assume the results of critical study as to the order of the documents. This implies, of course, that we base our sketch of the religion of Israel on the critical reconstruction of Israel's history. But, since this reconstruction is not yet universally accepted, it is necessary at this point to state in brief what it holds to be the actual process of Israel's development. The comparative study of religions shows with increasing clearness that the religion of a people bears an intimate relation to that people's political and social conditions. What these conditions were in Israel must be determined by the historian. As thus determined, Israel's development may be sketched as follows:

About thirteen hundred years before Christ a group of nomad clans was making its way into the cultivated country of Canaan, the district which lies between the Jordan and the Mediterranean. For some three hundred years the struggle went on between the older inhabitants and the newcomers. The result was the amalgamation of the two elements, with the desert blood predominant. David succeeded in uniting the heterogeneous sections into one people, though the unity was never very perfect, and the single kingdom was broken into two after less than a hundred years. The larger fraction maintained a semblance of independence for about two hundred years, succumbing at last to Assyria in 722. Judah, the smaller fraction, enjoyed the name of a kingdom for something over a hundred years longer. But it, too, fell before a greater power, becoming an insignificant province of the Babylonian Empire. Never again politically independent, the Jews yet learned to live among the gentiles without mixing with them, keeping their separate social and religious customs.

This bare outline shows that we may distinguish four

stages in the history of this people, and the presumption is that the religion will show four stages corresponding to these. First of all, the clans were nomads living on the milk of their flocks and the plunder taken from their neighbours. Their religious ideas must have been similar to what we find among the Arabs of the same region at the present day. Then came the stage of amalgamation with the Canaanites and the adoption of the agricultural life. The adoption of Canaanitish religion would naturally follow, and we have abundant evidence that it actually did follow. With the reign of Solomon the arts of life made an advance; commercial enterprises were undertaken; great buildings were erected; class divisions became more marked. The reaction did not come at once, but when, in the time of Ahab, foreign customs seemed about to prevail, a vigorous protest was made under the lead of Elijah. The succession of prophets thus introduced marks a new era for the religion of Israel. Their political revolution, which set Jehu on the throne, did not stop the march of events, but their influence lasted long after the fall of Samaria, which they so plainly foresaw. Their message was repeated with emphasis by Isaiah but was disregarded in the half-century that followed his death. The attempt of the prophetic party to effect a thorough reformation of religion under Josiah was of short duration, but, as was true in the case of the earlier prophets, the message had greater vitality than the men who formulated it. The remnant which survived the fall of Jerusalem felt the full force of the denunciations which the prophets had put on record, and their attempt to regulate their lives by the traditions which came from the fathers made the final period (that of legalism) the most strongly marked of all the stages of Israel's religion.

What is now clear to us is that in our history of the religion we must begin with the nomadic stage and end with the highly developed legalism which is characteristic of the religious community which we know as the Jews. For the nomadic stage we have to depend on indirect evidence, for the nomad does not preserve records of his experiences. In the agricultural stage written documents begin to appear. But it is only under the monarchy that literature in any real sense of the word takes form. And religiously the most important literary monuments of this period are the remains of the written prophets. Of course here, as in other departments of human history, no clear and sharp lines of division can be drawn. This is most distinctly seen in the case of Deuteronomy. The writers of this book supposed themselves to be putting the ideas of the prophets into definite form; yet they were, in fact, introducing a new period—that of legalism.

This instance is important as showing that the political development and the religious history do not exactly coincide. Politically, the fall of Jerusalem in 586 was the most important event in the history of Israel; religiously, the publication of Deuteronomy, nearly forty years earlier, was epoch-making. It may be well to note, however, that the legalism introduced by Deuteronomy would not have become effective had not Jerusalem fallen into the hands of Nebuchadrezzar. What stands out clearly is that our divisions of Israel's religion will be the following:

1. Nomadic religion.
2. Agricultural religion.
3. Prophetism.
4. Legalism.

CHAPTER II

NOMADIC RELIGION

According to the unanimous voice of tradition, the Hebrews were immigrants to Palestine, coming from the eastern desert or from the south. The tradition is confirmed by the monuments, according to which the Chabiri, a nomadic people, invaded Syria in the fourteenth century or earlier. We are entitled, therefore, at the outset to seek for religious phenomena akin to those presented by the desert-dwellers of the present day. Direct testimony, that is, accounts contemporary with the desert sojourn, we must not expect, for the literature in our hands dates from the time of the monarchy. But the conservatism of religion is such that we may expect survivals from the earlier stage of thought to show themselves in tradition. The tradition, as was just remarked, is to the effect that the fathers of the people were, if not nomads in the strict sense of the word, at least shepherds without fixed dwellings. This is the more striking because the ideal of the Hebrew writers for themselves was agricultural. What the Israelite of the ninth century desired for himself was to dwell in the shadow of his own vine and fig-tree, with none to molest or make him afraid. But when he pictured those ideal figures, the patriarchs, he represented them as shepherds wandering up and down the land accompanied by their flocks, living in tents, and not having title even to a burial-place until they had bought it from the earlier inhabitants.

What, then, was the religion of these fathers of the nation? It is almost superfluous to remark that it was not monotheism. The theory of Renan, according to which early Semitic monotheism was suggested by the sterile uniformity of the desert, so different from the engaging variety of the cultivated country, is no longer held by any one. In fact, to the nomad the phenomena of the desert are as varied as are those of any other region. And better acquaintance with nomadic ideas shows us that the early Semites, like all other peoples, did not hold a belief in one God. This is made evident by the Arab descriptions of the times before Mohammed as well as by the survivals of polydemonism among the Bedawin to-day. The idea of the unity of God came late to the Semite as it comes late to other peoples. The impression made by nature upon early thinkers is that of a multiplicity of powers, and religion consists in the worship or at least the conciliation of these powers whenever they make their presence known.

Since the decipherment of the Babylonian and Assyrian documents the endeavour has been made to discover in them a primitive monotheism, and to derive Hebrew religion from the dwellers in the Euphrates Valley. It is sufficient to notice here that if any monotheistic beliefs existed in Babylon they were the property of a few isolated thinkers and never moulded the popular religion. The whole impression made by the religion of Babylonia and Assyria is that of a highly developed polytheism. And that the early Hebrews worshipped a multitude of gods is affirmed by their own writers. The author of Joshua's farewell speech (Joshua 24 : 2) declares that the fathers served other gods before their migration to Canaan. Even as late as the time of Jeremiah the prophet could say that Judah's gods were as many as her cities (Jer. 2 : 28). The sacred writers did indeed believe, or at least some of them believed, that the polytheism which was so constant a phenomenon in their people's history was a declension from the purer faith of the fathers. But in this they were moved by the same sort of idealism which prevails in almost every period of history, an idealism which locates the golden age in the past. Careful consideration of the facts will free us from this prepossession.

Polytheism among the Hebrews seems to be indicated first of all, by the fact that the usual Hebrew name for God (*Elohim*) is plural in form. Various theories have been brought forward to account for this curious fact. For the early dogmaticians, who assumed that the Old Testament reveals all that is essential for Christian belief, it was an evidence of a trinity of persons in the Godhead. This will hardly be seriously urged to-day. More recent is the hypothesis that Elohim is a plural of majesty, akin to the formulæ in which monarchs speak of themselves as "we." Such plurals of majesty, however, are without parallel in Hebrew. The only view that can be urged with plausibility is that the word originally designated the whole group of divinities and was gradually narrowed down so as to be applied to the One. Vestiges of a belief in a group of divine beings have survived even in our present Bible. Yahweh himself says: "Man has become like one of us" (Gen. 3 : 22). The Creator takes counsel of his associates: "Let us make man in our image" (Gen. 1 : 26). We read also of sons of Elohim, who must themselves be of divine nature (Gen. 6 : 2). It is true that in our present text these other divine beings are thought of as subordinate to the chief God. But this shows only how the earlier belief was reconciled with the later.

More convincing is the variety of names which are used for God. Strictly speaking, the fact that any name besides "God" is used is evidence for polytheism. It would not occur to a man of our time to ask for the name of the divinity who reveals himself to him; yet this is what Moses does. And in Israel we find several names applied to God. Elohim we have just discussed. Then we have El (Gen. 31 : 13; 35 : 1; 49 : 25, and elsewhere), a name found among the other Semites. It has been traced among the Phœnicians and Arabs as well as in Babylonia. Among the Babylonians it seems to have been the most general name for God, but among the Phœnicians it was applied to a particular divinity whom Greek authors identified with Kronos.[1] Again we find a name, Shaddai, sometimes conjoined with El, but apparently once designating a separate divinity (Deut. 32 : 17). In poetic passages of comparatively early date it is brought into parallelism with Yahweh, as though an archaic equivalent of that name (Gen. 49 : 25; Num. 24 : 4 and 16). Further, we meet with Elyon, meaning Most High, usually combined with El, but sometimes independent (Num. 24 : 16; Deut. 32 : 8). In the former passage we have three of these names in parallel clauses: "Who hears the words of El, knows the knowledge of Elyon, and sees the vision of Shaddai."

The name Elyon (Elioun) was known among the Phœnicians, as we learn from Eusebius. This author quotes from Philo of Byblos, who in his account of the Phœnician religion says that Elioun was one of the gods who died and received worship after his death.[2] The theory that the gods are deified men, which underlies this statement, does not here concern us. All that we have now to do is to note the evidence of these various names for God. Although applied by the biblical writers to the one God of the Hebrews, they really attest a primitive polytheism.

It was at one time thought that the primitive ideas of religion could be discovered by tracing the etymology of divine names. Unfortunately, the meaning of almost all the Semitic names for God is obscure. Elyon, to be sure, is quite transparent, meaning the Exalted or the Most High. This meaning made it easy for the Hebrews to apply it to their God. Of the others, the name Yahweh, the proper name of Israel's God, has naturally been most discussed, but the discussion has led to no generally received result. The idea of the biblical writers, or at least of some of them, on this point will occupy us later. As to the other divine names we remark that it is still uncertain whether Shaddai means Mighty or El means Powerful (these meanings are

[1] A detailed discussion may be found in Lagrange, *Études sur les Religions Sémitiques*,[2] pp. 70–83.

[2] Eusebius, *Præparatio Evangelica*, I, 10.

usually attached to these names), although both words have been elaborately investigated by scholars.

These names for God have survived into the latest period of Hebrew religion. They do not directly give us light on the nomadic stage. From analogy we conclude that before a distinctly polytheistic stage of religion there was a somewhat vague polydemonism among the Hebrew clans, much like what is found in the desert to-day. Throughout Syria and the neighbouring wilderness there are countless divinities dwelling in trees, fountains, rocks, and hills. At the present day these superhuman beings are called *saints* or *prophets*, but both Christians and Moslems pay them the worship due to gods. A tree which grows before the door of a church is regarded as an incarnation of the saint to whom the church itself is dedicated; but a church building is not at all necessary to give sanctity to a tree. A story is told of a solitary tree standing in the open country under which a gazelle had taken refuge. A hunter fired at the animal but the ball turned and wounded the gunner. He at once recognised that the tree was inhabited by a saint who protected those who took refuge with him. Therefore, although no one had ever heard of a saint being buried at this place, the people of the nearest village agreed with the hunter's interpretation of the incident, and instituted a festival in honour of the hitherto unknown, offered a sheep, baked bread, cooked rice, and rejoiced before the sacred object. Other examples from the same region show that it is not always the grave of a saint which makes the tree sacred. The tree itself has supernatural power. He who cuts a branch from it will be punished, even visited by death. In the time of Mohammed "trees to hang things on" were common in Arabia, and the name was given because of the custom which is still observed, that of hanging a piece of one's garment on the tree to show it reverence or to secure its potent influence.[1]

[1] The above examples are taken from Jaussen, *Coutumes des Arabes au Pays de Moab*, but similar ones will be found in Curtiss, *Primitive Semitic Religion today*.

The people in Canaan did not, in the early period, differ essentially from those who dwelt in the desert. The literature in our hands mentions the tamarisk planted by Abraham (Gen. 21: 33), because the tree was venerated in the later period. The author probably did not think of it as divine in the strict sense of the word, but it was to him at least sacred, as he indicates in saying: "He planted a tamarisk in Beersheba and called there on the name of Yahweh, El-olam." The calling on the divinity showed his presence in that place. Since men at this stage of culture almost necessarily conceive of a god as dwelling in a material object, it is altogether probable that the earliest inhabitants believed Yahweh to inhabit the tree. So with the oak or oak grove at Mamre, also connected with Abraham (Gen. 13 : 18; 14 : 13, and 18 : 1–4). The uncanny or supernatural quality of such trees might be ascribed to idols buried beneath them. When Jacob took the foreign gods which were in possession of his family and buried them under the oak at Shechem the divinities who inhabited the images took up their residence in the tree (Gen. 35 : 4). Later we read of the Oak of the Pillar in Shechem and are inclined to identify it with Jacob's tree. It certainly was a sacred tree, for the pillar which is mentioned is one of the pillars which regularly stood at a sanctuary until the Deuteronomic reform. The oak in the sanctuary of Yahweh (Joshua 24 : 26) is apparently the same. In the same chapter with the Oak of the Pillar we read of the Oak of the Soothsayers (Judges 9 : 37), and in other places of the Oak of the Diviner (Oak of Moreh in our version, Gen. 12 : 6; Deut. 11 : 30). Such trees were probably oracular, like the oak of Zeus at Dodona. Then the pains taken to tell us that Deborah was buried under an oak is explicable only if the people believed the spirit of the dead to live in the tree (Gen. 35 : 8). Gideon's oak, which is spoken of as the place where the angel, or Yahweh himself, appeared to the hero, may be of the same nature with these others (Judges 6 : 11 and 19), and with it we may mention the Palm of Deborah (4 : 5). An omen is given by the rustling in the tree, indicating that the indwelling divinity is on the move to help his people (II Sam. 5 : 22–25), and the flaming bush in which Yahweh appeared to Moses belongs in the same group (Ex. 3 : 2). In fact, Yahweh is called in one passage, He who dwells in the bush (Deut. 33 : 16).

The polemic of the prophets reveals distinctly the form of the popular religion. Jeremiah tells us how the Israelites worship under every green tree (Jer. 3 : 6), and reproaches them with calling a stick their father (2 : 27). The word translated *stick* is the same that is elsewhere rendered *tree*, so that possibly the author has direct reference to tree-worship. The case would be little different if he meant a wooden idol, for the earliest wooden idols were pieces of a sacred tree rudely carved into human semblance. Isaiah gives us to know in unmistakable terms that oaks were objects of the people's affection (Isaiah 1 : 29).

Fountains are held in reverence by almost all peoples. To the Bedawin they are especially important because of their rarity. The fountain seems to have a life of its own, and it is beneficent to men and animals. The story of Hagar and the fountain Beer-lahai-roi is evidence of the Israelite feeling in the nomadic stage. It is, in fact, a survival from the time when the fountain was worshipped. In one form of the story, as we now read it (Gen. 16 : 7–14), it is the angel of Yahweh who reveals himself to Hagar. In the parallel it is Elohim (21 : 14 *ff.*). It is not too bold to suppose that in the earliest form of the story it was the spirit inhabiting the fountain who gave the revelation. In this, as in so many other cases, the *genius loci* has been displaced by the angel or by Elohim. In all probability the name of the fountain originally told who the divinity was, but this has now been purposely obscured. The name of the well at Beersheba was given by a sacred ceremony, and is interpreted to mean either the *Well of Seven* or the *Well of the Oath.* But, as we have traces of a divinity named Sheba in some of the Hebrew proper names, it is not unlikely that the well was his. There is no evidence that there were seven wells, and even if we take Sheba in its meaning of *seven* it is more natural to conclude that originally seven spirits were supposed to dwell in the well than that the name should have been given on account of the seven lambs used in an ancient covenant (Gen. 21 : 22–34). In the country east of the Jordan there is at the present day a cult of the daughters of the fountain. A simple wall with niches is erected over the fountain and here the people pay their devotions.[1] Among sacred fountains perhaps the most important was the one at Kadesh. The name itself indicates a sanctuary, and the other which was attached to it, *Fountain of Judgment* (En Mishpat, Gen. 14 : 7), indicates that an oracle was connected with the place. Massah and Meribah are names of places in the vicinity, and probably show that the divinity gave decisions in cases of dispute, and that this was done by the ordeal.[2] Moses was the minister of the oracle, and it is not improbable that the fountain was the place where he consulted the divinity. If this be so the tradition which made Moses bring water from the rock was the local tradition concerning the origin of this source. We find also a place name, Baalath-beer, the *Goddess of the Well*, which indicates another of these sacred sources (Joshua 19 : 8), and we may add to the group the well-known Dan, situated at one of the copious sources of the Jordan. Here also the divinity of the place was appealed to to decide cases of dispute, his name being *Judge*.

Two objections will be urged against this enumeration of divinities. One is that these are not nomadic sanctuaries, but are found within the borders of Palestine. The other is that we have no intimation in the Bible that worship was offered at any of these places. To the first the reply is that, with the exception of Dan, all these fountains are actually located in nomadic territory, that is, in the border of the cultivated country, where the people kept up the pas-

[1] Jaussen, *Coutumes des Arabes*, p. 302.

[2] Meribah is the *Place of Litigation*, and Massah the *Place of Testing*.

toral life all through their history. The answer to the other objection is that we must not expect the biblical writers to make record of practices which were proscribed in the later period of the history. When Abraham is represented as sacrificing at Beersheba and when Moses is pictured administering the oracle at Kadesh, this is as much as we could expect them to put on record.

Among the nomads of to-day we learn of sacrifice offered to a mountain.[1] The history of the Hebrews gives distinct parallels. Sinai and Horeb were the residence of Yahweh. At Kadesh the hill or rock from which the fountain flowed partook of its sacredness. Mizpah of Gilead was a hilltop sanctuary. Balaam sought Yahweh on the heights overlooking the Jordan Valley (Num. 22 : 41; 23 : 14 and 28). The Song of Moses congratulates Zebulun on the sanctuaries on the mountains (Deut. 33 : 19). It is probable that the location of Solomon's temple was decided by the sacredness of the hill on whose top it was built. In fact, the naked summit of the hill is the central object of the Moslem sanctuary which stands on the spot at the present day. The complaint of Jeremiah that the people sacrificed on every high hill as well as under every green tree is well known, and Ezekiel reckons eating on the mountains among the transgressions of Judah (Ezek. 22 : 9; *cf.* 20 : 28). Among the sacred mountains Sinai and Horeb certainly belong to the nomadic region, and the others show that nomads and agriculturists are at the same stage of religious thinking.

Sacred stones belong in the same class with sacred mountains. The classic example is the one which Jacob set up at Bethel (Gen. 28 : 10–22), and which was apparently an object of worship long after the settlement in Canaan. Such a stone is still pointed out as the residence of a divinity by a dream or revelation, as may be illustrated from recent observation. At Maan in the transjordanic region there is a rock seven feet high. One night a woman took shelter

[1] Jaussen, *op. cit.*, p. 359.

by it and in her sleep she saw a serpent emerge from the rock. At the same time a voice said: "I am the *Welieh* [female saint] of the rock." Soon after, another person sleeping here had a similar dream, only instead of a serpent he saw a woman. The reputation of the rock as the home of a spirit was thus established, and the women of the neighbourhood began to invoke the aid of the saint and to show their devotion to her by kissing the rock, by anointing it with henna, and by burning incense before it.[1] The parallel with the experience of Jacob is exact, except that the inhabitant of the rock is no longer called a god but a spirit or saint. In the Hebrew Scriptures we read that Joshua set up a stone under the oak which is in the sanctuary at Shechem and said: "This stone shall be a witness against us, for it has heard all the words of Yahweh which he has spoken among us, and it shall be a witness against you that you will not deny your God" (Joshua 24 : 26). It must be clear that if the stone hears all the words spoken it is animated by a spirit. Although here made a witness in the cause of Yahweh, this spirit must have been originally a divinity. So we must say of the stone which Jacob set up as a witness between himself and Laban (Gen. 31 : 45, 51). Owing to the combination of documents in this narrative, the stone is now supplemented by a heap of stones. One of the component documents made the single stone the witness; the other made it the heap of stones. This only shows that a divinity may inhabit a group of stones as well as a single stone. The circle of stones at Gilgal attributed to Joshua (Joshua 4 : 3 and 8) marked a sanctuary which is frequently mentioned in the history. There were images here also, as we read in one passage (Judges 3 : 19). In the book of Exodus a sanctuary is marked by twelve stones set up by Moses, and here the covenant with Yahweh is entered into (Ex. 24 : 4).

The single stone set up at an altar as the residence of the divinity was called a *maççeba,* and such a stone seems to

[1] Jaussen, *op. cit.*, p. 303.

have been set up at every altar of Yahweh until the promulgation of Deuteronomy. The earliest decalogue, when it prohibits *molten* images, seems tacitly to recognise these primitive pillars as legitimate. Such upright stones are still found in Palestine, and more have been uncovered by excavation.[1] There is nothing to show that these menhirs are specifically nomadic, but Arabic antiquity shows that the nomads shared the belief of their neighbours with regard to them, and the biblical evidence seems convincing. In connection with these monuments we should note that altars sometimes receive proper names as though identified with the divinity. Jacob called one El-God-of-Israel (Gen. 33 : 20), Moses named one Yahweh-my-banner (Ex. 17 : 15), and Gideon had his Yahweh-Shalom (Judges 6 : 24). Since the earliest altars received the blood of the victim directly from the hand of the offerer, they, like the pillars, must have been identified with the divinity himself. Otherwise we must suppose that the names ascribed to the altars in the passages just cited were originally given to the attendant *maççeboth*. An altar named Ed, that is, Witness, existed beyond the Jordan to a comparatively late date (Joshua 22 : 34).

In one of the early accounts of the covenant entered into by Yahweh and Israel we find that the blood was sprinkled on the altar and on the people (Ex. 24 : 6–8). The blood which unifies the parties should, of course, be applied to both, so that we have no doubt that the altar was identified with Yahweh himself. Possibly we should interpret the covenant between Jacob and Laban in this light. After the heap of stones was gathered, the two parties ate upon the heap. Yahweh was thus made, in the most realistic sense, a partaker of the food, and therefore a party to the covenant. Down to the present time it is the divinity localised

[1] One at Maan is pictured by Jaussen, *Mission Archéologique en Arabie* (1909), p. 9; those uncovered by excavation at Megiddo and Gezer are reproduced by Vincent, *Canaan d'après l'Exploration récente* (1907); those at Tell es-Safi by Bliss and Macalister, *Excavations in Palestine* (1902), plate 9.

in some material object who is invoked in case of an oath; "If a person accused of crime dares to go to a sanctuary, lay his hand on the grave or pillar (of the saint) and swear that he has not committed the crime he is regarded as innocent. The saint punishes more severely than a human judge."[1]

If we may judge by the nomads of to-day, the early Israelites worshipped not the material objects but the spirits which dwelt in them. The giving of such a name as Bethel (House-of-God) to the stone would indicate this. The Arabs believe the desert to be inhabited by a class of spirits whom they call the Ginn. These appear frequently in the *Arabian Nights.* Such spirits, as a rule, have not attained the dignity of gods; that is, they do not receive a regular worship. But they must be conciliated on occasion; for example, when their territory is invaded. When the tent is pitched in a new place a sacrifice is offered to the local Ginnee, or a meal is cooked for him. Even in the towns when ground is broken for a new building, a foundation-sacrifice is offered to the *genius loci;* else he will avenge himself by sending calamity on the occupants of the house. This was the custom in ancient Palestine also, as the excavations have shown. When a new family is established by the marriage of a young man and young woman who set up their own tent, a sacrifice is offered, and they beg permission of the "master of the place" to occupy it with a new home. The tent-pole is smeared with the blood of the victim; and where the Bedawy adopts the agricultural life and builds a more permanent dwelling the blood is smeared on the lintel, as was the Israelite custom at Passover.

The local genius may rise to the dignity of patron divinity to a family or clan by revealing himself and thus showing his friendly interest. In this case an altar or pillar is erected and sacrifice is brought at fixed intervals. The revelation, however, may be hostile rather than friendly, intended at least to warn the recipient that he must pay due respect to

[1] *Palestina-Jahrbuch* (1911), p. 103.

the proprietor of the ground. Some stories which are now imbedded in the Hebrew text are evidently based on traditions of this kind. The biblical authors suppose in every such case that the divinity is Yahweh. But the original stories probably attributed the revelation to a purely local divinity. The mysterious stranger who wrestles with Jacob (now called an angel, Gen. 32 : 24–32) was originally such a local divinity. In this instance Jacob's strength and valour are such that he comes off victor and even wrests a blessing from the hostile power, though not without receiving a wound. The ghostly nature of the visitant is made evident by his anxiety to be allowed to go before daybreak, for the night demons, like the ghosts of popular superstition, cannot endure the light of the sun. This is further evidence that the original tradition was not recounted of Yahweh or of his angel, since neither the one nor the other had reason to shun the daylight.

The origin of this saga escapes us. It may have been intended to explain the place-name Penuel (Face-of-El), or it may have been an old myth representing the dangerous temper of the Jabbok. In either case it throws light upon early beliefs. The divinities were near to men, so that they could be seen face to face, but the encounter was not always to be desired.[1] An even more striking illustration of the belief is found in the story of Moses and the circumcision of his son (Ex. 4 : 24–26). In this we read that at one of the camping places in the desert the divinity attacked Moses and would have slain him. Zipporah was quick-witted enough to remember that circumcision blood is a powerful charm. She therefore circumcised her infant son and touched her husband with the blood, whereupon the hostile God left him. As in the other case, our text identifies the mysterious enemy with Yahweh. But he has none of the features of Israel's covenant God, and his attack upon the prophet is passing strange in view of the fact that

[1] A Phœnician locality, *Face-of-God*, mentioned by Strabo (*Geog.*, XVI, ii, 15), is brought by Ewald into connection with Penuel.

Moses was a chosen instrument for the redemption of Israel. The only explanation is that a story of some local divinity has been adopted in the Yahweh tradition.[1]

In this connection we may notice further the fragment preserved in the book of Joshua (Joshua 5: 13–15), according to which Joshua at the invasion of the land met a strange apparition carrying a sword. The Israelite leader went boldly up to him and asked: "Art thou for us or for our enemies?" The reply was to the effect that the stranger was leader of the heavenly host, apparently coming to the help of Israel. The text, as we have it, only tells us that Joshua was commanded to put off his shoes in recognition of the sanctity of the place, and the thread is then abruptly broken. It is not too bold to suppose that this was a local saga, according to which the divinity of the place promised to help the Israelites in getting possession of the country on condition that they continue to honour him at this sanctuary.

These survivals are sufficient to show that the early Israelites worshipped a multitude of local divinities. Even very late authors complain that the desert demons (satyrs, *se'irim*) still receive the sacrifices (Lev. 17: 7), and we shall have occasion to note the tenacity of life shown by one of them, named Azazel. The question which will next suggest itself is whether the spirits of dead men were among the objects of worship. There is a growing consensus of opinion that the Hebrews, like all other peoples at a certain stage of thought, worshipped these spirits. We have already seen that among the natives of Syria at the present day the tombs of holy men are places of devotion, and that an oath taken in the name of a Wely is more binding than the one taken in the name of Allah. Not all deceased persons receive this honour; only men (sometimes women) who have been distinguished for sanctity during their lifetime. Like the wonder-worker Elisha the power of the saint continues after his death, and miracles are wrought at his grave. For this

[1] Jewish tradition holds that circumcision is a prophylactic against the demons.

reason he is honoured there by sacrifices and festivals. Parallel with the case of the local divinity cited above is the declaration of an inhabitant of Maan: "If one swears by Abdallah [a Wely buried at Maan] and the oath is false he is sure to die." [1] Among the saints who are thus honoured the prophets and patriarchs of the Old Testament still have a place. The tomb of Abraham at Hebron is one of the most sacred spots of the Mohammedans, and the Bedawin across the Jordan are sure that El-Halil (the Friend of God), as Abraham is called, visits and helps them in answer to their prayers.[2]

To appreciate the tenacity of religious belief and custom we need only remind ourselves that these examples are taken from a region where Islam has endeavoured to enforce a strict monotheism for thirteen hundred years. It is important to notice that the spirit of the ancestor or alleged ancestor of a clan is the one most sure to receive religious veneration. He is thought to accompany his descendants on their wanderings and to protect them in danger. He is therefore invoked by them in time of trouble. Unsettled as the life of the nomads is, all of the tribes have their regular places of resort for religious purposes, and these are generally graves of an ancestor. The place is marked by a heap of stones: "An Arab never passes by such a monument without making a brief prayer; if he is not in haste he stops and prostrates himself in token of veneration; and on occasion he makes a visit of more ceremony, when he offers a sacrifice in consequence of a promise or vow." [3] In addition to these private sacrifices there are also public occasions when the greater part of the tribe makes a pilgrimage to the tomb and holds a feast of some days' duration. At the return of a successful expedition also an animal is sacrificed at the tomb of the ancestor in recognition of his help.

Other testimony might be adduced. The reverence paid to the tomb of Mohammed is rightly regarded as polytheistic by the Wahhabees. Yet it is said that a pious Moslem

[1] Jaussen, *Coutumes des Arabes*, p. 311. [2] *Ibid.*, p. 308.
[3] *Ibid.*, p. 317; *cf.* p. 355.

living in the third century of the Hejra boasted of having offered twelve thousand animals in honour of the prophet. The obstinacy of popular beliefs was perhaps never more strikingly manifested, for Mohammed himself forbade such rites as savouring of heathenism. Among the Arabs it is still the custom to sacrifice a sheep at the death of a member of the tribe, and another seven days later. This latter is called the sacrifice of consolation, and the phrase reminds us of the cup of consolation spoken of by the Hebrew prophet (Jer. 16: 7). In one case the sacrificial feast, in the other the libation is supposed to benefit the soul of the departed. The blood of sacrifices offered at the tomb of a saint is still poured over the heap of stones or other monument, as it was poured or smeared on the stone altar or pillar in the old days. Oil is also poured on the monument. Another rite of worship is the rubbing of earth, taken from the tomb, on the face of the worshipper. The sacredness of such earth makes it effective for healing the sick, on whom it is rubbed in the same way.[1] Another custom is that of offering the hair of the mourner at the tomb: "The women cut their hair at the death of a husband, father, or near relative. The long tresses are laid upon the tomb or rolled about the stone placed at the head of the grave. I have observed a more curious custom; two stakes were driven, one at the head, the other at the foot of the grave, and a cord was stretched from one to the other. On this cord were tied the long locks of hair."[2] In the time of Mohammed we are told that when Chalid ibn al-Walid died all the women of his clan shaved their heads and laid the hair on his tomb.[3]

The fact to which allusion has already been made, namely, that Mohammed attempted to suppress such customs, is of importance, for it shows that he, who knew the thoughts of his countrymen so well, believed their mourning rites to be polytheistic. The prohibition of swearing by one's ancestors and the command to swear by Allah alone[4] must

[1] Jaussen, *Coutumes*, p. 310.
[2] *Ibid.*, p. 94.
[3] Goldziher, *Muhammedanische Studien*, I, p. 248.
[4] *Ibid.*, p. 230.

be motived in the same way. Other testimony from Arab antiquity might be adduced. For example, the ground around a tomb was, at least in some cases, a sanctuary and an asylum. The prohibition of marking off such ground except for God and the prophet, put into Mohammed's mouth by tradition, is doubtless apocryphal, but it shows the attitude of the theologians to be the same with that of the prophet himself. The stones erected at the grave are doubtless, both in Arabic and in Hebrew antiquity, sacred stones like those at the sanctuary of a divinity.

It is only by this review of Semitic custom outside Israel that we are able to understand survivals which are attested in the Hebrew Bible. First of all, the custom of marking the grave by a stone, which is recorded in at least one Old Testament passage: This is the grave of Rachel (Gen. 35 : 20; I Sam. 10 : 2). Rachel was ancestress of the two tribes Joseph and Benjamin, and her grave seems to have been located on the boundary of these tribes. Here her spirit lingers, for Jeremiah hears her lament over the approaching captivity of her children (Jer. 31 : 15). The pillar over the grave is called by the same name which is used elsewhere (*maççeba*) for the sacred stone set up at a sanctuary. The custom is further illustrated by the act of Absalom. The prince had no son, and for this reason he took and reared a pillar (*maççeba*) in the King's Vale (II Sam. 18 : 18). He justified himself by saying: "I have no son to keep my name in remembrance." The word translated "keep in remembrance" means to pay religious reverence to a divinity. The thought of the passage is that Absalom, despairing of a son (who alone could pay the regular religious rites) erected this pillar in order that charitable people might be reminded of him and to a certain extent give his soul the honour which the departed crave.[1]

We now see why so many tombs of heroes are mentioned

[1] The text of the passage is not in order, and it is possible that in the earliest account it was David who erected the pillar; but this would not make any difference for our present inquiry.

in the Hebrew narrative. The cave where Abraham and Sarah are buried is important to the writer because it was in some sense a sanctuary. That its sanctity has persisted until the present day we have already noted. Jacob took pains to secure that he be buried in the tomb of his fathers (Gen. 47 : 30). The bones of Joseph were brought from Egypt in order that they might rest among his descendants (Joshua 24 : 32). The burial-place of Joshua, of Eleazar and of each of the Judges is carefully noted. Absalom's pillar was not the only monument consecrated to this prince, for the heap of stones raised over his body where he fell served the same purpose with the pillar (II Sam. 18 : 17). Similar heaps of stones were raised over the slain Canaanites, the kings of Ai, and the five kings slain at Makkedah (Joshua 8 : 29; 10 : 27). And the criminal Achan received the same honour (Joshua 7 : 26).

Here modern ideas are in conflict with those of antiquity and we are shocked by the thought that the souls of bad men, like Absalom and Achan, should receive the kind of reverence paid the gods. But early religion gives a large place to fear, and, the spirit of a bad man being as truly supernatural as that of a good man, it must be placated even more carefully. This is illustrated by the Greek hero-worship, where all the dead are regarded as "blameless," whatever their previous record has been. Some of the shrines at which the Greeks paid reverence are distinctly affirmed to be those of men of violent lives. The spirit is especially dangerous if the body which it once inhabited is left unburied, and the Hebrew pains in caring for burial is explicable on this ground. David cares for the body of Abner and for the bones of Saul's descendants, as well as for those of the king himself (II Sam. 3 : 32 and 21 : 14). These last are laid in the ancestral tomb, a boon which was especially desired, since thus one was sure to receive attention from the living members of the family. The curious custom of burial in one's own house is occasionally recorded (I Sam. 25 : 1; I Kings 2 : 34). This is accounted for by the desire of the family to have the spirit of the ancestor as protector of the home.[1] The kings of Israel, we are expressly told, were buried in the palace or in an adjoining garden. The objection made by the prophet Ezekiel to this custom, owing to the proximity of the palace to the temple, sufficiently shows that there was a religious motive; and from this point of view we may interpret the burning made for these kings as a religious rite, either sacrificial or designed to destroy property which was taboo because it belonged to a superhuman being.

Supernatural power is attributed to the dead or dying. The Pentateuchal narratives give the dying Isaac, Jacob, and Moses power to predict the future and to determine the course of coming events (Gen. 27 and 49; Deut. 33). The yearly festival in memory of Jephthah's daughter was probably a religious rite in which the spirit of the dead maiden received comfort from the sympathy of the young women who gathered at the shrine, and possibly was gratified by the banquet of which they partook.

Just as the demon resided in the pillar erected to him, so the spirit of the dead man took up its abode in the pillar or heap of stones erected over his body. This conception we know to have been prevalent among the neighbours of Israel, for we have instances in which the gravestone is directly identified with the soul (*nephesh*) of the deceased.[2] This explains some texts which have puzzled the expositors. These texts speak of the soul as that which defiles the person who touches a corpse (Num. 5 : 2; 6 : 6; 19 : 13). If the soul has left the body we do not see how it can defile. But in Hebrew thought the soul still has its abode in the body, at least until the latter has been deposited in the tomb. Then it dwells in the tomb, for the touch of a grave makes one taboo just as surely as the touch of a corpse. Why the contact should produce defilement we shall inquire

[1] Ethnological parallels are numerous.

[2] Lods, *La Croyance à la vie future et le culte des Morts dans l'Antiquité Israélite*, p. 62.

presently. What now interests us is that the soul resides in the pillar just as any other divinity resides in the visible object which marks his sanctuary.[1]

The continued existence and the superhuman knowledge of the souls of the dead is implied in the practice of consulting the spirits. The classic example is that of Saul and the witch of Endor. There is no reason to doubt that the narrator believed in the reality of the apparition. The most significant thing is that the necromancer calls the ghost a god (I Sam. 28 : 13). The wide prevalence of spiritistic arts in Israel down to a late period is proved by the polemic of the prophets (Isaiah 8 : 19) as well as by legal prohibitions in late as well as early codes (Ex. 22 : 17; Deut. 18 : 10 *f.;* Lev. 20 : 27). The reason for the opposition is that the necromancer was priest or priestess of a religion which Yahweh would not tolerate; that is, they worshipped the spirits.

As has often been pointed out, the mourning customs of the Jews are survivals from the animistic stage. Besides the natural expressions of grief, such as weeping and crying out, we read of fasting, shaving the head or some portion of it, tattooing or cutting incisions in the flesh, rending the clothes, and strewing ashes or earth on the head. The majority of these are religious customs. The strewing of earth on the head is a sign of consecration, the earth being taken from a sanctuary—in this case the burial-place. The ashes are in like manner sacred, bringing the mourner into communion with the departed, probably being taken from a sacrifice (*cf.* Jer. 6 : 26). Mourning garments—sackcloth is usually associated with the ashes of mourning—are to be classed with the special robes which the worshippers donned at a religious ceremony. The rending of the clothes had some reference to the taboo imposed by the presence of a corpse.

[1] Jaussen points out that a stele in one of the Nabatæan inscriptions is distinctly said to be the residence of the god (*Mission Archéologique,* p. 416). The gigantic monoliths at Axum, in Abyssinia, are said to be called "souls," like the Phœnician monuments spoken of above (*Archiv für Religionswissenschaft,* XI, p. 567).

Some of these customs might be interpreted in such a way as not to be inconsistent with the Yahweh religion, but some of them, as we have seen, were strictly forbidden. The Deuteronomist prohibits tattooing and shaving the head: "You shall not cut yourselves nor make any baldness between your eyes for the dead" (Deut. 14 : 1). The priestly writer in repeating these prohibitions brings the forbidden practices into connection with enchantment and augury (Lev. 19 : 26–28) and is especially stringent with the priests (21 : 1–6). The Deuteronomist takes pains to have the faithful Israelite declare that he has not given any part of the tithes to the dead (Deut. 26 : 14), doubtless because there was strong pressure exercised by common custom to make the offerings to the dead a first charge on the sacred things. The desire of the legislators, therefore, was to separate everything connected with the worship of Yahweh from contact with the dead. But since death is a universal human experience every one at some time or other must come into the presence of a corpse. Such persons are pronounced by the law ritually unclean and are not admitted to the sanctuary of Yahweh until purified by a special rite. In the case of the high priest, in whom sanctity was most important, a stricter regulation was enforced and he was not allowed to approach any dead body whatever, not even that of his father or his mother (Lev. 21 : 10–13).

The fact that all of this testimony is from comparatively late documents only shows the strength of the belief in the demonic nature of the spirits of the dead. This belief has left its mark on the legislation, not only in the prohibitions we have noted, but in some positive regulations. The sacrifice of a red cow enjoined in Numbers (chap. 19) seems to be a sacrifice to the dead which has survived in the ritual system because it could not be eradicated. The sacrifice is unique in the priestly system in that it is not offered at the sanctuary. The colour of the animal and the manner of its offering remind us of the sacrifices brought to the dead in other religions, and the fact that the man who handles the ashes is unclean points to the same conclusion. Further, the heifer strangled near the spot where a man has been murdered by an unknown hand seems to be a similar survival (Deut. 21 : 1–9). The ghost of the dead man must be propitiated lest he do harm to the people of the neighbourhood.

Mention has already been made of the burnings for the kings of Judah (Jer. 34 : 5; II Chron. 16 : 14; 21 : 19) and of Ezekiel's protest against the burial of these kings in immediate proximity to the temple (Ezek. 43 : 7). The importance attached to male offspring throughout the Old Testament is intelligible if a man's sons were the ones to pay him worship after his death. It has even been suggested that the command to honour father and mother has reference primarily to the payment of the funeral rites. This, however, is problematical. The patriarchal family, which we find fully developed in Israel, usually rests on the religious basis of ancestor-worship. What is certain is that we have enough evidence to warrant us in saying that the worship of the dead existed in Israel throughout its history and that it dates back to the time of the wilderness sojourn.[1]

The nomad does not clearly distinguish the wild animals from the spirits which in his imagination people the desert. Traces of animal worship, therefore, do not surprise us when we meet them in the Old Testament. The serpent had the reputation of superhuman knowledge, and sacrifice was brought to a bronze serpent in the temple down to the time of Hezekiah (II Kings 18 : 4), a striking example of religious conservatism. This serpent was ascribed to Moses, and our narrative sources represent it to have been a harmless talisman by which those bitten by serpents were healed. But it is clear that Hezekiah would not have destroyed so innocent and so venerable a monument had this been all that he be-

[1] The recollection of this fact finds expression even in the Psalter, where eating the sacrifices of the dead is brought into connection with the worship of Baal-peor (Psalm 106 : 28). An elaborate discussion of the whole subject will be found in Lods, *La Croyance à la vie future et le culte des Morts dans l'Antiquité Israélite*, Paris, 1906.

lieved it to be. It must have been an idol representing the serpent-god, to whom one might appeal for protection from his subjects. A sanctuary in the vicinity of Jerusalem bore the name "Serpent's Stone" or "Dragon's Well" (I Kings 1 : 9; Neh. 2 : 13). Other direct evidence of the worship of animals, except that of the bull, which will occupy our attention later, there seems to be none. But indirect testimony is given by the abhorrence of the Yahweh religion for "unclean" animals. The reason for this abhorrence is the fact that these animals were associated with other gods than Yahweh. Probably they were not only consecrated to these divinities but were regarded as incarnations of them. We have already seen that down to a late period the desert demons were worshipped. These demons are called *Se'irim,* which means *goats* (Lev. 17 : 7). The divinities were, therefore, wild goats, or goat-like in form, resembling the satyrs of Greek mythology. Egypt, the classic land of animal-worship, shows numerous parallels.

The reaction of Yahweh-worship against these superstitions is itself an evidence that they once prevailed. Even so late an author as Origen, and one so comparatively enlightened, thought that every animal is in some manner akin to a demon, and Plutarch speaks of the ass as an unclean and demonic beast.[1] But demons are only gods of inferior rank, or who have been proscribed by more advanced religious belief. The close connection of uncleanness and sanctity in ancient thought gave rise to the gentile opinion that the Jews worshipped an ass.

Summing up what has been said, we may say that the early Hebrews worshipped the spirits which they supposed to animate trees, fountains, and rocks; they reverenced the animals, also, or at least some of them, and they paid religious adoration to the spirits of the dead at the places where they were interred. Yahweh was himself originally the god of a mountain or, according to one account, of a cave (I Kings

[1] *De Iside et Osiride,* 30. Origen, *Contra Celsum,* IV, 72. I owe this citation to Kalisch, *Leviticus,* II, p. 72.

19:9–14). The Hebrew writers who have recorded these evidences would doubtless have been glad to ignore them had they had less fidelity to tradition. This makes their evidence all the more convincing. The survival of so many of these beliefs into the later period shows what the religion of the nomads must have been.

It is evident that the religious emotion which dictates worship of these divinities must be that of fear. The *fear of Yahweh* was, in fact, the Hebrew definition of religion down to the New Testament period. Later documents, indeed, emphasise the love of God, and there are expressions of trust and affection in the higher stages of this religion. But the nomad was moved more by fear than by love. This is true to the present day, for the Palestinian Arab still speaks of a pious man as one that fears Allah, and reverence for the local saint of which we have spoken as the most vital religion of these people has always behind it the idea that he will be swift to avenge an insult. The oath by the saint, as we have seen, is inviolate just for this reason, and the laxity in swearing by Allah is due to the belief that he is a God of mercy who will not be so particular.[1] It is not without reason then that Yahweh is called the Fear of Isaac, and that Jacob swears by him under that name (Gen. 31:42 and 53).

Fear of the gods expresses itself in the ascription to them of a quality for which we have no good name in English, but for which we may provisionally use the word *sacredness*. The gods, as inhabitants of a different sphere from that in which men are found, or rather as having a different nature from that of men, possess in themselves this uncanny quality —to call it *holiness*, as is so often done, is misleading, for to us this implies moral perfection. On account of this mysterious quality it is dangerous to approach the divinity without certain precautions; to handle what belongs to him is also dangerous. To protect oneself from this dangerous power is one object of religious rites. But to ward off the

[1] Jaussen, *Coutumes*, p. 292.

baleful influence of one god we may put ourselves under the protection of another. The use of charms and spells is intended to enlist a divine protector. The earliest ornaments used by men were not designed to make the person attractive; they were amulets in which supernatural power resided. In other words, sacredness has two sides to it; it may be either helpful or harmful. When Aaron asked for the earrings of the Israelites and made them into an idol of Yahweh, he was moved by the reflection that these objects were already sacred, that is, they had already something of divinity in them. They were therefore fit material for his purpose (Ex. 32 : 2–4). Micah made an image out of some of the silver which he had taken from his mother because she had laid a curse upon it, that is, she had made it taboo by dedicating it to the divinity, and it was thus withdrawn from secular use (Judges 17: 1–5). Gideon in like manner used the earrings of the Midianites for an image of Yahweh (Judges 8: 25–27). In this case the earrings were probably originally devoted to another god. But if so, the way to render them innocuous was to dedicate them to Yahweh, for the sacredness imparted by the more powerful God would overcome that of the weaker. Here is the secret of the whole opposition of clean and unclean which is so prominent in the ritual of the Hebrews, and which survives in orthodox Judaism to the present day. The sacredness of Yahweh is strongly opposed to the sacredness of another divinity; this therefore becomes uncleanness for the Yahweh religion. It is probable that we have here the reason why David's music was expected to cure Saul's madness. Music has in it something of divine power; the musician may, in fact, be inspired by Yahweh, as we see in the case of the early prophets. He is therefore able to drive away the evil demon, who is the cause of madness. Plato believed that the sacred dance and music would cure those who were possessed.[1]

This idea of sacredness as an uncanny power runs through the whole history of Hebrew religion. A curious illustration

[1] *Laws*, VII, 790, cited by Rohde, *Psyche*, p. 336.

is found in a late law (late in the literary formulation, that is), which must be a survival. In the ordeal for the woman suspected of adultery it is commanded that the accused drink of a cup which contains sacred water (probably from a sacred spring) in which some of the dust from the floor of the sanctuary has been dissolved as well as the ink in which the curse was written. If she is guilty it will punish her (cause her to miscarry), but if she is innocent it will not harm her (Num. 5 : 11–31). The sacred water, reinforced by the sacred dust and the sacred formula, has supernatural power to discover and punish guilt. The dust of the sanctuary has the same uncanny power that we have discovered in dust from a grave, as believed by the Bedawin down to the present day. The whole theory of ordeals, which plays so prominent a part in the history of religion, is based on this sacredness of material that belongs to a god or demon.[1]

This matter of exorcism and magic is important because, crude as it seems to us, it opened the way to a higher conception of religion. The idea that we may secure the aid of the friendly divinity by an alliance or covenant is on this side of the line which divides magic and religion. This idea of alliance or covenant became fundamental in the religion of Israel and has become one of the leading ideas in Christianity also. What now interests us is that it originated in the nomadic stage. Among the nomads the relations of man and man are regulated by covenant. Clans are, in fact, made by covenants between smaller groups, and clans coalesce into tribes by the same process. But, as we have seen, the covenant is made binding by making the local divinity a party to it. This divinity, thus brought into the compact, became not only the guardian of the oath, but a member of the clan. And as the earliest covenants were blood covenants, the divinity was made a blood-brother by the same sort of rite with the one used when two men made an alliance.

From this point of view we must explain the rite of

[1] *Cf.*, further, Goldziher, *Muhammedanische Studien*, II, p. 260.

circumcision, which doubtless goes back to ancient times. This rite was practised in Egypt, as we know, and is still observed by almost all African tribes, by the Australians, and in parts of North and South America. Among the most primitive tribes it seems to be a rite of initiation. The boys of the tribe are not thought to attain manhood until they have undergone this operation, which is usually performed at puberty, and which admits them to full membership in the tribe, releasing them from the control of their mothers. The admission is by a blood covenant, the blood which flows at the operation being applied to the men of the tribe, and their blood at the same time being caused to flow over the initiates. The account of the circumcision of Moses' son, already considered, shows the power of the blood, and, as the divinity is made a party to all the solemnities of the tribe, we see how circumcision was not only the sign but the seal of the covenant. It is, in fact, so regarded in the latest documents. As for the bodily organ which was operated upon, we must remember the importance of reproduction in all early societies, where the life of the clan depends upon the number of fighting men. Because of the importance of having many sons born to the clan, the whole sexual life was under the protection of the divinity, and entrance on the marriageable age was the most important event in the life of the individual. In the later stages of Hebrew society circumcision was performed in infancy, but there are traces of the earlier custom which connected it with the age of puberty.

Since this rite brought the boy into covenant with the clan and with the clan-god, we understand why it is called a purification and why the uncircumcised are called the unclean. All tribal marks and mutilations seem to be religious in their origin, and this could be no exception. If it be objected that we have no evidence that human blood was ever used to bring the Israelite into communion with the divinity, we must remember that in the later stages of this religion pains were taken to ignore those features of early custom which had become repulsive to advancing thought. If human sacrifice was practised in the early stages—and that it was admits of no doubt—human blood must have been regarded as the most potent means of sanctifying the covenant. The priests of Baal cut themselves with knives as they danced about the altar, thus appealing to the god by the covenant relation which gave them a claim on him (1 Kings 18 : 28); and Hosea intimates that the Israelites also cut themselves at the altar of Yahweh (Hosea 7 : 14, emended text). The prohibition of cutting oneself for the dead is emphasised by the Deuteronomist because such mutilations bring one into communion with the departed.

These survivals show that the use of human blood to ratify the covenant was not unknown, and we may suppose that in the prehistoric stage circumcision blood was applied to the altar or pillar which represented the divinity. In our records animal blood has taken the place of human blood, and we find the covenant ratified by sacrifice of an animal. The earliest account of the covenant made between Israel and Yahweh tells us that the blood was sprinkled on the altar (representing Yahweh) and on the people. The blood cements the union; the parties become of one blood (Ex. 24 : 6–8). To the present day some of the Arabs give solemn sanction to a betrothal by a blood covenant: "When an Arab has secured a bride for his son by a promise from the young woman's father, he takes a sheep or goat to the tent and slays the animal there, sprinkling a little of the blood on the fiancée. She is thereby irrevocably promised to the young man. She and all her kin are bound by the contract." [1]

Circumcision, covenant rites, and sacrifice, then, go back to the nomadic period of Israel's history. And the communion meal is naturally a part of the sacrificial rite. When the blood had ratified or renewed the covenant the flesh of the animal was eaten by the members of the clan. It is well known that among the Arabs to this day eating with a man establishes peace with him, so that you are safe from

[1] Jaussen, *Coutumes*, p. 345.

his hostility as long as the food is in your body. Jacob and Laban establish peace by the common meal, to which apparently the divinity is also invited. The covenant between Israel and the Gibeonites was ratified by the parties eating together (Joshua 9 : 14). Whether the Hebrews ever conceived the sacrifice as the slaying of a divine animal in order that his life might strengthen the members of the clan by entering into them cannot be definitely made out. Such a conception does not seem to have been entertained in the historic period.

A sacrifice which differs in some respects from the others adopted in the later ritual is the Passover, and we may perhaps assume that this goes back to nomadic times. What was peculiar about it was its performance at the home instead of at a sanctuary. The blood, instead of being poured upon an altar, was smeared on the door-posts and lintel, and it was required that the whole flesh should be consumed before morning. This seems to be the original clan sacrifice. The unity of the group is shown by their gathering in one house. In the nomad period the social unit is the circle of tents pitched at one spot, and all the members of the group easily find accommodation in the tent of the sheikh. The smearing of the blood on the tent-pole (the earliest method) serves a double purpose: it keeps off the demons which prowl around, and which are especially active at certain seasons of the year; at the same time it brings the clan into renewed covenant with the divinity. The fact that the spring was the season for this festival makes us associate it with present Arab custom. The lamb which was slain was probably the first one yeaned that season. For this lamb is still considered sacred, and must be sacrificed to a saint.[1]

The Hebrew authors found a historic occasion for the Passover in the slaying of the first-born in Egypt, but the documents themselves allow us to discover that the festival is older than the exodus. Moses asks Pharaoh that the

[1] Jaussen, *Coutumes*, p. 366.

people may go three days' journey into the wilderness to observe the feast to Yahweh. The natural supposition is that this was the season when such a sacrifice should be observed, and that the God would be angry if it was omitted. The festival is spoken of as if it were some known and established thing. In the mind of the earliest writer, therefore, the exodus was demanded in order that the Passover might be observed. When Pharaoh refused his assent, Yahweh took the first-born of the Egyptians as a substitute for the sacrifices which were wrongfully withheld. The fact that after the settlement in Canaan the Passover was amalgamated with another festival, that of unleavened bread, does not now concern us.

The covenant sacrifice implies that the god becomes a member of the clan. The numerous Semitic proper names which affirm that the divinity is a kinsman become intelligible when we bear this in mind. It is not always as father that he is presented; he is often brother or uncle of the clansman. Possibly this points to a time when the father was of less importance to the child than the uncle or brother.[1] The totemistic clan, that is, the one in which gods, men, and animals are all kinsmen, is matriarchal, or, perhaps better, matrilinear. The women of the clan do not leave their kinsmen to join the group to which the husband belongs, but remain among their own people, receiving visits from the man from time to time, but keeping the children for their own group. The greater importance of the uncle or brother in such a society is evident. Although there is no clear and decisive evidence that such a system ever prevailed among the Hebrews, there are some facts which find their best explanation on the hypothesis that the Hebrews, like so many other peoples, have passed through the totemistic stage. Thus the mother is the one who names the child in many cases (Gen. 4:25; 16:11; 29:32; 30:24; I Sam. 1:20). This is hardly conceivable in a strictly patriarchal society.

[1] The subject is considered at length by W. Robertson Smith, *Religion of the Semites*, Lecture II.

There are also some cases of exogamous marriage which look in the same direction (Samson, Judges 14, and Gideon, Judges 8 : 31). Animal proper names might be adduced as further arguments. Yet it is clear that at the entrance into Canaan the Hebrews had left the totemistic system behind.

At what point of time the worship of the heavenly bodies entered the religion of Israel is impossible to determine. Later writers have much to say in opposition to this worship, but it is possible that they have in mind rites that were introduced from Assyria or Babylon (Deut. 17 : 3). It does not seem violent, however, to suppose that the moon was an object of adoration in the nomadic period. The new moon was a festival from early times, and among the Arabs the new moon is still greeted with song or prayer at its appearing.[1] The fact that the Sabbath is often mentioned in connection with the new moon leads us to suspect that it also was a lunar festival. Sun-worship was common in all the more advanced religions of western Asia, and the story of Samson indicates that it had some hold among the Israelites, but whether this was true in the nomadic stage is not clear.

On another point we are compelled to admit our ignorance. This is whether the early Hebrews had goddesses as well as gods. The other Semites paid great attention to a goddess of fertility whom the Babylonians called Ishtar, the Canaanites Astarte. Her worship in Israel in the historic period is well attested, but whether it is earlier is not known. The goddess of fertility would naturally flourish in the cultivated country, but the phenomena of the oases may well have associated her with certain spots in the desert as well. It has recently been argued with much ability that a goddess of the oases, perhaps embodied in the palm-tree, was the original divinity of the Semites.[2]

[1] Jaussen, *Coutumes*, p. 294; Doughty, *Travels in Arabia Deserta*, I, 366, 455.

[2] Barton, *A Study of Semitic Origins*.

We are on more certain ground when we say that the most fundamental social institution of the nomadic life is blood-revenge. The solidarity of the clan brings with it the duty of revenge. "Our blood has been spilled," they say, when any member of the group has been injured or slain. If the murderer cannot be identified, some member of his clan must pay the penalty. The consequence is that some tribes are at constant feud. The logic of the system is well set forth by the woman of Tekoah, who complains that the whole family will be exterminated by strict adherence to custom (II Sam. 14 : 4–11). What now concerns us is that the institution is religious because the god is a member of the clan, and the duty of blood-revenge devolves upon him as well as upon the human kinsmen. Where there is no human avenger the god will assume the obligation. In case of murder within the clan the punishment is not death but banishment, which, as we see in Cain, is worse than death. All that now concerns us is that the divinity protects the blood, and so long as it is unavenged it cries to him from the ground. To the latest times the Israelites called Yahweh their *go'el,* that is to say, the next of kin, on whom the duty of revenge devolves. The oft-quoted passage, "Whoso sheds man's blood by man shall his blood be shed," is the expression of clan custom, and in immediate connection with it Yahweh declares that he will avenge if man does not: "Surely your blood will I require; at the hand of every beast will I require it and at the hand of man" (Gen. 9 : 4). Joseph's brothers felt that the hand of God was avenging their treatment of their brother when their lives were threatened in Egypt (Gen. 42 : 22). Solomon felt himself justified in slaying Joab even at the altar, because as the instrument of Yahweh he was thus returning the man's blood-guilt on his own head (I Kings 2 : 32), and Elijah did not hesitate to declare that Yahweh would require the blood of Naboth from Ahab (I Kings 21 : 19). Even in the nomadic stage, therefore, Yahweh was a God of justice, the protector of the clansman's life.

His attitude toward strangers, however, was that of a thorough partisan. The nomad is at perpetual war with his neighbours, and raids upon the neighbouring tribes are the regular way by which the means of subsistence are obtained. The divinity stood in such close relations with the clan that he took part in their wars. This is illustrated by Mesha, who tells us that Chemosh delighted in the victories of his people. A tribe might pay its devotion at any of the shrines which lay near the route of its wanderings, but its own tutelary divinity stood in closer relation to it than any of the others. To secure his presence on their campaigns it was natural to carry the visible object in which he was supposed to reside. Hebrew tradition speaks of a tent which accompanied the people in their wanderings, and also of an ark or chest which secured the presence of the divinity. This tradition speaks of two stones placed in the ark, and we are inclined to suppose that these were sacred stones, *bethels* in which the God had his residence.

Recently it has been argued that the ark was a seat or throne on which the divinity was invisibly present, and parallels are adduced from other religions. But it seems pretty clear that the Hebrew word means box or chest. It seems more probable, also, that the nomads would carry a fetish than that they would conceive of the deity as invisibly present. In any case the ark was so closely identified with Yahweh that its presence secured his presence. Moses invoked it in the morning with the words: "Rise, Yahweh, and let thine enemies be scattered, and let thy haters flee before thee!" And when it rested at night he said: "Return, Yahweh, to the myriad thousands of Israel" (Num. 10 : 35). Because the ark secured the presence of Yahweh the Israelites carried it into battle against the Philistines, and the Philistines themselves, when they heard of its presence, said: "God has come into the camp" (I Sam. 4 : 7). David, in dancing before the ark, danced before Yahweh (II Sam. 6 : 5 and 16). All these examples are from the later period, and it is not certain that either ark or tent actually existed in the nomadic stage, but at least there is nothing improbable in supposing that one or the other dates from that time. Egyptian influence is sometimes assumed here as elsewhere, and it is true that in Egypt the gods were carried about in chests, though more often in boats. It is precarious, therefore, to assume Egyptian influence. Portable gods are mentioned in the story of Rachel's stealing the teraphim of her father (Gen. 31 : 19).

Fragmentary as our information is, we have been able to make out a fairly good outline of what Israel believed in the nomadic period. How the people advanced from this rudimentary stage we have now to discover.

CHAPTER III

MOSES AND HIS WORK

Priestly tradition makes Moses the giver of the Law and therefore the founder of the religious institutions of Judaism. Deuteronomy puts into the mouth of Moses the statutes and ordinances which it wishes to see observed in Israel. The older narratives ascribe to the same leader a code of civil regulations or at least a decalogue of commands given by his mouth at Horeb or Sinai, as the case may be. All that we can with probability conclude from this stream of tradition is that a man named Moses had a marked influence on the religious development of early Israel. That he was not a legislator in the later sense of the word seems obvious. For in the first place the Bedawy tolerates no statutes. What regulates his relations with his fellows is tribal custom. And that tribal custom prevailed in Israel as late as the time of David is shown by the protest of Tamar against her brother's violence. She appeals to no law; all she says is that it is not so done in Israel (II Sam. 13 : 12). This and other cases show that no authoritative code was recognised in the earlier period. Not even a decalogue is appealed to by the prophets in their arraignment of Israel for its sins. One has only to reflect on the impressive use which these preachers might have made of an ethical decalogue, divinely given (if they had known of such a decalogue), in order to realise that no such decalogue had yet been promulgated. To this we may add that the character of the earliest code ascribed to Moses forbids us to suppose it to have been given in the desert. To impose a code intended for an agricultural people on tribes not yet in possession of a cultivable country would have been both impracticable and irrational. Moreover—and this is the most convincing of all the considerations that present themselves—the earlier prophets did not believe that a ritual law had been given in the desert. They, in fact, categorically deny that sacrifice was either commanded or offered in the wilderness (Amos 5 : 25; Isaiah 1 : 11–15). Jeremiah declares that Yahweh had given no directions concerning sacrifice or offering, though he admits that Israel had been charged with the duty of obedience to its divinely sent teachers (Jer. 7 : 22).

These prophets did not deny that Moses had existed; much less did they deny that there had been a great deliverance at the beginning of Israel's history. It is assumed by all the Old Testament writers that there had been such a deliverance. Amos says: "I brought you up from the land of Egypt and led you forty years in the wilderness to possess the land of the Amorites." Even more striking is the declaration: "Hear the word that Yahweh has spoken to you, O sons of Israel; against the whole family that I brought out of the land of Egypt, saying: You only have I known of all the families of the earth; therefore will I visit upon you all your iniquities" (Amos 2 : 10; 3 : 1 *f.*). Hosea alludes to the exodus a number of times and says specifically: "When Israel was a child then I loved him, and called my son out of Egypt." And in another passage the prophet declares that the relation between Yahweh and Israel was constituted at the time of the exodus (Hosea 11 : 1; 12 : 10; *cf.* 2 : 17; 9 : 3). He adds that it was by a prophet that Yahweh brought his people out of Egypt and by a prophet that he guarded them (12 : 14).

While the literature outside the Pentateuch is thus aware of the importance of the exodus, it is to the Pentateuch itself that we must look if we are to get an idea of the place which Moses had in the thought of the people at all stages of their history. The extreme complexity of the critical problem with reference to these books must not prevent our attempt to get an historical view. The first thing that impresses us is that the documents here united agree in ascribing to Moses the foundation of Israel's religion and of Israel's nationality. One writer conceives of him as civil ruler; another describes him as the great liberator; a third emphasises his magical power as far superior to what Egypt could show. Still another thinks of him as the minister of the oracle and declarer of the will of Yahweh. Finally, he becomes the inaugurator of the priesthood and the originator of the theocracy. Various as these views are, they testify unanimously to the greatness of the man whom they glorify. They create a considerable probability, therefore, that such a man once existed and that he did an important work for Israel. What that work was, however, is not so easy to define. Its historic basis must be found in the sojourn in Egypt.

Reconstructing the oldest narrative, we may present the case somewhat as follows: In the course of their migrations, probably driven by famine, one or more of the clans which sojourned in the desert south of Canaan took refuge in the border-land of Egypt. Here they kept their flocks in the ancestral manner in the district called Goshen. The friendly relations which at first existed between them and the Egyptians became strained when the Pharaoh tried to force them to labour for him (as did his other subjects) on his great public works. One of their own number aroused the enmity of the king and was forced to flee the country. Finding a refuge among the tribes to the east of the Red Sea, he was adopted into one of them and married the daughter of the priest of the local divinity. Religious by temperament, and brooding over the misfortunes of his brothers in Egypt, he invoked the aid of this divinity on behalf of these kinsmen. One day, approaching a sacred tree or thicket, he heard the voice of the God calling him and warning him of the sanctity of the place. Then came the wished-for promise of aid. The God commanded him to lead his people from Egypt to this sacred spot that there they might pay him worship (Ex. 3 : 1–12).

The sequel of the account tells how Moses, in order to assure himself of the genuineness of the revelation, asked the name of the divinity, and the name Yahweh was revealed to him (Ex. 3 : 13–18). There is here a conflict in the narrative, for the new name would be that of a new divinity and not that of the god of the fathers. His identification with the God of Abraham, Isaac, and Jacob is, in fact, a theological attempt to carry the Yahweh religion back to the time of the patriarchs. One of the documents goes so far as to make the name Yahweh invoked as early as the antediluvian period. But earliest must be the theory that Moses, as the inaugurator of Israel's religion, brought to his people a hitherto unknown God. This is implied also in the account of the covenant entered into after the deliverance, for no such compact would have been necessary had Yahweh been the God of the Hebrews from the earliest times.

In accordance with the commission given him, Moses went to Egypt and demanded of the Pharaoh a furlough for his people, that they might go three days' journey into the wilderness and observe the festival of this God. The request was the mildest that could be framed and was thus framed to test the Pharaoh's attitude. It was stated in a way that should have appealed to him. The Hebrews were afraid that, if they neglected the festival which was due the divinity, he would visit his wrath upon them in the form of a pestilence (Ex. 5 : 3). The refusal of the king was followed by a contest between the God of Moses and the gods of Egypt, or between the supernatural power of Moses and that claimed by the Egyptian magicians. For at the revelation at the bush Moses had received a magic staff which enabled him to outdo the celebrated wonders of the Egyptian sorcerers. The series of plagues by which the obstinacy of the king was broken culminated in the death of the first-born among the Egyptians, the flight of the Israelites, and the great deliverance at the Red Sea. What basis in fact the narrative has can no longer be discovered.

Whatever took place was interpreted by the people as the direct intervention of the new God on their behalf.

The earliest account seems to have stated that the people journeyed the three days in the wilderness and thus reached the sanctuary at which they had come to worship. The first thing done here was to make a covenant with the God who had so signally favoured them. The account, now imbedded in other matter, deserves citation in full. It reads as follows: "Then Jethro, Moses' father-in-law, came with his [Moses'] wife and his sons unto Moses into the wilderness where he was encamped at the mount of God; and he said unto Moses: I, thy father-in-law, am come unto thee. . . . And Moses told his father-in-law all that Yahweh had done unto Pharaoh and to the Egyptians for Israel's sake, all the trouble that had come upon them in the way, and how Yahweh had delivered them. And Jethro rejoiced for all the goodness which Yahweh had done to Israel in that he had delivered them out of the hands of the Egyptians. And Jethro said: Blessed be Yahweh who has delivered you out of the hand of the Egyptians and out of the hand of Pharaoh. Now I know that Yahweh is greater than all gods, for exactly in that in which they dealt arrogantly with you he smote them. Then Jethro, Moses' father-in-law, took burnt-offerings and peace-offerings for Yahweh, and Aaron came and all the elders of Israel and ate bread with Moses' father-in-law before the God." (Ex. 18 : 5–12.)

The fact of a foreigner's officiating at a sacrifice at which Aaron and the elders of Israel are only guests is so extraordinary and so much out of harmony with later Hebrew thought that we are compelled to see in this account a very ancient tradition. According to it the chief men in Israel are received into covenant with Jethro's God at a sacrificial meal. Moses is not mentioned, probably because, being already in covenant with Yahweh, he acted as acolyte for his father-in-law. It is possible that in the original account he was stated to be a pupil of Jethro at this function, learning the ritual proper for the sacrifice to Yahweh.[1] In any case this narrative shows that Yahweh was formally introduced to Israel by a Midianite priest. It is sometimes assumed that Jethro's admiration for Yahweh's power is admiration for the God of Israel. But in that case we should expect him to avow his conversion to this God before sacrificing to him, and even then he could hardly assume to act as priest. The only explanation is that Jethro was gratified at the evidence of his own God's superiority to all the gods.

Later in the narrative we read of the ratification of the covenant between Yahweh and the people as a whole. Here Moses acts as leader. After submitting to the people the question whether they will obey the voice of Yahweh, and receiving their affirmative answer, he erected an altar at the foot of the mountain and twelve pillars (*maççeboth*) for the twelve tribes. Then he chose out the young men of the sons of Israel and they offered burnt-offerings and sacrificed bullocks for peace-offerings. Then Moses took half the blood and poured it into bowls, the other half he sprinkled on the altar; and when the people promised, "all that Yahweh has commanded will we do" he sprinkled the people and said: "This is the blood of the covenant which Yahweh has made with you on the basis of all these commandments" (Ex. 24 : 3–8). In the text we have a book spoken of. This is because the author supposed the earliest written code to have been given by Moses. The important thing is that the document before us, like the other, asserts that Moses became the founder of Israel's religion by bringing the people into covenant with Yahweh after the deliverance from Egypt.

Another view of Moses as founder of the religion of Israel is given by the account of his administration of the oracle. Jethro appears in his company here also. In the chapter from which we have already cited we read that Jethro was astonished at the burden which Moses took upon himself in

[1] As supposed by Gressmann, *Mose*, p. 168.

judging the people. He therefore counsels him to relieve himself of part of the labour by appointing judges to hear the minor cases, reserving for himself the more important ones, which he shall decide by bringing them before the divinity (Ex. 18 : 13–27). The narrative presupposes a somewhat permanent settlement of the people (probably at Kadesh) where they have leisure for litigation. Moses is the arbitrator between man and man, but in his attempt to hear all the cases that are brought before him he is wasting his strength. Jethro's advice is twofold: first, Moses should have helpers; secondly, he should make use of the oracle to decide the more difficult cases. It is not hazardous to conjecture that in the earliest form of the story Jethro instructed Moses not only in the civil administration (indicated by the appointment of the minor judges) but also in the manner of using the oracle of Yahweh. For Jethro, as priest of Yahweh, must know how to ascertain the will of the God.

We can hardly doubt that Kadesh was the seat of an oracle, for one of its names was En Mishpat (*Fountain of Judgment*). Further, as was said above, it is not improbable that its prerogatives in this respect are indicated by the names Massa and Meribah, both of which are located at Kadesh. One name, *Place of Testing*, would indicate that the ordeal was applied to those who were brought into judgment; the other name, *Place of Litigation*, needs no explanation. As the only tribunal to which the nomad or half nomad submits is that of a divinity, the tradition in this case is just what we should expect.

According to the earliest sources at our command, therefore, Moses is not only the deliverer of the people from Egypt; he is the minister of the oracle, the priest of the sanctuary at Kadesh, and also the civil ruler so far as any nomad people endures the yoke of a ruler. The sources further indicate that his position was not secured without conflict. At one time he calls for volunteers in the cause of Yahweh, and the young men who rally to him put to death their own nearest relatives in defence of the Moses religion (Ex. 32 : 25–29; confirmed by Deut. 33 : 9). The result was to organise the priestly guild of Levites. The protest of Korah against the limitation of the priesthood, on the ground that all the people are sacred, is another evidence of the conflict waged against these innovations. The revolt of Dathan and Abiram, now read in connection with that of Korah, seems to have been directed against the civil power exercised by Moses, for his answer is that he has not been guilty of receiving bribes (Num. 16 : 15). Protest against the prophetic assumptions of Moses made by Aaron and Miriam (Num. 12) is additional evidence of the struggle which the new religion had to undergo.

Some motive must have been presented to the people to induce them to adopt a God hitherto unknown. What this motive was is not difficult to discover. The state of early society being a state of war, the divinities are sought in order that they may give their aid in battle. Yahweh, therefore, is consistently presented to us as a God of war. And since the covenant with the God of Midian meant a covenant with the people of Midian, the fact would seem to be that Israel and Midian entered an alliance for defence, and perhaps also for offence, against their enemies. Midian nowhere appears in the later history as an ally of Israel, but we read concerning the Kenites that they entered Canaan with Israel. The Kenites were counted a subdivision of Midian, according to some of the documents, and Moses' father-in-law or brother-in-law (here called Hobab) was asked by Moses to journey with Israel. It was his clan, in fact, that went with the tribes (Judges 1 : 16), and later a member of this clan was camped near the scene of the battle with Sisera, who met his death at the hands of the wife of the sheikh (Judges 4 : 11; 17–22). Later in the history the Rechabites—zealots for the religion of Yahweh—were also assigned to the Kenites (I Chron. 2 : 55).

These scattered indications allow us to conclude that the fundamental fact of the sojourn at Kadesh was the formation of an alliance between Yahweh, Midian, and Israel against hostile neighbours. And who these were can hardly be doubtful. In one of the earliest stages of the wilderness wandering we read of a conflict with Amalek ending with a declaration on the part of Yahweh that he will be at war with this tribe from generation to generation (Ex. 17 : 8–16). Dramatic use of this declaration is made by the writer who tells of the rejection of Saul (I Sam. 15), so that the fact of the enmity is strongly attested. The lasting feud here alleged between Amalek and Israel is explicable if we suppose the object of the alliance between Israel and Midian to have been a war for the possession of the oasis of Kadesh, to which the Amalekites asserted a claim. The fountain of Kadesh is the most copious in all the region and it would evidently be an object of desire to all the desert tribes. We might even suppose that the Kenites had been worsted in an attempt to get possession of the coveted spot and had sought the help of Israel by the mediation of Moses.

While the advantages offered by the new religion were material in their nature, we have no reason to doubt the sincerity of the religious impulse by which Moses himself was moved. In the account of the battle with Amalek he appears as the religious leader, not as the military commander. His position is not unlike that of Mohammed in a later time. And as in certain stages of social development the religious motive is the only one strong enough to produce united action in any community, the whole history becomes intelligible on the supposition that Moses was one of those religious natures to whom the divinity is a present reality. Such a nature in the solitude of the desert, brooding over the wrongs of his countrymen, impressed by the power of the God of the flaming mountain, may well have heard the voice out of the bush commanding him to deliver Israel from bondage. The idea of revelation lies at the basis of all religion, and we have seen how powerful it is down to the present time. It is by revelation of himself, or, as earlier thinkers expressed it, by revelation of his *name*, that a divinity showed his friendliness to man. For it is only when one knows the name of the divinity that he can effectively call him to his aid. A certain reluctance to reveal his name is, indeed, ascribed to the divinity in some Old Testament stories, as though he were afraid of thus placing himself in the power of man. The wrestler with Jacob in his night experience refuses his name; the superhuman being who speaks to Manoah says that his name is wonderful, that is, that it is a mystery which should not be made known to men. But these are exceptional cases. Yahweh's affection for Moses is shown by his full revelation of his name and by his frequent appearances to him, in which he speaks with him face to face as a man talks to his friend. And that this friendliness is extended to Israel of the later time is indicated by the declaration of the earliest legislative code: "In every place where I make my name known I will come to thee and bless thee" (Ex. 20 : 24). The same text shows that the friendly relation was to be recognised on the part of man by his building of an altar and bringing his offerings to the God, thus graciously revealing himself.

If our attempt to find the earliest tradition is successful, we see that Moses was actually the founder of the Yahweh religion for Israel. From this time the people never altogether lost sight of the fact that in some sense Yahweh was their God and that he had a unique claim to their allegiance. What Yahweh was as God of the Kenites or of Midian is not known to us. The theophany at Sinai suggests that he was God of one of the volcanoes which within historic times have been active along the east shore of the Red Sea. In the consciousness of the people he was the God of Sinai or Horeb long after the settlement in Canaan. The pillar of smoke and fire which some of the documents assert to have led the people in their exodus, and afterward in their wanderings, is a reflection of volcanic phenomena. Since there are no volcanoes in the Sinaitic peninsula, it is clear that the tradition which connects the giving of the Law with one of the peaks in this region is without foundation. The tradition is, in fact, of Christian origin. Whether a volcanic tidal wave was not connected in some way with the passages of the Red Sea it is useless now to inquire.

The priest and the prophet (and Moses appears in both characters, as we have seen) must be a wonder-worker if he is to command the allegiance of his people. Moses doubtless appeared to his contemporaries as a man possessed of supernatural power. The rod which he carried was the visible organ of this power. By it he wrought the plagues in Egypt and by it he parted the sea so that the people passed through. In the battle with Amalek he lays a spell on the enemy by holding up the rod (Ex. 17 : 8–13). With this rod he smites the rock and the water gushes forth. Whatever the historical fact behind these narratives, we have no reason to impugn Moses' good faith. He himself must have supposed that he could do wonders, and without powers apparently supernatural he could not have enforced his authority on a half-savage people. How powerful is the belief in the ability of the diviner to work weal or woe is well illustrated by the story of Balaam, whose curse was invoked in order that Israel might be destroyed. The account implies that the curse would have had the desired effect had not Yahweh turned it into a blessing. Deborah, the prophetess, owed her influence over the tribes to the belief that her song had magic power and would throw the ranks of the enemy into confusion. Comparison with these characters shows the nature of the influence which Moses was able to acquire and which he used so as to give his people a new impulse. Making all allowance for the exaggerations of later tradition, the work of Moses seems intelligible and the substratum of the narrative has probability in its favour.

It remains to inquire in what respect the religion introduced by Moses was an advance on that which he found already in existence. Our first impulse is to seek a reply from the name Yahweh, the name by which the divinity made himself known. The account itself lays stress on the meaning of the name and has naturally called forth much speculation. Unfortunately, the recorded reflections on the meaning of the name are of much later date than the name itself, later even than the time of Moses. The meaning *I am that I am*, which has become part of the Christian tradition, does not adequately render the Hebrew original. Such a phrase is much too abstract for Moses' day, and if the people had apprehended this as the meaning of the name they would have had little interest in it. What they wanted was a god who would give them help in a given exigency —some assurance of his sympathy and of his power would meet their need. Such assurance was given them, but not by any definition of the divine name. The Hebrew phrase we are considering would perhaps be more adequately rendered: "I will be what I will to be." It would then indicate that Yahweh is the self-determining one, the one who has mercy on whom he will. But such a revelation would have been superfluous to the Israelites, for it would not occur to them to doubt the freedom of the divinity to act according to his own good pleasure. This text, then, is of no use for our present purpose.

It is unnecessary to recount all the speculations of later scholars on this head. They will appeal with different force to different minds. No one of them seems to have occurred to the Hebrew writers, and no Old Testament allusion can be quoted in their favour. Only one of them need be mentioned. This is the one which derives the name from a verb meaning to cast down. Yahweh would then be the one who casts down his weapons—the lightnings or the thunderbolts or the stones thrown up by the volcano. A certain force is given this conjecture by the fact that Yahweh in many passages appears as the God of the storm. Volcanic phenomena, such as are indicated in the accounts of the sacred mountain, would suggest that the divinity of the place was active in the thunder-storm. The connection of mountains and storms is so obvious that we are not surprised to find the God of the storm at home on the mountain top. The case of Zeus is strictly parallel.

The storm god is also a god of war, and that Yahweh appealed to Israel in his character of war-god needs no demonstration. The carrying of the ark into battle is explicable only on this theory, and the exhortation spoken at the beginning of the day's march, "Rise, Yahweh, and let thine enemies be scattered and let them that hate thee flee before thee," is significant enough. The belief that even after the settlement in Canaan Yahweh had his home on one of the southern mountains, whence he came to the help of his people in their conflicts, is dramatically set forth in the Song of Deborah:

> "Yahweh, as thou camest forth from Seir,
> Marchedst from the field of Edom,
> The earth trembled, the heavens dropped,
> The clouds dropped down water;
> Mountains shook before Yahweh,
> Before Yahweh, Israel's God."

There is no reason to doubt that the poet meant this to be taken literally. In later stanzas of the same poem we read that the stars from their paths fought against Sisera and that the river Kishon swept away the slain Canaanite warriors. What actually occurred was a cloudburst in which the people saw the direct intervention of the storm god on their behalf. It is probable that the title Yahweh Zebaoth (*Yahweh of Armies*) expresses the same faith—that the celestial powers are under the command of Israel's God and that he marshals them for the help of his people in battle. Another poem of early date describes the theophany at Sinai in similar terms:

> "Yahweh, who came from Sinai,
> And rose upon his people from Seir,
> Shone forth from Mount Paran,
> And appeared at Meribath-Kadesh:
> The people of Jacob became his possession;
> He became king in Jeshurun."
>
> (Deut. 33 : 2–5).[1]

[1] Sinai is read in the present text of the Song of Deborah (Judges 5 : 5), but is apparently not original there. The text of Deut. 33 is

Yahweh appears as God of the storm in other passages, also, as where he throws down hailstones on the Canaanites (Joshua 10 : 11), and where, in answer to Samuel's prayer he sends thunder and rain (I Sam. 12 : 17*f*.). Even in the latest period Yahweh appears as God of the thunderstorm whose voice shakes the forest (Psalm 29).

On the basis of the accounts which have come down to us, critically treated, it seems fair to say, then, that Moses was the founder of the particular religion of Israel. Himself religiously impressed by the phenomena of the mountain region in which he sojourned, and able to interpret the experiences of his people from this point of view, he aroused in them a faith that the God whom he had met in the desert had chosen Israel as his special charge. As God of the storm he was able to fight on their behalf against their enemies, and his willingness to do this was indicated by the covenant into which he entered. The promise he gave in this covenant was that he would lead them into Canaan. In the texts now in our hands the promised presence is described in various ways. At one time it is said that an angel will accompany the people; in another the Face of Yahweh is spoken of. Moses is dissatisfied with the promise of the angel and will content himself with nothing less than the Presence of Yahweh in person.[1] The promise of the Presence is confirmed and the faith of the people strengthened by the material symbol of the ark. For the ark a tent was provided, in which Yahweh appeared and gave revelations to his servant.

There is no evidence that Moses wished to abolish the worship of the minor divinities, the clan and family gods, which were already naturalised among the people. The demand that Yahweh alone should be worshipped belongs in the later period. The conflict with the Baal religion, which

not free from suspicion, but what is given above has probability in its favour.

[1] The angel in whom the Name dwells can hardly be distinguished from Yahweh himself (Ex. 23 : 21), but the entreaty for the Presence (Face) seems to indicate that the latter is superior (33 : 2, 14).

is set forth in the story of the golden calf, is also of later date. Yet the impression must have been made on the people that Yahweh is the superior divinity, to whom the first devotion must be paid. The covenant between Yahweh and the clans was also a covenant between the clans themselves; and by this union of discordant elements, and by the common devotion to Yahweh, not only was the sense of nationality awakened, but the basis was laid for future progress. And it is probably true, as has been urged by others, that there was a valuable ethical element in the thought that Yahweh and Israel were united not by nature but by an act of free choice. The god of the fathers might have been supposed to be by nature bound so closely to the descendants that he was compelled to take their part, whatever their behaviour to him. But when the people reminded themselves that there was an act of free choice on Yahweh's part, they realised more distinctly that they were under obligation to live up to the covenant. The germ of the prophetical appeal for righteousness may be found here. The point of view is given by one of the late writers in the words: "Now therefore if you will obey my voice indeed and keep my covenant you shall be my possession from among all peoples—for all the earth is mine—and you shall be unto me a kingdom of priests and a consecrated nation" (Ex. 19 : 5 *f.*). Moses would not have used words of such sweeping import, but he had in germ the idea which here finds such full expression.

We have already had occasion to notice that the local divinities were made parties to oaths and agreements between men. In several cases it is evident that Yahweh showed his ethical character by holding men to their engagements. The most conspicuous instance is that of the Gibeonites who suffered through Saul's zeal for Israel (II Sam. 21 : 1–14). The strong predilection of Yahweh for his own people seems to have suggested to the king that his transgression of the ancient covenant would be condoned just because it was motived by zeal for Israel and therefore for Yahweh. But the sequel impressed upon the people the idea that Yahweh is a God of righteous judgment. This same idea must have been fostered by Moses' use of the oracle to settle disputes among his people. A good while after Moses' time it was customary to bring a man suspected of breach of trust to the sanctuary and there test him by some sort of ordeal or by an oath of purgation (Ex. 22 : 7–11). The tradition that Moses referred the cases brought before him to the decision of God indicates that this was ancient custom. It probably indicates also that Moses himself was a righteous man, for he could not have retained his hold on the confidence of the people if he had not administered the oracle according to justice.

It would be too much to say that from our point of view the Yahweh of Moses' time had a perfect moral character. That he was a thorough partisan so far as Israel's relations to other peoples was concerned is shown by his taking part in the wars. The enemies of Israel were also the enemies of Yahweh. Even within the bounds of Israel itself he might have his favourites. If his action seemed arbitrary no one could call him to account, and he had full freedom to act according to his good pleasure.

Although the founder of the religion of Israel, Moses was not in our sense of the word a monotheist. Probably he never considered the question whether there was one God for the whole universe. The problems which confronted him were practical problems, and for the solution of these it was enough to say that Yahweh was powerful enough to secure Israel in possession of all that he had promised them. Sufficient to that day was the faith that Yahweh was a God of war and that Israel was his special care. Except that he was more powerful, he did not differ essentially from Chemosh of Moab, who also delighted in the slaughter of his enemies, who were the enemies of his people as well. Like Moab, Israel devoted its enemies to destruction, and Yahweh insisted on the carrying out of the vow, as we see from the case of Agag. The consecration of warriors by a special service when going on a campaign was customary in Israel as among her neighbours. In these respects the religion of Moses was crude and cruel like the other religions of the time. But the religion of Moses had in it the promise of development which cannot be truly asserted of these others. How the development came about we have now to see.

CHAPTER IV

THE TRANSITION

FROM about 1200 B. C. until the time of David the Israelites were making their way into Canaan. Tradition is no doubt correct in representing the conquest of the country east of the Jordan as first accomplished, though it is wrong in making the occupation the result of a single battle, or rather of two battles. East of the Jordan the people were always half nomads, so that amalgamation with the earlier inhabitants, or gradual absorption of them, was easier here than across the river. The impression made by our narratives is to the effect that for centuries the land of Gilead retained much of primitive Israelite life and manners. It is for this reason, perhaps, that Ishbaal and David found a refuge in Mahanaim when hard pressed by enemies in Canaan—the tie of blood, so strong among the nomads, was here in full force as in the old desert days. But the political centre of the country was west of the Jordan, and our sources tell us little of the religion and manners of the transjordanic region.

In Canaan proper, at the time of the invasion, the agricultural life was fully established except in the country bordering on the Dead Sea, and the change brought about by amalgamation with the earlier inhabitants was marked—though perhaps not so marked as we are accustomed to think. Israelites and Canaanites were of the same blood and spoke the same language. The later biblical writers preferred to disguise this fact, making Canaan the son of Ham while Israel was derived from Shem. But there can be no doubt from the evidence in our hands that the two peoples were closely related. Their customs were very similar; their names for God (except that of Yahweh) were the same; intermarriage was early tolerated. The main difference was the one already mentioned—the Canaanites were agriculturists and lived in walled towns. Since it was difficult for the nomads to reduce fortified places, the process, which is usually thought of as a conquest, was really an amalgamation in which the superior vigour of the Israelite stock asserted itself, making an Israelite nation out of the combined elements. The Israelite authors are conscious that amalgamation has taken place, for the more rigid of them allege intermarriage with the Canaanites as the reason for all the misfortunes which befell the people. Indirectly they testify to the same thing when they make certain tribes sons of Jacob by slave girls. The names of at least two of the tribes (Gad and Asher) point in the same direction, for they are the names of Syrian divinities. Judah marries a Canaanitess—that is, the tribe of Judah was made up from the two separate races. In the testament of Jacob Issachar is under task-work (Gen. 49 : 15). This means that the Israelite tribe is the inferior part of the composite community. A commentary on the statement is given by the earliest account of the conquest (Judges 1), in which the author tells us frankly that in most of the cities the Canaanites were too strong to be dispossessed and that they and the Israelites dwelt together, sometimes one element being the predominant one, sometimes the other. The most that the Israelites could do in the majority of cases was to reduce the older inhabitants to the position of serfs, and this was not done until the time of Solomon.

The religion of the Canaanites was not very different from that of their nomad neighbours. There was, therefore, no violent break when the immigrants adopted the sacred places of the country and attributed their foundation to Abraham, Isaac, and Jacob. These sacred places were on the hilltops and under the evergreen trees, and were associated with the local divinities just in the way in which the desert rocks and trees were. When the people of Shechem consecrated Abimelech as prince they did it at the Oak of the Pillar which is in Shechem (Judges 9 : 6). These people were Canaanites, and the *maççeba* at this sacred tree was probably an object of worship before the Israelite invasion. Yet it had now become the dwelling of Yahweh, for one author supposes it set up by Joshua (Joshua 24 : 26), and if by him it must have been sacred to the God of Israel. It is, perhaps, not without significance that the divinity of this city is called El-berith or Baal-berith (Judges 8 : 33; 9 : 4 and 46), for the name means God-of-the-covenant or Lord-of-the-covenant. The name was given to the God because he had become the guardian of the treaty by which the two peoples bound themselves to live together in peace.

The examples of sacred stones, already discussed under the head of nomadic religion, need not again be cited, though the most of them, from the nature of the case, were found on the soil of Canaan. To later writers they were uncongenial, and the effort was made to disguise their original cultic significance and to make of them historic monuments. The stones from which the sanctuary of Gilgal took its names are thus to the writer of the book of Joshua simply memorials of the crossing of the Jordan (Joshua 4 : 3), and the stone Ebenezer appears as a similar monument of an Israelite victory (I Sam. 7 : 12). The sacred stones on Ebal (originally Gerizim, Deut. 27 : 2) are made into stones of record on which the Deuteronomic law is written. But the mention of the altar in the same connection indicates that the place was a sanctuary. Numbers of such simple sanctuaries may have been founded after the Israelites entered the country, for, as we have seen, the earliest law encouraged the erection of altars wherever some extraordinary event indicated the special presence of the divinity. At the close of a day of battle Saul had a great stone set apart as a place of sacrifice, and the account indicates that this king showed his piety by erecting a number of such altars (I Sam. 14 : 35).

Excavation seems to show that the Canaanite sanctuaries

were for the most part open-air spaces with pillars and altars such as are indicated in the Hebrew accounts. But there are indications also that in the more advanced communities the god was represented by a metal image, in which case a building was needed for the protection of the sacred object. The God of Israel had only an ark or a tent, and permanent structures such as we find at Shiloh must have been taken over from the Canaanites. The comparatively late author who ascribes to David the intention to build the temple affirms that Yahweh had sojourned in a tent up to that time (II Sam. 7 : 6). This was true only in a limited sense, for the temple at Shiloh, though probably Canaanite in origin, had been appropriated by Yahweh after the conquest. That it became customary to represent Yahweh by an image is also evident from the narratives, for the later reaction against molten images indicates that the Israelites had yielded to Canaanite influence in this respect.

All that we know of the Canaanites and their kinsmen leads us to believe that they worshipped a multitude of divinities, *genii locorum,* such as we have already discovered among the Hebrews in the nomadic stage. The name most frequently applied to one of these gods was *Baal,* originally not a proper name but an appellative meaning *possessor.* It seems to have been a primitive Semitic word, for in Babylon it was applied to one of the older divinities in the form *Bel,* and afterward it was transferred to the chief god of Babylon, whose proper name was Marduk. In the Old Testament it occurs in the plural to designate the whole group of local divinities, or else with the article showing the consciousness that it was not strictly a proper name. In a number of place-names it shows that the local divinity was regarded as the proprietor of the place. Thus we have Baal-peor, the divinity of the mountain Peor (Num. 25 : 3–5), Baal-hermon, the god of Mount Hermon (Judges 3 : 3), parallel to which is Baal-lebanon in an inscription. Baal-perazim is in our narrative connected with a manifestation of Yahweh (II Sam. 5 : 20). Baal-tamar is evidently the Baal who inhabits a palm-tree (Judges 20 : 33). In some cases the spirit is feminine—something which the later religion of Israel rejected. Thus the Baalath-beer is the Naiad of the well (Joshua 19 : 8; other Baalahs are mentioned in 15 : 9, 11, and 19 : 44). Finally, we have Bamoth-baal and Kirjath-baal, both of which indicate that the Baal is lord or possessor of the heights or of the city (Num. 22 : 41; Joshua 15 : 60).

The conception of the divinity as possessor of a place or district implies private property in land, something unknown to the nomad but essential to the agriculturist. A man cannot cultivate successfully unless he has undisturbed title to his land. This is conspicuously true in the cultivation of those crops for which a considerable part of Canaan was famous—the fig, the olive, and the vine—since these crops require a series of years before they repay the care of the cultivator. Moreover, the success of the farmer depends upon the water supply, and in the border of the desert irrigation is necessary to bring the land into fruitfulness. This labour will not be expended unless the gardener is tolerably certain that he will receive his reward. But the water supply, whether it comes from the sky or from the underground reservoir which wells up in springs and fountains, is evidently given by the gods. Hence the idea of the nomad is that the oasis where the water flows out of the ground and causes a luxuriant vegetation is the garden of God. Private property in land was first ascribed to the divinity, and the agriculturist thought of himself as tenant of this proprietor. The farmer who had subdued the wild land, therefore, held that he owed something to his landlord. His agriculture was interwoven with religious rites designed to conciliate the god, and the first-fruits of the crop were paid to him in recognition of his rights. Not all the Baals were gods of agriculture, but those who most distinctly appealed to the Israelites when they were learning to till the soil must have been those who had it in their power to give or to withhold the harvest. Hosea correctly represents the popular belief when he makes Israel justify her worship of the local Baals by saying: "I will go after my lovers who give me my bread and my water, my wool and my flax, my oil and my drink" (Hosea 2 : 7). It is probable that the larger part of Canaanitish religion consisted in rites designed to propitiate the Baals to whom the soil belonged.

It follows that Baal was not a sun-god. That the sun was worshipped in Palestine is indicated by the place-names Beth-shemesh and En-shemesh. But he was not the god of the cultivator, for the sun in Syria is hostile to the crops rather than favourable to them. Even the Baal-shamem of the Phœnicians (Baal of heaven) seems to have been a sky-god rather than a sun-god. From a sky-god the rain might be expected, and this Baal might be the husbandman's patron divinity. Baal-hamman, whom we meet in Phœnician inscriptions and possibly once in the Hebrew Scriptures (Cant. 8 : 11), is probably not the Baal of the sun, as has sometimes been maintained, but the Baal of the pillar, for the *hammanim* were pillars or obelisks like the *maççeboth.* The translation "sun-images" given in the Revised Version (Lev. 26 : 30; Isaiah 17: 8 ; 27 : 9) is based on conjecture only. What seems clear is that Baal was worshipped as the god of fruitfulness and the giver of the crops. Associated with him was his female counterpart.

We have already found traces of goddesses in some place-names. Parallel with these Palestinian divinities is the Baalah of Gebal who was the chief object of worship in that city. She is called simply the Baalah or Mistress of the city. What her proper name was is not certain, but it is probable that she was one form of a female divinity widely worshipped throughout the Semitic world. This goddess bore the name Ishtar in Babylon, Astarte (Ashtart) in Canaan. Among the Hebrews her name was undoubtedly the same that we meet in Phœnician, though the Hebrew punctuators have vocalised it differently (Ashtoreth, plural Ashtaroth), perhaps to avoid pronouncing a name offensive to them. As to the nature of the divinity there can be no doubt; she was the goddess of animal fruitfulness and therefore of sensual passion. In the Babylonian myth she is represented as having had many lovers upon whom she has brought misfortune. Evidence of her worship in Palestine is given by some place-names, though these are not numerous. Thus we read of an Ashtaroth (Deut. 1 : 4; Joshua 9 : 10) and of a Beeshtera which may be abbreviated from Beth-ashtart (Joshua 21 : 27). East of the Jordan was Asteroth-karnaim, which means Ashtart-of-two-horns (Gen. 14 : 5). Because of the two horns Ashtart has been supposed to be a moon-goddess, but there is no direct evidence to connect her with the moon. Her planetary embodiment in Babylon was the celestial body which we still call Venus, translating the Babylonian name into its Latin equivalent. In accounting for a horned goddess we may suppose that the horns are those of her sacred animal, the cow, or perhaps the ewe. Ashtart was worshipped in one of the chief Philistine towns (I Sam. 31 : 10).

The best evidence of the attraction which Canaanite religion had for Israel is given by the constant protests of Hebrew writers against the Baals and Ashtarts. These protests show that these were generic names for the various local divinities. The proper names of some of them have come down to us. Thus we read of Hadad-Rimmon, the Syrian god of the thunder-storm; of Anath, a Syrian (originally Babylonian) goddess; of Nebo, who undoubtedly came from Babylon; of Dagon, one of the chief gods of the Philistines, but who also had a sanctuary, Beth-dagon, in Israel; and of the sun-god as already mentioned. Whether the horses dedicated to this divinity, which were kept in Jerusalem as late as the reign of Josiah, were originally Canaanite or whether they were Assyrian importations cannot be made out with certainty (II Kings 23 : 11). The cult of the sun and moon and constellations which is mentioned in the same connection (II Kings 23 : 5) and against which the Deuteronomist inveighs (Deut. 4 : 19) may have come in with the Assyrian domination. But enough remains to show that the Israelites did not think of displacing the multitude of divinities which they found in possession of the country when they entered it. What they did at first was to worship these local divinities along with Yahweh, and we may suppose the reaction against this practice is indicated by the command: "Thou shalt not have any other gods *in my presence*." Late writers are reluctant to admit that other gods were actually associated with Yahweh in the same sanctuary, but various hints to the effect that they were are contained in the history of the Jerusalem temple. One class of divinities—the teraphim—was found in the sanctuary of Yahweh from the time of the judges (Judges 17 : 5) down to that of Hosea (Hosea 3 : 4). The fact that Canaanite altars, pillars, and images had been adopted by the Israelites is clearly seen by the Deuteronomist, and this explains his bitterness against the country sanctuaries (Deut. 12 : 2 *f*.).

The association of various gods in the same sanctuary was apparently followed by identifying the several divinities as so many forms of one God. In the case of Yahweh and Baal this was made easy by the fact already noticed that Baal means simply possessor or owner and might be applied to any god. It was inevitable that the Israelites should think of Yahweh as the Lord (Baal) of Israel. In the same way the divinity named Melek (in our text Moloch) would be identified with Yahweh the King (*melek*) of Israel. A god of this name was, as we know, worshipped by the Phœnicians; under the name Milcom he was the chief god of the Ammonites and had a sanctuary at Jerusalem (I Kings 11 : 5–7). His worship among the Israelites is indicated by a number of personal names, for there seems no reason to doubt that as the name Elimelek, among the Phœnicians, indicated the worship of this divinity, so it did among the Hebrews. The notoriety of this god came from the fact that he was worshipped by human sacrifice in the Valley of Hinnom just under the walls of Jerusalem. Jeremiah leaves no doubt in our mind that by the people at large this service was thought to belong to Yahweh, for speaking in the name of Yahweh he says: "And they built the high-places of Baal which are in the Valley of the Son of Hinnom to cause their sons and their daughters to pass through the fire to Melek, which I commanded not, neither came it into my mind" (Jer. 32 : 35). It is impossible to see why Yahweh should protest that this sort of sacrifice had not come into his mind unless the people supposed it to be offered to him. In another passage the prophet speaks of the high places of Baal being built "to burn their sons and their daughters in the fire for burnt offerings to Baal, which I commanded not, neither spoke it, nor did it come into my mind" (19 : 5). The citations make it clear that the people of Jerusalem offered these sacrifices to Yahweh, whom they called both Baal and Melek. With these passages we should combine the prohibitions in Leviticus (18 : 21 and 20 : 2–5) which speak of sacrifices to Melek as defilements of the sanctuary of Yahweh and profanation of his name. They could not effect this defilement unless they were brought into Yahweh's own sanctuary.

The amalgamation of Yahweh with Baal and Melek is probably only one example of a process which went on through a long period. It was, in fact, inevitable that the amalgamation of peoples should bring syncretism in religion. Even where hostility was acute Canaanite families might go over to Israel and be adopted, as is made plain by the story of Rahab (Joshua 6 : 25). The town of Gibeon and its allies secured a treaty which gave them standing in the Israelite commonwealth, and Yahweh protected their rights against the aggressions of Saul (II Sam. 21 : 1–14). This case is particularly instructive because it shows that the divinity worshipped at Gibeon was Yahweh; the transgressors of the covenant were impaled before the Yahweh of Gibeon. The Gibeonite sanctuary became in fact one of the most prominent of those dedicated to the God of Israel, for in the time of Solomon it was "the great high place" (I Kings 3 : 4). Intermarriage between Israelites and Canaanites was common. A certain amount of preference for marriage within the clan is indicated by the patriarchal stories, but the very mild protest of Samson's father against his son's proposal to take a Philistine wife shows that the opposition cannot have been very intense (Judges 14 : 1–3). Gideon married a Canaanitess. In fact, it was only in the time of Deuteronomy that the prohibition was uttered: "Thou shalt not give thy daughter to his son, nor take his daughter to thy son; for this will turn away thy sons from following me" (Deut. 7 : 3).

To the strict worshipper of Yahweh there was a real danger in such alliances, for the religion of the women of the family is pretty certain to be instilled into the children. It is probable also that the rites which were supposed to secure fruitfulness were practised by the women, and the newcomers, in learning agriculture, would feel it necessary to adopt these rites. If, as we have supposed, the clan and family gods were worshipped along with Yahweh there could be no effective protest against the adoption of the Baals and Ashtarts. These were at least gods near at hand, while Yahweh's proper home was the desert. Nor must we underestimate the influence exerted by the more ornate ritual which was performed at the Canaanite sanctuaries. The essence of the agricultural festivals was eating and drinking and rejoicing before the god, with music and dancing and in some cases sexual indulgence such as the primitive mind supposes acceptable to the divinities of fruitfulness. Sacred prostitutes were found at the high places, and appeared even in connection with the temple at Jerusalem down to the time of Hezekiah (I Kings 14 : 24; 15 : 12; II Kings 23 : 7). The unbridled licence of the great festivals, so unsparingly denounced by the prophets, was taken over by the religion of Yahweh from that of Baal and Ashtart. Like these divinities, Yahweh was now honoured by gifts of wine and oil—the most valued productions of the agricultural life (Judges 9 : 9 and 13).

In proportion as Israelites and Canaanites became one people Baal and Yahweh would become one God. And since Israel was the more vigorous stock, the composite divinity was called Yahweh. He was doubtless called Baal, also, as is made known by proper names compounded with Baal even in the family of devout worshippers of Yahweh. We need only notice Jerubbaal, one of the heroes identified with Gideon by tradition; Ishbaal, son of Saul (the correct reading has been preserved in I Chron. 8 : 33; elsewhere the scribes have distorted the name to Ishbosheth); Baaliadah, son of David (I Chron. 14 : 7); and Ishbaal, one of the champions in David's army (I Chron. 11 : 11, emended text). Jonathan's son, who appears in most passages as Mephibosheth, was really named Meribbaal (I Chron. 8 : 34; 9 : 40), and we find Baalhanan (I Chron. 27 : 28), and Baaliah (I Chron. 12 : 5). This last name is particularly instructive, for it distinctly affirms that Yahweh is Baal, and there is some evidence that the equivalent name Jobaal was once found in the text (Greek manuscripts of Judges 9 : 26).

In the time of David, then, Yahweh has become identified with the Baal—he is the Baal of Israel, we may say, and the land of Canaan is his land. David complains that his banishment from the cultivated country is banishment from the presence of Yahweh (I Sam. 26 : 19). The older sanctuaries have been adopted by Yahweh. The most conspicuous instance—that of Gibeon—has already been mentioned; but this was not an isolated case, for Gilgal seems to be another, and even the site of the Jerusalem temple may have been determined by the previous worship of the local divinity. The adoption of earlier sacred places by a new religion is one of the commonest phenomena in religious history. The reconsecration of the church of Saint Sophia by the Moslems, and its use as a mosque down to the present day, is a case in point. The great mosque of Damascus was a church before it became a mosque, a temple of Zeus before it became a church, and probably a temple of Rimmon before it was assigned to Zeus.

The biblical narrative seems to have preserved the memory of such a transfer in the story of Gideon and his altar. The narrator represents Gideon receiving a divine command to break down the altar of Baal and erect one to Yahweh on the same spot (Judges 6 : 25–28). Probably the original text stated that the new altar was made of the stones taken from the old. For fuel Gideon used the wood of the asherah. If the narrator means that the altar of Yahweh is erected on the same spot and with the same material as the old, he is far removed from the later abhorrence of Baal-worship; for the later point of view would have been that the spot once devoted to Baal was for ever unclean, and that the stones of the altar as well as the wood of the asherah were an abomination to Yahweh. The historic fact underlying the narrative must have been that the original sanctuary of Baal at Ophrah was taken over by Yahweh.

Though Yahweh was now fully naturalised as god of Canaan and god of agriculture, he did not lose his warlike character. This is shown by the use of the ark in war. In one instance, indeed, this use led to disaster, and the palladium passed into possession of the Philistines. But the sequel showed the superiority of Israel's God. He humiliated Dagon and afflicted the people with a pestilence, so that they were obliged to send the hostile guest back to his own country, sending also a votive offering. The historicity of the account does not here concern us. It shows the popular idea of the superiority of Yahweh. His close association with the ark led David to bring that sacred object to Jerusalem and to carry it with him on his campaigns. Yet the idea persisted that Yahweh retained his home at Horeb, so that Elijah sought him there when in need of special encouragement. Yet Elijah sacrificed at Carmel, just as the people did at the local high places. So close is the association of Yahweh with the soil of Canaan that Naaman begs some of that soil that he may erect a private altar upon it in Damascus (II Kings 5 : 17). The danger that the Yahweh of each locality would be regarded as different from all other Yahwehs was not remote. Solomon would hardly have gone to Gibeon to worship had he not supposed the Yahweh of Gibeon to be more ready to answer prayer than the one at Jerusalem. When Absalom was in exile he vowed a vow to the Yahweh of Hebron, and David found it quite natural that the vow should be paid at that sanctuary (II Sam. 15 : 7*f*.). Whether Absalom's statement was according to fact or whether it was only a pretext makes no difference for our present purpose.

The number of places at which Yahweh was worshipped during the early monarchy is not realised by the casual reader of the Old Testament. We have already had occasion to mention Gibeon, Gilgal, and Ophrah. At Shiloh was a notable sanctuary, in charge of a family of priests, who possibly claimed to descend from Moses. Moses was also claimed as ancestor by the priests of Dan (Judges 18 : 30). At Nob was a sanctuary, in possession of a priestly clan, all the members of which except one were massacred by Saul (I Sam. 22 : 18). Bethel traced its foundation to the patriarch Jacob, and other sacred places were associated with the patriarchs. We may be sure that in this period every village had its high place, located by preference on top of a hill. No objection seems to have been raised to the representation of Yahweh by an image, for Gideon set up an ephod, which was certainly an object of worship, in his native place, making it out of gold taken from the enemy (Judges 8 : 24–28). At Dan was also a molten image captured from its original owner. Images seem, however, not to have been common in the earliest period of the occupation, and it is likely that the Canaanites themselves were usually content with the rude stone pillar, such as the one raised by Jacob at Bethel. A sacred tree was pretty sure to be planted at each altar, as we have discovered. With the tree, or perhaps in some cases a substitute for it, was a wooden pole or post—the asherah, whose origin and significance are obscure.

The hostility of the Deuteronomist to both pillars and

asherahs indicates that in his opinion they were idolatrous. That the pillar was regarded as the residence of the god has been made sufficiently clear. Whether the asherah was dedicated to Ashtart, as has sometimes been supposed, whether it was the impersonation of a goddess Asherah of which we have some evidence, or whether it was, like the pillar (*maççeba*), dedicated to Yahweh himself, is still undetermined. Poles or posts seem to have been dedicated to various divinities among the Assyrians and Babylonians, and, as we read of prophets and sacred vessels of Asherah (or of the asherah) among the Hebrews (I Kings 18 : 19; II Kings 23 : 4), the idolatrous nature of the object can hardly be doubted.

The earliest form of worship was apparently the presentation of a gift, the material of which was applied directly to the sacred stone. Thus Jacob poured oil upon the pillar at Bethel (Gen. 28 : 18). Libations were poured on the altar down to the latest times—usually of wine which rejoiced God as well as man. The idea was the primitive one that the divinity residing in the stone absorbed the food or drink. In the case of animal offerings the earliest method was to pour the blood on the sacred stone, and this was done in Israel even when the use of fire became customary. In the account of the sacrifice of Isaac we read that the boy was bound and laid on the wood, before the act of slaying. The evident purpose was that the blood of the victim should flow directly upon the stone. In the account of Gideon's sacrifice it is said that he brought out his gift and laid it upon the stone, then the angel touched the flesh, and fire burst from the rock and consumed the offering (Judges 6 : 21). This is a poetic way of describing the transition from fireless offerings to those burnt on the altar. Originally the food was simply laid upon the sacred stone. At a later time it was sublimated by fire and the divinity partook of it in the form of a sweet-smelling savour.

A separate order of priests was not necessary to this sort of worship. Any man could sacrifice, though it would be the father of the family who would usually officiate. When Moses made a solemn covenant the sacrifice was performed by the young men of the clans (Ex. 24 : 5). Where there was a sacred object of value, however, it would be necessary to have a guardian for it. Thus at Shiloh the ark was in the keeping of Eli and his sons, and Samuel, the attendant, slept in the sanctuary (I Sam. 3 : 3). When Micah made an image he secured a priest to guard it. In proportion as a sanctuary became a place of resort it would devolve upon the priest to keep order among the worshippers and see that the service was rightly performed. It was in order to do this that Eli sat at the gate of the temple. The reproach directed against his sons is to the effect that instead of looking to the orderly performance of the service they thought only of their own advantage (I Sam. 2 : 12–17). Hosea's complaint against the tyranny of the priests (Hosea 5 : 1) receives light from this passage.

The primary office of the priest was not to offer the sacrifices but to attend to the oracle. Saul and David take a priest on their campaigns that they may know the will of the divinity. This will is revealed by means of the ephod, whose nature and working are still obscure. It is clear, however, that the use of this implement was an art which required special knowledge and training. The man who had this special knowledge was called a Levite. Keeping this in mind we understand the self-gratulation of Micah on having a Levite for his priest. This particular Levite traced his descent to Moses, and Moses, as we have seen, was primarily the minister of the oracle at Kadesh. While we are led to suppose that there was a tribe of Levi in early days—which in some obscure way was nearly exterminated—the Levites in historic times are rather a guild than a clan. The poem ascribed to Moses intimates, as does the account of the golden calf, that the members of this guild had disregarded the ordinary ties of kindred in order to devote themselves to the worship of Yahweh (Deut. 33 : 9). For this devotion they are rewarded by the gift of the Urim and Thummim, the implements of the oracle (probably used in connection with the ephod). The priesthood, however, was not strictly limited to the guild of Levites, for the people of Kirjath-jearim consecrated one of their own number to have charge of the ark (I Sam. 7 : 1), and David appointed Zadok, a man apparently not of priestly descent, and also made priests of some of his own sons as well as a certain Ira the Jairite (II Sam. 8 : 18; 20 : 25).

With the increasing magnificence of the court after the building of the temple, the Jerusalem priests enjoyed larger emoluments and greater prestige. In order that these royal officers should be relieved of the menial parts of the service it became the custom for the kings to present slaves to the sanctuary. Ezekiel seems to have been the first to protest against this custom, on the ground that the persons thus brought into the sacred place were not duly consecrated. Certain experiences of the priests themselves led them to emphasise this matter of consecration. Thus one Uzzah was smitten with death because he took rash hold of the ark (II Sam. 6 : 7). Although the details of the process escape us we must suppose that there was a gradually increasing stringency in drawing the line between the sacred and the profane, until in the exile it was resolved not to allow any but duly consecrated persons to enter the sanctuary.

Priests, however, were not the only persons who in the earlier period enjoyed the special favour of the divinity. Special gifts of sight were granted to some men, and those who received them were called seers. Such a man was supposed to tell where lost articles could be found. Samuel not only satisfied Saul about the lost asses, but also informed him of the divine purpose to make him king. It is probable that Samuel blessed the sacrifice for his townsmen not because he was priest but on the general ground that he was in special relations with Yahweh as his seer (I Sam. 9 : 5–13). The seer's divine equipment was sufficiently defined in his title of "man of God." Because of his special relation to the divinity he was able effectively to bless or to curse. Among the Arabs at the present day certain men are believed to have the same power. They are sought after to recover articles lost or stolen, to detect the thief, and to heal the sick.[1] The title of seer fell into disuse in later times, and the Old Testament writer who gives us the account of Samuel supposes that the seer and the prophet were the same (I Sam. 9 : 9). But the prophet was, at least in the earlier period, distinguished by his abnormal enthusiasm and also by his associating himself with others of like temperament in a religious society (I Sam. 10 : 5–16; 19 : 18–20). This enthusiasm was contagious and infected the bystanders who thereupon joined in the religious exercises of the band (music and dancing), even becoming so frenzied as to fall down in a cataleptic fit.

The reputation of madmen given the prophets by the people (II Kings 9 : 11) is explicable on the ground of these extravagant manifestations. Madness was thought to be possession by a spirit or demon, and it is possible that in the earlier days the prophet (*nabi*) was so called because possessed by the divinity of revelation, the Babylonian Nebo. In the period of which we have record the Hebrews attributed the possession to the spirit of Yahweh. The spirit was the organ by which the God of Horeb was able to work at a distance. While at great national crises the divinity himself came on the thunder-cloud to help his people, his influence on individuals was by means of the spirit. Thus the spirit "clothed itself" with Gideon and drove him to his heroic deed (Judges 6 : 34); it impelled Othniel (3 : 10), and afterward stirred or rushed upon Samson and Saul (Judges 15 : 14; 14 : 6; 13 : 25; I Sam. 11 : 6). The spirit might be a spirit of evil in that it wrought evil to men. Yahweh sent a spirit of evil between Abimelech and his subjects, whose mission was to stir up strife and thus avenge the brothers whom Abimelech had slain (Judges 9 : 22 *f*.).

The best illustration of this belief is found in Saul the

[1] Jaussen, *Coutumes des Arabes*, p. 386.

King. If we may interpret the account according to our lights we shall conclude that the unfortunate man was afflicted with melancholia, becoming at times acute mania. The popular explanation would be that he was possessed by a demon, as the Arabs at the present day call an insane man *majnûn*, that, is possessed by a *jinnee*. The piety of the Hebrew writers, which ascribed all that takes place to the direct action of Yahweh, saw the cause of the phenomenon in a spirit sent by Yahweh, an evil spirit only in so far as it was an instrument of harm to Saul (I Sam. 16 : 14*f.*). In another passage we read that Yahweh did not hesitate to deceive men by the spirit, which in this case was allowed to become a lying spirit in the mouth of the prophets in order to lure Ahab to his death (I Kings 22 : 21–23). Since, according to this representation, the spirit assumes a distinct personality we may call him an angel. But in most cases he seems more like an effluence from Yahweh than a person distinct from him. Our authors did not take pains to define their idea more exactly. What now interests us is that this theory of the spirit may well have been Canaanitish as well as Israelite, for the phenomena of prophetism seem to be the same in both religions.

The result of the process we have been studying was to amalgamate the religion of Israel and the religion of Canaan. But from the beginning the process met with something of protest. The complex civilisation of the cultivated country involved evils against which the more thoughtful of the desert-dwellers revolted. Evidence of this is given by the institution called the Nazirate. The only early example is that of Samson, and in his case the historicity of the account is not above suspicion. As we now read it, the hero's mother was, during her pregnancy, to eat nothing that came from the vine, to drink no wine or fermented drink, and was to avoid all that was ritually unclean. The purpose was to devote the child to this sort of abstinence during his prenatal life. He himself followed the same course and in sign of his devotion he let his hair grow long.

Similar abstinence is narrated of Jonadab ben Rechab, of whom we read that he enjoined upon his clan not to eat anything that came from the vine, not to build permanent houses, and not to engage in the cultivation of the soil (Jer. 35 : 6–10). The reason for this strict rule was opposition to the agricultural life and devotion to the simpler manners of the desert. Since the Rechabites were Kenites, that is, original worshippers of Yahweh, their devotion to the ancestral mode of life was really devotion to the ancestral God. In the time of Jehu they were known to be members of the strict Yahweh party and opposed to the Baal of Jezebel and her family (II Kings 10 : 15–17). The later legislation allows Nazirites to consecrate themselves for short periods of time, but in the case of Samson the vow is assumed to be lifelong.

The only explanation of the phenomena is to recognise the fact that to the strictest worshippers of Yahweh the vine was taboo, and this was because it was sacred to the Baal of the cultivator. This Baal, then, was felt to be hostile or at least uncongenial to Yahweh. The rigorists who took Yahweh seriously could not adopt the cultivation of the soil, since this was under the patronage of the Baals. The opposition was heightened by the Philistine oppression when Israel was rallied against its enemies by leaders who invoked the help of Yahweh. The history of the period is unfortunately obscure, but the appearance of the enthusiastic prophets, and the Nazirate of Samson, possibly also of Samuel, indicate a revival of devotion to the national God. Saul himself, the leader of the revolution, seems to have received his impulse from Samuel, and his zeal for Yahweh, though a zeal not according to knowledge, was manifested by his attempt to exterminate the Gibeonites because they were not of Israelite blood. That the national movement was a religious movement is indicated by the title "Anointed of Yahweh" given to Saul and afterward to David, for unction was a distinct rite of consecration, as we see from the story of Jacob at Bethel. David's reluctance to lay hands on the "Anointed of Yahweh" arose from the fact that such an act would be sacrilege. The sacred character of the act of anointing is made evident also by the sanctity of the person by whom the act was performed (prophet or priest), by the place where it was performed (usually a sanctuary), and by the oil itself which was taken from the sanctuary.

The conflicts in which Israel engaged in the first period of the monarchy thus served to emphasise the importance of Israel's God, Yahweh. David's devotion was shown by the great political stroke of bringing the ark to Jerusalem. The ark had never been connected with the Baals. It was the leader of Israel in the desert wandering and in subsequent battles. Its installation at Jerusalem was eloquent testimony to the fact that David was devoted to Yahweh and relied upon him to support the throne. This is intelligible when we remember that David's tribe was more nearly related to the Kenites than were those in the northern part of the country, and that they had perhaps assimilated less of the Canaanitish life than had the others. Not that we should think of Yahweh as the God of Judah who was forced upon the other tribes by David, for there is no reason to doubt the tradition which connected the ark with Shiloh, and in the time of David Yahweh was already naturalised at Gibeon.

Nor can we suppose that David was a monotheist. He had the teraphim in his house in his early days, and we hear nothing of his attempting to abolish the Canaanitish sanctuaries in any part of the kingdom. The most that can be asserted with safety is that by the establishment of a regular cultus at Jerusalem, under the direct protection of the royal house, Yahweh was given a certain pre-eminence over the local divinities. Yahweh, in the language of Jethro, was acknowledged to be the greatest of the gods. Even this pre-eminence seemed to be endangered in the time of Solomon, for this king prided himself on being cosmopolitan in his tastes and beliefs. Only thus can we account for his building shrines for many divinities in Jerusalem or at least in its immediate vicinity. The present text evidently endeavours to state the matter in the way most favourable to Solomon, but it admits that he erected sanctuaries for Chemosh and Melek on the mount east of Jerusalem, immediately facing the temple, "and so for all his wives who burnt incense and sacrificed to their gods" (I Kings 11 : 4–8). The worship was not confined to the foreign wives and their households, for Solomon himself took part in it. It is not improbable, therefore, that foreign deities were introduced into the temple itself. Phœnician models seem to have been followed by the artisans who erected this building, and the mythological imagery would certainly have polytheistic suggestions for the worshipper. The two brazen pillars in front of the building might be regarded as *maççeboth*, such as were found at every sanctuary of Yahweh in this period. But they were paralleled by the two pillars which stood at the entrance of the sanctuary of Melkart, in Tyre, and by the two in the temple of the Syrian goddess at Hierapolis. They would naturally be associated in the minds of the people at large with Baal rather than with Yahweh, and the fact that they received proper names would imply that they were embodiments of separate divinities.[1]

Attendant divinities are the cherubim which embellished the inner sanctuary and protected the ark with their overshadowing wings. From Ezekiel we know that these were composite animal figures like the winged bulls and lions of Babylon and the sphinx of Egypt. The Yahwist makes them the guardians of the Garden from which the first man was expelled (Gen. 3 : 24), and Ezekiel also stations them in paradise (Ezek. 28 : 14, 16). They are, therefore, mythological figures, and to this extent inconsistent with a strict monotheism such as we attribute to the Hebrews. Further we find in the temple court the great sea, which is something

[1] Their names, Jakin and Boaz, are not yet satisfactorily explained and have perhaps been changed so as to disguise their original significance.

more than a reservoir for the use of the priests. Its twelve bulls represent the twelve signs of the zodiac, and the sea itself is a symbol of the celestial store of waters from which come the rains.

Consideration of all the phenomena, then, seems to authorise us in saying that in Solomon's temple we have a picture of the amalgamation of elements from various sources. The chief divinity was Yahweh, but he was confused with the Canaanite Baal and was attended by minor divinities imported from Phœnicia, Syria, Babylon, and Egypt. Moreover, the temple probably stood upon the spot made sacred by the earlier inhabitants, for the original native rock, the summit of the hill on which the fortress was built, would be the spot at which the Jebusites worshipped the local deity. Of jealousy on the part of Yahweh we have as yet no trace.

The division of the kingdom made no difference in the religious beliefs and customs of the people. In the northern kingdom the monarchs were devoted to the God of Israel and fostered his worship at the two great sanctuaries of Bethel and Dan. Bethel was of venerable antiquity, its foundation being attributed to Jacob. Dan was of more questionable origin, having been founded by the tribe of Dan when they captured the city and furnished by them with an image taken by violence from its owner. Probably the site in each case was sacred before the Israelite occupation, the one at Dan being located at a copious fountain, the one at Bethel showing a curious rock formation such as the imagination attributes to the activity of the gods.[1] Both these sanctuaries were redecorated by Jeroboam I and furnished with golden bulls as objects of worship. The account makes it clear that the king had no idea of introducing new gods, for he expressly says that this is the God who led Israel out of Egypt (I Kings 12 : 28).

[1] A description of the site is given by Peters, in *Studies in the History of Religion*, dedicated to Crawford Howell Toy (New York, 1912), pp. 239 *f.*

Yahweh was already worshipped, then, under the image of a bull, and, in fact, this is clear from the account in Exodus, which condemns the usage, for the significant thing in that account is that the bull (calf it is called in contempt) was made by Aaron, the father of the legitimate priesthood (Ex. 32 : 2–4).

At the same time this worship of the bull is the plainest evidence of the syncretism which we are discussing. For it is evident that the nomads, who had only sheep and goats, would not think of paying homage to the bull. This animal, on the other hand, is so necessary to the husbandman that its worship in an agricultural community is inevitably a part of agricultural religion. The introduction of a bull god from Egypt is not probable, for we know that Egyptian influence is not traceable in the early religion of Israel. On the other hand, there is evidence that Adad, the storm god of Syria, was represented riding on a bull. As Yahweh, like Adad, was a storm god, it would be easy to transfer to him the attributes of Adad. Moreover, recent excavations at Samaria have brought to light the proper name Egelyo, meaning Calf-of-Yahweh,[1] parallel to the Palmyrene Egelbol, Calf-of-Baal. Other traces of bull-worship in Canaan and Syria have been found, and it is well known that the chief god of Heliopolis (Baalbek) was a bull god.[2] The evidence seems sufficient to justify the conclusion that the identification of Yahweh with the bull was the result of his fusion with Baal.

It was nearly a hundred years after this union of Yahweh with the Canaanite god that the reaction became acute. Even then the reaction was not directed against the Canaanite Baal but against a new divinity. Ahab had married a Phœnician princess and thus allied himself closely with the Phœnician court. Jezebel doubtless thought the civi-

[1] Lidsbarski, *Ephemeris*, III, pp. 153 *f.*; *cf.* König, *Geschichte der Alttestamentlichen Religion*, p. 210.

[2] Gressmann, *Altorientalische Texte und Bilder zum Alten Testamente* (1909), II, p. 76.

lisation of her own country superior to that of the Israelite peasants, and introduced her religion, with the manners of her father's court, into Samaria. Her own god was the Baal of Tyre, whose proper title was Melkart, and to him a sanctuary was erected at the Israelite capital; and here, we may suppose, Ahab himself was polite enough to pay occasional reverence. The opposition of the people was called out not by the new rites but by new methods of administration. The old Israelite legal precedents were disregarded by the foreign woman, for she suborned perjury and instigated judicial murder in order to gratify her husband's whim.

The reaction, which was necessarily political as well as religious, was led by Elijah. The legends which have attached themselves to his name do not obscure his character or leave us in any doubt as to the kind of man he was. He was a true child of the desert, native of that transjordanic region where the people retained much of the old nomadic life and thought. He was possessed by the religious passion which makes a man intolerant of any gods but his own and leads him to fierce action where that god's rivals invade his territory. We may attribute to him the first formulation of the statement, so frequent in later times, that Yahweh is a jealous God. It is evident that Elijah had no prejudice against the other gods on their own territory. He went to Sidon, where the very Baal whom he opposed in Israel had his home, and remained quiet under his protection. His theory was evidently that each nation has its own god and that for Israel this God is Yahweh. And to this was added the belief that Yahweh is the protector of the individual Israelite against the aggressions of unscrupulous rulers, and that he is the avenger of blood when blood has been unrighteously shed. The alternative which he set before the people was plain: "If Yahweh be God serve him; if Baal, then serve him!" The disciples of the great prophet were reinforced by the clan of Jonadab ben Rechab, already known as zealots for Yahweh, and the result was the extermination of the house of Omri and the seating of Jehu on the throne.

With the extermination of the party of the Phœnician Baal the attempt to introduce new divinities into Israel seemed to come to an end. But Yahweh continued to unite the attributes of Israel's war-god with those of the Canaanite Baal. The festivals were those of the agricultural life; the sanctuaries continued the old orgiastic worship of Canaan. Morals were on the plane of tribal custom tempered by the decision of the king. The claim of blood-revenge was stronger than the king's peace, as we see from Joab's murder of Abner. The customs of war were barbarous. The Judaites cut off the thumbs and great toes of their captive Adonibezek, as he himself had been accustomed to do with his captives. The foreigner was entitled to no consideration except where a formal treaty had been entered into. The Danites sought for no pretext when they attacked Laish (Judges 18). Rahab betrayed her countrymen and was highly praised for the act (Joshua 6 : 22–25). Assassination was one of the means of ridding the land of a tyrant, and the assassin became a hero (Judges 3). It continued to be the custom to devote a hostile city or tribe to the divinity and to carry out the vow by extermination, and in the belief of the people this was required by Yahweh himself (I Sam. 15).

The evidence of archæology shows that human sacrifice was practised by the Canaanites, and it certainly was not foreign to the Israelites, though whether they adopted it from their predecessors or whether it was a part of the desert religion is not yet clearly made out. That the god Melek was worshipped in this way we have already noticed, and we have noted also the probability that he was in some cases at least merged in Yahweh. But that not all cases of human sacrifice can be laid to the charge of Melek seems evident. The thought of human sacrifice to Yahweh as something grateful to him underlies the story of Jephthah's daughter. The grief of the people narrated in this connection did not at all arise from the thought that such an extraordinary fulfilment of a vow was contrary to the religion of Yahweh but from the fact that a family was extinguished by the death of the virgin. The calamity consisted in this—that neither Jephthah nor his daughter would have any one to pay honour to them after their death. The case of Agag was somewhat different; he was devoted to death by the ban placed on his people by Saul. His death "before Yahweh" was therefore a gratification to the divinity, in that it assured him that the vow had been carried out, but whether the slaying was regarded as a sacrifice is not clear. Probably it was, for the Deuteronomist speaks of the burning of "devoted" property as a whole burnt offering to Yahweh (Deut. 13 : 17). The foundation-sacrifice alluded to in connection with the rebuilding of Jericho (I Kings 16 : 34) may not have been offered to Yahweh. But there is no question that his claim on the first-born was understood to require sacrifice of infants. Ezekiel believed that this had been commanded in the early period: "Moreover I gave them statutes which were not good and ordinances in which they should not live, and I polluted them by their own gifts in that they caused to pass through the fire all that opened the womb, that they might know that I am Yahweh" (Ezek. 20 : 25 *f.*). The prophet believed that the sacrifice was commanded by Yahweh as a punishment of the people. The testimony of Jeremiah on this subject has already been considered, and comparison of the passages shows that the people construed literally the command: "The first-born of thy sons shalt thou give unto me" (Ex. 22 : 28).

The sacrifice of children by other Semites is well attested. The Carthaginians are said to have offered two hundred children from their noblest families when hard pressed by their enemies. The case of Mesha, king of Moab, is parallel. This king, when besieged, sacrificed his first-born son on the wall of the city and thus roused his god to activity so that the besiegers were forced to retreat

(II Kings 3 : 27). Excavation in Palestine has brought to light a great number of infant remains, for the most part those of new-born infants. Their proximity to the altars indicates that they were sacrificed, though not all of them have passed through the fire. The prevalence of the custom in Israel is indicated by the fact that Ahaz, king of Judah, sacrificed his son (II Kings 16 : 3), and Manasseh, who revived the ancient religious customs, included this among them (21 : 6). The story of the sacrifice of Isaac and the acceptance of a ram as substitute for the child (Gen. 22) is therefore a protest against rites actually practised in the time of the writer, that is, in the eighth century B. C.

What becomes clear, as we trace the history of the twelfth, eleventh, and tenth centuries B. C., therefore, is the transformation of Israel's religion under the influence of the agricultural life. The nomads brought with them the rite of circumcision, which they continued to observe, and the festival of the Passover, which was now united with the agricultural observance of unleavened bread. They adopted the harvest festivals of the earlier inhabitants. Local seasons of rejoicing are mentioned at Shiloh (Judges 21), at Bethlehem (I Sam. 20 : 29), and at Shechem (Judges 9 : 27). The enthusiastic exercises of the prophets who raved about the Canaanite altars were adopted by the devotees of Yahweh (I Sam. 10 : 9–12). Sitting under one's own vine and fig-tree, with none to molest or make afraid, became the ideal of the Israelite. The old tribal organisation persisted but was gradually overshadowed by the kingship, which received the divine sanction. Yahweh was worshipped as in some sense the patron deity of Israel, but he often shared his sanctuary with the local Baals or more frequently took on their features. The sanctuaries were the original rock altars of the Canaanites, and at some of them molten images represented the God, though for the most part the object of reverence was the primitive stone pillar. The more ornate ritual of the Canaanites was taken over, marked at certain seasons by lavish indulgence in eating and drinking and by immoral excesses. This was the state of things when the early narratives were composed to which we must now give attention.

CHAPTER V

RELIGION IN THE EARLY LITERATURE

It can hardly be doubted that a considerable literature existed in Israel from the time of Solomon at least. But from that and earlier times only fragments have come down to us. It was apparently in the ninth century that it occurred to religiously minded men to write a connected story of the earlier traditions of their people. Their work has been preserved embedded in the books of the Hebrew canon from Genesis to II Samuel inclusive. Critical analysis restores these early documents to us in the J and E strata of the Pentateuch, and in the hero stories of Judges and Samuel. The religious motive of the authors is evident: they desire to record the evidences of Yahweh's goodness to his people in the past and thus to stir the gratitude and stimulate the fidelity of their contemporaries. The authors sympathised with the prophetic party which, under the lead of Elijah, was strenuous in opposing the innovations of Jezebel. In their opinion the best vindication of Yahweh was the record of his dealings in the past. They therefore embodied in their narratives some of the ancient poems which glorified the God of Israel. By common consent the oldest of these is the Song of Deborah. This is a song of triumph composed to commemorate a signal victory over the Canaanites. The victory is ascribed to the direct intervention of Yahweh who, from his distant home in the south, came on the thunder-cloud to deliver his people. The various tribes are praised or blamed according to the part which they took or refused to take in the conflict. Patriotism and religion are one—to take the part of Israel is to come to the help of Yahweh. The conclusion is a vigorous curse against the enemies of Israel as the enemies of Yahweh: "So let all thine enemies perish, Yahweh! But let them that love thee be as the sun in its strength!" (Judges 5 : 31.)

Similar religious and patriotic faith is revealed by the testament of Jacob (Gen. 49). The author will encourage the tribes by giving them a sense of Yahweh's protecting care or else warn them of the danger of going contrary to his righteous will. The low estate of Simeon and Levi is attributed to their cruelty, upon which Yahweh has visited a penalty. Reuben has lost his birthright because of an act of lawlessness committed by the ancestor of the tribe. On the other hand, the tribes most prosperous are the objects of Yahweh's favour. Joseph is under the direct protection of the God of Bethel, who strengthens him for war and gives him the blessings of fruitfulness: "Blessings of the heaven above, blessings of the depth below, blessings of the breast and of the womb." Here Yahweh is evidently the God of the rains, of the underground reservoir, and of animal fruitfulness. So he appears in the other ancient poem, the one called the Blessing of Moses. In this the felicity of Ephraim is ascribed to Yahweh, to whom is addressed the prayer: "The best that the sun brings forth, and the best that the moon causes to spring up, the treasures of the ancient mountains and the precious things of the eternal hills, the best of the earth and its fulness and the good pleasure of him that dwells in the bush, come upon the head of Joseph and on the crown of the crowned one among his brothers" (Deut. 33 : 14–16). The favour of Yahweh, however, is not extended to Judah, in spite of the fact that the Jerusalem temple is in possession of this tribe, for the author is able only to pray that Yahweh may fight for him and restore him to the unity of the tribes. Yahweh, therefore, is present in the northern kingdom and at the local sanctuaries. Zebulon and Issachar are happy in that they are in possession of sacred places to which they invite the neighbouring clans: "They call peoples to the mountains; there they offer righteous sacrifices" (v. 19). Levi is especially blessed (in sharp contrast to what is said in the older poem) in that he is in full possession of the priesthood: "Thou hast given to Levi thy Thummim, and thy Urim to thy beloved, whom thou didst try at Massah, didst contend with at Meribah; who said of his father: 'I know him not'; he considered not his brothers nor his children; for they obeyed thy commandment, and kept thy instruction; they teach Jacob thy testimonies, and Israel thine oracle; they bring sweet savour to thy nostrils and whole burnt offerings on thine altar."

The tone of this poem and by consequence the tone of the writer who included it in his narrative is in sharp contrast with that which we find a little later in the written prophets. The poem shows an optimistic faith in the God of Israel. This God is not thought of as dwelling in the temple at Jerusalem but manifesting himself at the many sanctuaries of the northern kingdom. The tribe or guild of Levi is not the Jerusalem priesthood but the company of ministers of the high places. Yahweh smiles upon them and upon the nation for whom they minister: "There is none like the God of Jeshurun, who rides on the heavens for thy help, and in his majesty on the clouds. Thy refuge is the eternal God, and underneath are the everlasting arms; he drove the enemy before thee and commanded to destroy them" (vss. 26*f.*).

The poems from which I have cited have been preserved for us by the two Pentateuchal writers whom we have called J and E and by the author who collected the hero stories of the book of Judges. The motive which led to the preservation of the poems moved the writers also in their choice of material from early tradition. Three classes may be distinguished in this material. There is, first, that which makes up the greater part of the book of Genesis and in which the forefathers of the nation are the actors; then the account of the wilderness wandering or the beginnings of the national life; and, finally, the stories of the heroes who secured Israel in possession of the land of Canaan. For the first period the material must have been drawn from folk-lore and, as we shall see, from early mythology. The authors had a much larger material to draw from than they actually put on record, as is seen from some of their briefer notices. For example, we are told how, as Jacob went on his way, the angels of God met him and he said: "This is God's camp; so they call the name of the place Camp" (Mahanaim, Gen. 32 : 2*f.*). This is a reference to the local tradition which accounted for the name of the place; the author might have given it at length, as he did so many others, had he been so minded. In like manner the account of Jacob's purchase of a piece of ground at Shechem (Gen. 33 : 18*f.*), the death of Deborah (35 : 8) and of Rachel (35 : 19), might have been expanded, but the author dismisses them with brief mention. The reason is probably that they did not serve his religious purpose.

In the lives of the patriarchs this religious purpose is twofold. First, the stories set forth the divine guidance of Israel, beginning with the forefathers; secondly, they show these same forefathers as models of piety and obedience. When we come to the wilderness wandering the same thought of divine guidance is prominent, but the people are not models of obedience. Rather they are held up in their frequent unbelief and murmuring as warnings for later generations. In the lives of the heroes again we see the power of Yahweh manifested in giving his people victory and securing them in possession of the land which he had promised to the fathers. It is evident that the writers are not interested in history for its own sake but for its revelation of the power, the love, and the forbearance of Israel's God. The contrast between these narratives and such a piece of plain historical writing as we find in the account of Absalom's rebellion is sufficiently striking to show what I mean.

The Pentateuchal writers take their material from a great variety of sources, and some of it is of great antiquity. Our present knowledge enables us to say that a part of it comes from Babylonia, a part of it bears the marks of the early nomadic or half-nomadic life of the Israelites, another part is the product of the soil of Canaan, and in some cases at least there may be Egyptian influence. A question which has been much mooted of late years is: How much of this material can properly be called mythological? The answer will depend on our definition of myth. If by a myth we understand a story which pictures the processes of nature as actions of anthropomorphic gods, there are no myths in the Old Testament. The story of the twelve labors of Heracles, if it be a poetic representation of the progress of the sun through the twelve signs of the zodiac, is a myth in the proper sense of the word. But it has no parallel in the Hebrew Scriptures. The tendency to discover ancient divinities in the persons of the patriarchs—Joseph a sun-god, Jacob a moon-god—has no warrant in our present text. Even if it could be proved that some of the incidents in the lives of these patriarchs are parallel to some things narrated of the sun-god and the moon-god, we must still recognise the fact that to the writers Joseph was not a divinity of any kind, but a man of Hebrew race whose life was like that of any other man except for the distinct providential guidance which it illustrates. Abraham may have been a local divinity once worshipped at Hebron. In the narratives we are considering he is only the ancestor of Israel, a man of extraordinary piety, no doubt, but still a man.

Except in the early chapters of Genesis (to which we shall return presently) myths do not form any important part of the material with which our authors deal. Legends or sagas, however, are distinctly traceable. A saga is a story which represents a nation or tribe as an individual. The growth of saga in Israel, as among the Arabs, was helped by the fact that the name of a clan or tribe was often used as a collective, that is, as though it were the name of an individual. Thus in the first chapter of Judges, Judah is said to have invited his brother Simeon to come with him into his portion. The narrator is well aware that Judah and Simeon are clans and not men, but the language might lead the reader to think of them as individuals. In many cases therefore when the Hebrew writers used the tribal names, we may be sure that they were aware that they were speaking of the collective body. But in other cases they were not clearly conscious of the historical nucleus which was concealed under the tradition, because the popular imagination had already personified the clans as individuals, and had told their adventures as those of so many ancestral heroes. It was doubtless the universal belief in this period, and indeed until recent times, that the tribes were actually descended from the eponyms whose names they bore. For our present purpose, however, this is not of prime importance. What interests us is not the family history of Abraham, Isaac, and Jacob, but the ideas of the writers of this history.

The lesson that these writers have most at heart is that Israel became the people of Yahweh in the earliest period by a divine act of choice; Yahweh was God of Israel because he was the God of Abraham. Moreover, this God revealed his righteous character by his actions in relation to these ancestors of the people. The pledge of Yahweh gave Israel its title to the land of Canaan. Even when the land was in possession of strangers Yahweh walked with Abraham and Isaac and protected their rights. The plan of God, thus traced back to the earlier period, gave the sort of assurance to believers which later was derived from an abstract theory of the divine election. The transfer of local legends to Yahweh is made in order to emphasise the main lesson. The divinity who appeared to Joshua, originally one of numerous local deities, as we have seen, now appears as the angel warrior who leads Israel's armies against the older inhabitants. The mysterious being who wrestled with Jacob is identified with the God of Israel, for Jacob says: "I have seen God [*Elohim*] face to face." The name of God here used is the one regularly denoting the God of Israel in the document E. The polytheism of these early stories is thus somewhat violently changed to monotheism, or rather to monolatry, for, as we have had occasion to notice, it did not occur to the Hebrews at this stage of their development to deny the existence of other gods than Yahweh. The most interesting case of transfer is the one which relates how the local demon fell upon Moses and would have killed him for intruding upon his territory had not Zipporah rescued her husband. The cruel night demon who thus throttles strangers has little in common with the covenant God who sent Moses to deliver his people, yet the account identifies them, calling the hostile being by the name Yahweh.

It is probable that the authors in adapting these stories to the thought of their own time have made more extensive changes than at first sight appears. The three who appear to Abraham and eat with him may have been three divinities in the early form of the story (Gen. 18). They may even have been the *numina* who inhabited the sacred trees under which Abraham pitched his tent. Other cases where the angel of Yahweh appears seem originally to have spoken of Yahweh himself. The angel who speaks to Hagar was, as we have seen, the spirit who inhabited the well; in the present form of the story he appears as the angel of Yahweh, and at the close of the account we discover that it was Yahweh himself (Gen. 16 : 13). The story of the discovery of Bethel plainly indicates that the divinity dwelt in the sacred stone. But the author of the story in its present form assumes that Yahweh dwells in heaven, and that the spot was sacred because the ladder rested there by which one could ascend to the Presence.

The authors we are discussing, therefore, with all their piety toward the old legends which they preserve for us, mark a distinct advance in religious thought. Although Yahweh is localised in Canaan, yet he is not bound to the soil. He is able to protect Joseph in Egypt; he goes with Jacob in his wanderings and encourages him to go down to Egypt, promising him protection (Gen. 46 : 4). He appears to Abraham in Mesopotamia and calls him to emigrate to a new land. Yahweh therefore is able to act within the jurisdiction of other gods. This is most strikingly brought out in the account of the exodus, where Yahweh enters into a formal conflict with the gods of Egypt and shows himself, as Jethro says, greater than all gods. The narrators did not reflect logically on the omniscience of Yahweh; enough for them that in every emergency Yahweh was able to protect his own. Even the Egyptians are made to recognise that Joseph is inspired by God (Gen. 41 : 32–39), but this, of course, they might do and still believe in their own divinities.

We must expect to find anthropomorphism at this stage of religious thinking. Even the latest of the Pentateuchal writers thinks of Yahweh as existing in human form, for there is no reason to understand the statement that man was made in the image of God and after his likeness in any other than the literal sense. In the older narratives we read of Yahweh's eye, his hand, his mouth, his ears, his lips, his nostrils. A striking passage tells us that after an interview with Moses Yahweh refused to show his glorious form to the prophet, but he added: "When my glory passes by I will put thee in a cleft of the rock and cover thee with my hand until I have passed by; and then I will take away my hand and thou shalt see my back, but my face shall not be seen" (Ex. 33 : 22 *f.*). The allegorists, no doubt, attempt to explain away the meaning of the passage, but its original sense must be plain. Equally human is the passionate nature of the divinity, which comes to view in many passages. His anger burns against his enemies, and he keeps hatred in his heart throughout the generations, as in the feud with Amalek (Ex. 17 : 16). He does not always see the end from the beginning, and has sometimes to repent of what he has done. Seeing the violence of the generation before the deluge, he repented that he had made man upon the earth, and it pained him to the heart (Gen. 6 : 6). Saul's disobedience leads Yahweh to confess to Samuel: "I repent that I made Saul king" (I Sam. 15 : 11).

Even in his dealings with Israel Yahweh has occasion to change his mind. The murmuring of the people causes him to threaten them with destruction, but he yields to Moses' intercession. The plea of Moses is to the effect that the Egyptians will hear what has been done, and will say that Yahweh has not been able to fulfil his promise. It is this very human thought of the damage to his reputation which finally prevails with the divinity (Num. 14 : 13–16). In another passage, where the situation is similar, Moses argues that the Egyptians will say that Yahweh had no purpose of mercy toward Israel, but brought the people into the wilderness on purpose to destroy them (Ex. 32 : 12*f.*). This idea of Yahweh's care for his reputation was entertained as late as the time of Ezekiel. The account in Exodus is significant as showing that Yahweh can be moved by his affection for individual men. It is when Moses offers to be blotted out of Yahweh's book that he finally yields to the entreaty and spares Israel. Elsewhere his mercy is shown for the sake of Abraham, Isaac, and Jacob (Ex. 32 : 13 and 32).

Doubtless the body of Yahweh was conceived of as ethereal, not material like ours. It is a body of luminous matter, a "glory," so that the offerings must be sublimated by fire in order that he may receive the agreeable odor (Gen. 8 : 20–22). He is gratified also by libations of wine and oil, and even to a comparatively late period he was thought to absorb the blood poured upon the altar. That he originally dwelt in the sacred stone we have already remarked, but in the period before us he is gradually dissociating himself from such material objects and taking up his residence in the sky. Thus he *goes up* after speaking to the patriarchs, or if he wishes to see what is going on on the earth he *comes down* to investigate (Gen. 11 : 5, 7, and apparently 18 : 20*f.*). But this point of view is not consistently held.

Certain ethical attributes are predicated of Yahweh, though we shall not be surprised to find the conceptions somewhat defective from our more advanced point of view. Yahweh is first of all faithful to his promises. It is the purpose of these narratives to emphasise this fidelity. Love for the fathers moves him to be gracious to the descendants.

This affection rises or sinks to partiality at times. Pharaoh and Abimelech are rebuked for their attempts upon Sarah, but nothing is said to Abraham concerning his prevarication, which was the occasion of the trespass (Gen. 12 : 10–20 J; 20 : 1–18 E; the same story is told of Isaac, 26 : 6–11 J). The incident is even made of advantage to the patriarch, for each monarch gives him rich presents. The belief in the unwavering favour of Yahweh toward Israel is well brought out in the story of Balaam. Although a foreigner, this seer has power to destroy men by his curse and to give them prosperity by his blessing. Hence the king of Moab sends for him to pronounce a curse on Israel. But Yahweh cannot be induced to curse his chosen people, and the inclination of the seer is overborne so that he utters a blessing:

> "God is not a man that he should lie,
> Nor the son of man that he should repent;
> Shall he promise and not perform?
> Or speak and not keep his word?
> Behold to bless is my mission,
> Therefore I bless and do not hold back.
> Evil is not seen in Jacob,
> Nor guilt in Israel
> Yahweh his God is with him,
> And the shout of a king is his." (Num. 23: 19–21.)

In saying that Yahweh does not repent the author was conscious of no inconsistency though he had said that in some cases Yahweh does actually change his mind. What he is here affirming is the fidelity of Yahweh to his chosen people. And while we may suppose that the election of the nation is an act of free grace, yet at the same time an ethical justification for it is found in the corruption of the older inhabitants. Yahweh's delay in giving Abraham full possession of Canaan is accounted for on the ground that the guilt of these nations is not yet sufficient to require their expulsion (Gen. 15 : 16). The local legend which related the destruction of Sodom is made to teach a lesson concerning moral corruption and its just punishment. It is the fear of God's justice which keeps men from sin. Abraham excuses himself for deceiving Abimelech on the ground that he thought there was no fear of God in the place and consequently no moral restraint. The story shows that even the Philistines were amenable to this motive, and Abimelech pleads his innocence of evil intent as a reason why he should not be punished for his trespass. The gentile, in fact, turns the tables upon Abraham by reproaching him for bringing him into unwitting sin and thus endangering his kingdom by exposing it to the wrath of God (Gen. 20 : 9–11). The most distinct expression of this connection of religion and moral conduct is in the story of Joseph, who refuses the solicitations of his mistress because he will not do a great sin in the sight of God (Gen. 39 : 9).

Even from earlier times Yahweh was the guardian of social custom and the avenger of blood. He watched over oaths, also, and punished their violation. Almost all the Hebrew authors, therefore, account for calamity by supposing it a punishment for sin. The extermination of the house of Ahab, for example, was regarded as a penalty for the sins of this king. This is not to say that the punishment is always fitted to the crime. Yahweh sometimes seems capricious or arbitrary in his dealings with his subjects. When the men of Beth-shemesh rejoiced at the coming of the ark one of their families did not share the joy. Yahweh, in anger at their indifference, smote seventy of their number with death (I Sam. 6 : 19, according to the Greek text). Uzzah, although a consecrated person, was smitten with sudden death because he rashly took hold of the ark, and this with the best of motives[1] (II Sam. 6 : 6 *f.*).

Yahweh's action is, therefore, often unaccountable. David cannot explain Saul's wrath against him except on the ground of a slander uttered by men or of a suspicion in-

[1] In like manner the man who took hold of the Palladium at Ilium was smitten with blindness, though his motive was to save the sacred object from the fire (Reinach, *Cultes, Mythes et Religions*, II, p. 316).

stilled into the king's mind by Yahweh (I Sam. 26 : 19). Yahweh even incites David to commit a sin in order that he may have an excuse for punishing the people (II Sam. 24). He leads Rehoboam to give a foolish answer to the representatives of the tribes in order to punish Solomon in the person of his son (I Kings 12 : 15). But in most cases, as has been said, the motive is distinctly ethical. Thus David's violation of the marriage rights of his subject Uriah is punished because the king has despised Yahweh (II Sam. 12 : 9–13). The calamity of Eli's house came because the priests despised the offerings and thus insulted the divinity (I Sam. 2 : 17; 3 : 13). The line is not clearly drawn between offence against an abstract moral code and personal affronts against the deity. In the case of Pharaoh the hardening of his heart, which is ascribed to Yahweh's direct action, is a means of vindicating the power of Israel's God (Ex. 4 : 21; 10 : 1 J). Samson's love for a Philistine woman is Yahweh's way of humiliating his enemies (Judges 14 : 4). The very partiality thus shown toward the favourites of the God is a reason for appealing to him in time of stress.

As between members of the nation, however, the appeal is made to the justice of Yahweh. "If a man sin against a man God will intervene," says Eli in expostulating with his sons (I Sam. 2 : 25). This is the force of the imprecation: "God do so to me and more also if I do not thus and so." The taker of the oath calls on God to punish in case he is unfaithful, and against the deity, if offended, there is no appeal. "If a man sins against God, who will judge the matter?" says Eli. Cases of what we should call poetic justice are favourite material for these authors. Thus Ahab's son is killed at the vineyard of Naboth (II Kings 9 : 24–26). Joab's guilt comes upon his own head although he is too powerful to be punished by David (I Kings 2 : 32). Adonibezek recognises the justice of God in meting out to him the same suffering which he had inflicted upon his captives (Judges 1 : 7). It is by the decree of Yahweh that Absalom adopts the advice of Hushai and thus brings ruin upon himself (II Sam. 17 : 14). The evil spirit who stirred up strife between Abimelech and the men of Shechem was the instrument by which Yahweh returned the sin of Abimelech on his own head (Judges 9 : 23). David leaves his cause in Yahweh's hand just because he trusts in the righteousness of his God to vindicate him (I Sam. 24 : 13). He even refuses to take vengeance when it is in his power, not only on Saul but afterward on Shimei (II Sam. 16 : 10–12). The fate of Nabal is construed as God's justice acting on behalf of David in a case where the hero had refrained from taking vengeance for himself (I Sam. 25 : 39).

In these examples we have not confined ourselves to the narratives of the Pentateuchal J and E, but have given illustrations from other literature whose point of view is similar. Looking more narrowly at the earlier strata of the Pentateuch we notice first that the Yahwist did not hesitate to make use of material from foreign sources. For it must be clear that his account of the creation and of the deluge are not purely Israelite in origin. The deluge story is known to be Babylonian; the account of the creation (the one contained in Gen. 2 : 4 to 3 : 24) has not yet been traced to a Babylonian source and probably came from Damascus. It presents the primeval chaos, not as a mixture of water and earth such as is indicated in the first chapter of Genesis, but as a desert, an arid plain in which nothing could live for lack of water. On this soil Yahweh first sent a mist to soften it and then planted it with trees pleasant to the eye and good for food. And since a garden in the desert quickly reverts to wilderness unless it has care, man was made to be the gardener. Man, as in a Babylonian document,[1] is made of clay and animated by Yahweh's breath.[2]

It seems clear that our author did not rise to the concep-

[1] The Gilgamesh epic. Parallels are found also among the Egyptians and among the Greeks. Ungnad, *Das Gilgamesh Epos,* pp. 8 and 101.

[2] In one Babylonian myth the kinship of man with the gods is indicated by making Bel cut off his own head and create man by mingling the blood with earth.

tion of creation out of nothing and, indeed, that he did not mean to describe the creation of the universe. The crude material existed before Yahweh laid hand upon it, but it needed his vivifying water before it could be made habitable. The phenomena of the oasis which presents a mass of living green to the eye wearied by the intolerable glare of the desert must have given rise to the story. Where this paradise was located we need not inquire. Since the expulsion of man it is no longer accessible to mortals, though the cherubim show that it is still the garden of Yahweh. Our present interest is to notice the vivid anthropomorphism of the story. Yahweh inhabits the garden and takes his pleasure in walking there in the cool of the day. He is surprised at Adam's hiding himself, and questions him to find out the reason. He threatens man with death on the day in which he eats of the forbidden tree, and then neglects to carry out the threat. Above all, he is jealous of man's aspiring to the rank of a god, or rather he discovers that man has reached that rank and fears that he may aspire further and become immortal. Hence the expulsion from the garden and the stationing of the cherubim to guard the tree of life. This jealousy of the divinity is shown in another story preserved by this author—the story of the tower, according to which Yahweh fears that men will not be restrained from the most lofty ambitions unless extraordinary measures are taken against them (Gen. 11 : 1–9). Parallels in Greek literature will occur to every reader.

Although this author shows a theology very primitive in many of its features, yet he has reflected on some of the fundamental problems of human life. He finds the lot of the cultivator a hard one—compelled as he is to wring his subsistence from an ungrateful soil. He is perplexed by the difficult parturition of woman, so different from the easy delivery of animal mothers. He must account for the serpent's abnormal figure and mode of progression, all the more astonishing in view of the animal's cunning. This narrative, therefore, comes from the first social philosopher, painfully impressed by the problems of human life, and compelled to account for them by an act of God, which was the just punishment for an act of disobedience on the part of man. Probably in the early myth which he has adapted to his purpose the serpent was a divinity. He is now reduced in power and made unable to resist the sentence imposed by Yahweh, though not too impotent to plot against him. That the garden is a mythological survival seems evident from what has been said of its being the residence of the divinity. Yahweh appears as the owner of the soil to which he has obtained title by irrigation and cultivation. He shows, therefore, the features of the Semitic Baal, the god of agriculture, who gives or withholds the crops. So late as the time of Ezekiel we find allusions to this garden of God.

Ezekiel addresses the king of Tyre thus: "Thou wast in Eden the garden of God; every precious stone was thy covering, the sardius, the topaz, the diamond, the beryl, the onyx, the jasper, the sapphire, the emerald and the carbuncle. . . . On the day thou wast created thy dwelling was with the cherubim; in the midst of them I set thee. Thou wast on the mountain of God, walkedst in the midst of the sons of God" (Ezek. 28 : 13 *f.*). We can hardly doubt that the prophet had in mind the story from which the author of Genesis has drawn. One thing comes out more clearly in Ezekiel's text; this is that the garden was located on the great mountain of the north, where, according to the Babylonians and other nations, the gods had their residence, like the Olympus of the Greeks. But our author was less interested in these details than in the relation of man to Yahweh, and the human lot of toil and suffering. For this he tries to account, and for the enmity which has always existed between men and serpents.

In the same way in which the story of Eden explains the fate of mankind by a transgression of its first father, the story of Cain accounts for the nomad life of a portion of the race. Doubtless a local saga, current in Palestine and motived by the mode of life of the Kenites, has here been preserved for us. It reflects the attitude of the cultivator toward the Bedawy. The poverty of the desert compared with the abundance which the farmer enjoys makes the latter believe that the desert life was adopted by Cain because he had been driven out of the cultivated country in punishment for crime. The religious side of the story comes out in the representation that expulsion from the cultivated country is expulsion from the presence of Yahweh, as was believed by David. The blood shed in the land of Yahweh cries to him for vengeance and does not cry in vain.

The division of society indicated by this story is into three classes. Abel is a shepherd and his offering is the one acceptable to God. This is, therefore, the calling preferred by the author. Cain is at first a farmer, but is compelled to become a nomad. He is the earlier representative of the class to which Ishmael belonged—the robber class—whose hand is against every man. The shepherd is reproduced in the patriarchs, although the transition to cultivators is hinted at in the case of Isaac, who sowed the soil and reaped a hundredfold because Yahweh blessed him (Gen. 26 : 12). Joseph sees himself and his brothers binding sheaves in the field, another indication that the author thought of the patriarchs as cultivators. The explanation is that the Yahwist reflected the condition of things in the border of the desert, where the shepherd is becoming a cultivator but is not yet closely attached to the soil.

Yahweh is a God at hand and not a God afar off. He therefore reveals himself to his chosen ones either by theophanies or by dreams. Such dreams may come even to gentiles like Abimelech and Pharaoh. But they are most frequently sent to Israel. Jacob receives one at Bethel and thus discovers the sacredness of the place. Where Yahweh reveals himself once he will probably reveal himself again. So the sanctuaries become places of incubation. Solomon went to Gibeon in order to seek a revelation, and this came to him in a vision of the night. It is the hope of Jacob's descendants that Yahweh will speak to them at the sanctuary where he once spoke to the great ancestor of the nation. The chief sanctuaries of the land were founded because of some revelation of the divinity. The earliest legislation assumes that Yahweh may reveal himself at any time and any place, and that the place will thereby become a sanctuary at which sacrifice may be brought and find acceptance (Ex. 20 : 24).

The best commentary on this command is found in the stories of the patriarchs that we have been considering. Abraham, Isaac, and Jacob, when they receive a revelation, at once erect an altar and call upon the divine name (Gen. 12 : 7; 26 : 25; 35 : 1). That many of the sacred places were ancient Canaanitish places of worship we have already had occasion to notice. But this does not alter the fact that the popular conception was that Yahweh might come near to a man at any time and that then the proper thing to do was to consecrate the place and make it a place of sacrifice. For sacrifice was the known and recognised method of approaching the divinity. The calling on the name of Yahweh was the way in which he was invited to partake of the gift. The practical result was to establish sanctuaries at innumerable sites, so that every village had at least one.

Since the earliest decalogue prohibits molten images of Yahweh we may suppose that in this period the reaction against Canaanitish religion had already set in. And one of the local sagas preserved to us confirms this impression, at least so far as Canaanitish morals are in question. This is the story of the destruction of Sodom and Gomorrah (Gen. 19 J). This was in origin simply a local saga which attempted to account for the formation of the Dead Sea. The Yahwist makes it an eloquent protest against the corruption of Canaanitish manners, which would even violate the rights of the guest in order to gratify unnatural lust. The justice of Yahweh would not tolerate such practices, and to the religious mind the sea became a standing witness to this fact.[1] That Israel itself was not free from such vices is indicated in another narrative, and this shows the practical intention of the author.

In spite of the protest against molten images of which we have spoken, one allusion to the golden bull of Bethel seems to have survived in the early literature, and that one not hostile. In the Testament of Jacob, now embodied in the work of J, we read:

> "By the hands of the Bull of Jacob,
> By the name of the Shepherd, the Stone of Israel;
> By the God of thy father—he will help thee,
> By El-Shaddai—he shall bless thee." (Gen. 49 : 24 *f.*)

If this reading be correct the reference is to the two sacred objects at Bethel, the sacred stone attributed to Jacob and the golden bull of Jeroboam. The author of the poem can hardly have been acquainted with the prohibition of molten images. The compiler in adopting the poem may have interpreted the language as poetic imagery only, or he may have condoned the image at Bethel because of its association with the most venerable sanctuary of the northern kingdom.

It is a matter of common knowledge that the story of the deluge adopted by J comes from Babylonia. And at the date we have assigned to this author we must recognise the probability that Babylonian literature was making its way to the west. What interests us here is not the closeness of the parallel between the Babylonian and the Hebrew account, but the way in which the Hebrew writer has removed the original polytheism. Instead of the many gods and their unseemly quarrels we have Yahweh alone sitting in judgment on mankind and inflicting punishment for their corruption. The anthropomorphism undoubtedly remains —Yahweh repents that he has made man; he shuts the door after Noah; he smells the sweet savour of the sacrifice and is moved by it never again to destroy mankind. But

[1] On the numerous parallels in folk-lore, see Gunkel, *Genesis*,[3] p. 214.

throughout the story he remains the only God and it is he who does his will in heaven and on earth.

That our author is more than a mere compiler is shown by the use he makes of the little bit of mythology concerning the marriage of the sons of God with the daughters of men (Gen. 6 : 1–8). We have already noticed that this was originally a story of divine beings who took human wives, begetting giants like the Titans of Greek mythology. The skill of the Yahwist is seen in the way in which he makes this fragment lead up to the story of the deluge. These giants are not only prodigious in strength but prodigious also in wickedness. They bring about such a state of things that only by their destruction can the earth be cleansed. The deluge receives thus an ethical motive, and the divinities of the early text are made wholly subject to Yahweh.

Yahweh's power is further illustrated by the story of the tower of Babel (Gen. 11 : 1–9). This seems to be a folk-story which circulated among the desert tribes in the vicinity of Babylon. The great temple of Marduk attracted their attention, since it was a conspicuous feature of their landscape. Wondering at the shape of the tower they supposed that it had never been completed and that it was arrested by the act of a god. When they ventured into the city, moreover, their ears were assailed by a polyglot mixture of tongues. This also they thought the result of a divine interposition. As in the other material we have considered, the polytheism of the original account has disappeared though the frank anthropomorphism remains. Yahweh goes down to see what is going on; he fears that mankind will become too powerful unless he intervenes; he finds unity of effort to be the secret of men's strength, and he therefore disunites them by confounding their speech. After this they are unable to proceed with their high designs. Whether according to the original account men actually planned to invade the heavens and so to storm the seat of the gods, we can no longer make out. Some parallels in other religions lead us to suspect this. If it were so, the author has toned down the story so as to preserve the dignity of Yahweh.

The religious interest of all these authors is seen in their treatment of the covenant between Yahweh and Israel. Historically, this covenant was entered into under the leadership of Moses. But faith antedated it and connected it with Abraham. The story of its solemnisation given by the Yahwist is interesting because of its analogies in Semitic practice to-day. The account in Genesis says that Abraham was instructed to slay a cow, a goat, a ram, a dove, and a pigeon. The two halves into which the animals were cut were laid apart, and after the sun had gone down, Yahweh, in the form of a burning torch, walked between the pieces. We are not told that Abraham also walked between the pieces, though that was probably the primitive idea. Among the Arabs east of the Jordan it is still customary to sacrifice an animal when a treaty is made. The body of the slain animal is cut in two and the parts are suspended on two stakes before the tent door. The parties then pass between them.[1] The idea as interpreted by those who take part in the rite is that the blood of the victim will drive away evil. Our author does not reflect on the reason for the rite. He makes Yahweh conform to the custom of the times, a custom to which we find a reference as late as the time of Jeremiah (Jer. 34 : 18; *cf.* Gen. 15 : 17).

The covenant with Abraham thus narrated binds Yahweh to give Abraham's descendants possession of Canaan but says nothing of obligations undertaken by the patriarch in return. It must be obvious that some such obligations formed a part of the agreement between Yahweh and Israel which these writers really have in mind. Historically, the covenant was entered into in the time of Moses, and it is interesting to see that the authors we are studying regarded it as a real covenant, an agreement by which each party bound itself to certain specific things. On the part of Yahweh there was an undertaking to give Israel possession of

[1] Jaussen, *Coutumes des Arabes*, p. 362.

the promised land; on the part of Israel there was a definite undertaking to give a part of the produce of the land to Yahweh. The obligation is formulated in ten commands to which the people promise obedience, and this decalogue in its most primitive form contains the following:

Thou shalt worship no other God.
Thou shalt make thee no molten gods.
The feast of unleavened bread shalt thou keep.
All that open the womb are mine.
Six days shalt thou work but on the seventh day thou shalt rest.
Three times in the year shall all thy males appear before God.
Thou shalt not offer the blood of my sacrifice with leavened bread.
Neither shall the sacrifice of the passover remain all night until the morning.
The first of the fruits of thy ground shalt thou bring to the house of Yahweh thy God.
Thou shalt not boil a kid in its mother's milk.[1]

The appropriateness of such a series of commands for an agricultural people needs no demonstration. It expressly recognises Yahweh as God of the soil, to whom the first-fruits belong. The three feasts which are enjoined are connected with the harvest. At each of these the farmer is to appear at the sanctuary, recognising Yahweh as the giver of the grain, the wine, and the oil. The God of animal fruitfulness is honoured by the gift of the firstlings of cattle and even by the consecration of the first-born of men. The idea of religion here presented is that which prevailed in Israel during its most flourishing period, as is shown by the testament of Jacob. Worship is the presentation of tribute to the God of the soil with the expectation of thus securing his continued favour. Jacob voices the idea of these authors when he vows that if Yahweh will give him

[1] Ex. 34. Several of the commands are given also at the conclusion of the Covenant code, Ex. 23 : 10–19. The present text of Ex. 34 gives twelve commands, but the explicit declaration that the ten words were written on tables of stone indicates that the original number was ten, and tradition speaks uniformly of a decalogue.

bread to eat and clothing to wear Yahweh shall be his God, and he will give a tenth of his gains to him. The covenant we are considering recognises the obligation assumed by the great ancestor of the people and formulates it in these commands.

The idea of the sacrificial service as something gratifying to Yahweh and the means of securing his favour was the one against which the prophets found themselves obliged to protest. The writers we are considering show that it was not a mere vulgar error but that it was held by the most thoughtful Israelites in this period. To the Yahwist, certainly, sacrifice was the natural method of approach to the divinity. For this reason he dates it in the earliest times. Abel's presentation of the firstlings of the flock secures the favour of Yahweh, whereas Cain's vegetable offering is not regarded. In the time of Noah, again, the aroma of the sacrifice moves Yahweh so that he resolves never to send another deluge, and this sacrifice is provided for by the presence of an extra number of clean (that is, sacrificial) animals in the ark. Even a non-Israelite like Balaam may hope to secure the help of Yahweh by offering a sacrifice (Num. 23 : 1 *f.*).

Sacrifice of children was not foreign to the early religion of Israel as we have had occasion to notice. The first protest against this custom, so far as we know, is due to the Elohistic author of the Pentateuch. The right of the divinity to test the faith and obedience of his servants in any manner that seems good to him is assumed. In the case of Abraham the test is the more severe in that Isaac is the only child. What the original form of the story was is not clear. Some scholars suppose that it told how Abraham was obedient even to the extent of sacrificing his only son. But the life of Isaac is so essential to the existence of Israel that we can hardly suppose this probable. Nor can we now discover the local saga which formed the nucleus of the story. In its present form it teaches that at least in cases where the sacrifice of the first-born would exterminate the family Yahweh will accept a substitute. The lesson would not have been needed unless the actual sacrifice were in vogue.

An important step was taken by this author when he stated that the covenant with Yahweh was embodied in a book, the so-called Covenant code (Ex. 20 : 22 to 23 : 32). This codex shows on the surface that it is a compilation from different sources. A part of its enactments, if we may call them so, are legal precedents, as: "If a man smite the eye of his servant or of his maid he shall let him go free for his eye's sake." Some are in the form of direct commands, as: "Thou shalt not let a sorceress live." The idea of the compiler is that all civil as well as all ritual custom is under the direct care of Yahweh and that the covenant with him is based on the whole social order. Moreover, as the origin of the nation was traced to the Mosaic age, and as the Decalogue already embodied the will of Yahweh in specific commands, it was natural to suppose that Moses was the recipient of a code which he published in written form. This idea of Moses as the great lawgiver was effectively used by the author of Deuteronomy and finally coloured the whole thought of the people. That the Covenant code, like the earliest decalogue, was the product of the agricultural age needs no demonstration.

In this code no line is drawn between civil and religious duties, or rather, we may say, that all duties are religious in their nature. Israel is a people consecrated to Yahweh, and must avoid all that is offensive to him. That which is torn by wild beasts must not be eaten because it had been infected by the taboo of a demonic being (Ex. 22 : 30). In approaching the presence of the divinity men must put away all strange gods, must wash their clothes, and must keep from women (Ex. 19 : 14 *f.*). This consecration is indicated in the passage which speaks of Israel as a kingdom of priests, as a sacred nation, and as Yahweh's own possession (Ex. 19 : 5 *f.*). This formulation may be of comparatively late date, but the idea is primitive. And, since Yahweh is the guardian of the social order, legal questions may be decided by him.

Thus the slave who decides to remain with his master is brought before God in order that his status may be sanctioned (Ex. 21 : 6). An oath of purgation taken before Yahweh is sufficient to establish a man's innocence (22 : 8, 10).

The code marks an ethical advance by its treatment of the manslayer. According to tribal custom, blood calls for blood whether there be evil intent or not. In this document it is provided that the unintentional slayer may flee to a place of refuge. Whether the author thinks of every sanctuary as such a place of refuge is doubtful. The more prominent sacred places would be better able to protect the suppliant, and historically we read only of the temple of Jerusalem as affording asylum (I Kings 1 : 50; 2 : 28). What is remarkable in the Covenant code is that the sacredness of the place is not to protect the intentional murderer: "Thou shalt take him from my altar to put him to death" (Ex. 21 : 14).

Neither in the Covenant code, nor anywhere else in these early narratives, is there any allusion to a life beyond the grave. The happiness of the patriarchs consists in a long life and a peaceful death. Nevertheless, the soul in some sense survives the death of the body. Jacob says that he will go down to Sheol to his son Joseph (Gen. 37 : 35). It is evident that Sheol is not the grave, for he could not hope to be joined with Joseph in a tomb. Samuel predicts that Saul and his sons will be joined with him, though they are not buried but lie on the field of battle (I Sam. 28 : 19). These passages indicate clearly enough the unimportant place which a belief in a future life took in the thought of the times. There was the notion that the immaterial part of man goes to an underground region where it leads a shadowy existence and whence it may be called by the necromancer. The ancestral animism which paid some sort of worship to the shades is already felt to be inconsistent with the religion of Yahweh, and for this reason the whole subject of the state of the dead is kept in the background.

Summing up what has been said, we may affirm that in the ninth century B. C. Yahweh has taken full possession of the land of Canaan. He has dispossessed the local Baals and taken their place in the sanctuaries. He is still Israel's God of war, but he is also the God of the agriculturist and the giver of the fruits of the ground. In dispossessing the Baals, therefore, he has taken on some of their features. The land of Israel is his land, as the Philistines imply when they propose to send the ark back to its own place. Yahweh himself confirms their view in that he forces the cows to go up the road to Beth-shemesh (I Sam. 6 : 9, 12). Joab's attempt to besiege Abel-beth-Maacah is an attempt to destroy the heritage of Yahweh (II Sam. 20 : 19). The land of Israel is consecrated by the presence of Yahweh so that even to later authors it is different from all other countries. Both Amos and Hosea think of other lands as unclean (Amos 7 : 17; Hosea 9 : 3). Even in the exilic period an author was able to say of Jonah, that he thought to escape the presence of Yahweh by fleeing from Canaan (Jonah 1 : 3). Foreigners coming into the territory of Yahweh are expected to pay him worship. Doeg, the Edomite, was undergoing purification at Nob when David came thither (I Sam. 21 : 8); Uriah, though a Hittite, declares his devotion to the ark (II Sam 11 : 11); Ittai, a Philistine just enlisted in the service of David, swears by Yahweh (II Sam. 15 : 21); and the colonists sent by the Assyrian king have no rest until they learn how to pay their respects to the God of the land (II Kings 17 : 24–28).

If the more advanced thinkers were satisfied with this religion, we may suppose the mass of the people to be equally so. They enjoyed the favour of Yahweh when the crops were bountiful and when they had peace from their enemies. They believed that the payment of the dues at the sanctuaries and the eating and drinking there secured a continuance of Yahweh's favour. If the political situation sometimes caused anxiety and there seemed to be danger from hostile neighbours, the Israelites comforted themselves with the thought that Yahweh was a man of war, and as he had overcome the Canaanites and Philistines so he would take the field against any other foe. There was apparently a tradition that a great day of Yahweh was not far away, in which he would signally vindicate himself upon invaders of his territory. This optimistic hope lulled the conscience of the people into a false security. Some aggressive movement was needed, more aggressive than was contemplated by the writers of the early narratives, if the religion of Israel was to make any real advance. Such a movement came in the preaching of the great prophets.

CHAPTER VI

THE EARLIER PROPHETS.

ACCORDING to ancient conceptions the gods are not far from any one of us, and they take an interest in the affairs of individual men. Hence the history of religion shows a variety of ways in which men have tried to discover the will of the divinity. Some of these ways were not in vogue in Israel. Observation of the flight of birds or of the conduct of animals, for example, is not alluded to in the Old Testament. Taking the auspices from the entrails of sacrificial animals is also conspicuous by its absence from our documents. Since divination by the liver of an animal slain at the temple was commonly practised in Babylon this absence of allusion in the Hebrew Scriptures is the more remarkable. The Hebrew ritual law enjoins that the liver be burnt on the altar (Lev. 3 : 15, etc.), probably in conscious opposition to gentile practice. Moreover, astrology, so sedulously cultivated in Babylon, does not seem to have gained a foothold in Israel. There is nowhere in the Bible any allusion to the theory of a close correspondence between what takes place in the visible heavens and what goes on on the earth. Although Yahweh is God of the heavenly armies, prognostication by observation of the constellations is not attempted. The sole exception is the assertion of Deborah: "This is the day in which Yahweh has given thine enemy into thy hand; has not Yahweh gone out before thee?" (Judges 4 : 14.) Even here the prophetess does no more than express the belief that Yahweh has indicated an auspicious day; in what method we are not told.

The reason why the systematic observation of the heavens

is discouraged by the Hebrews is evidently the fact that such observation was closely connected with the worship of the planets and constellations. A late writer has inserted in the book of Jeremiah a warning against being afraid of the signs of heaven as the other nations are afraid of them (Jer. 10 : 1*f*.). The Deuteronomists frequently exhort Israel to keep from this superstition which was rife among the nations, even tolerated in them by Yahweh's own appointment (Deut. 4 : 19, etc.). Yahweh's complete control of the heavenly bodies is indicated by the assertion that he has made them to regulate the calendar (Gen. 1 : 14) and by his making the sun reverse its course (Isaiah 38 : 7*f*.). But no *prediction* is associated with any of these texts. Where the Babylonian star-gazers are alluded to it is in tones of open contempt. Addressing Babylon and anticipating its imminent destruction, the prophet says: "Let now the dividers of the heavens, the star-gazers, the monthly prognosticators, stand up and save thee from the things that shall come upon thee" (Isaiah 47 : 13). These passages seem to show that astrology, so far as it was practised in Israel at all, was a foreign importation, and, taken with the silence of the documents concerning auspication by the liver, they make it clear that the religion of Israel developed independently of that of Babylon.

This does not mean, however, that various other methods of inquiring the will of the divinity—methods which we call superstitious—were unknown in Israel. The polemic of the Deuteronomist is sufficient evidence: "When thou comest into the land which Yahweh thy God gives thee, thou shalt not learn to do after the abominations of these nations; there shall not be found in thee any that makes his son or his daughter to pass through the fire, who uses divination or practises augury, or a sorcerer, or a charmer, or a consulter with a familiar spirit, or a wizard, or a necromancer. For whosoever does these things is an abomination to Yahweh thy God" (Deut. 18 : 9–12). The continuation of the passage shows that these ways of ascertaining the will of the divinity are contrasted with the word of the prophet as the false contrasts with the true. The author indeed regards these not only as false but also as foreign superstitions, but the tenacity with which they were held in Israel, returning after each attempt to suppress them, shows that they were a part of the popular religion. Though violently repressed by the reforming party, they came back into view as soon as pressure was withdrawn, as in the time of Manasseh (II Kings 21 : 6).

It is not always easy to discover the nature of the arts denounced by the Deuteronomist. Divination by the sacred lot is certainly one of them. From Ezekiel we learn how this was done. A bundle of arrows was shaken in the presence of the god, and one was drawn from the bundle. Nebuchadrezzar is undecided whether to march against Rabbath-Ammon or against Jerusalem. At the parting of the ways he consults the teraphim, looks on the liver, and shakes the arrows to and fro. The arrow which comes into his hand is marked "Jerusalem," and this decides the route of the army and the fate of the city (Ezek. 21 : 26–28, E. V., vss. 21–23). This passage would not prove that diviners were found in Israel, but in other passages Ezekiel intimates that they were active among his own people, and even brings them into close connection with the prophets (13 : 9, 23). Isaiah classes them with the judges, prophets, and elders, as pillars of the state (Isaiah 3 : 2). Reaction against them is shown by Jeremiah, who, however, mentions them in connection with the prophets (Jer. 27 : 9; 29 : 8), and the classic expression of this opposition is found in the verse:

> "For rebellion is as the sin of divination,
> And like the teraphim is obstinacy." (I Sam. 15 : 23.)

Another kind of divination is designated by the word which we have rendered *augury*. Manasseh is accused of it (II Kings 21 : 6), and Isaiah reproaches Judah with being full of it, "like the Philistines" (Isaiah 2 : 6). Jeremiah warns the people against the augurs who prophesy a lie (Jer. 27 : 9). It is prohibited by the Law (Lev. 19 : 26). With it we may class *soothsaying.* The only distinct clue to this form is given in the story of Joseph, where the value of the stolen cup is said to consist in its use for this art (Gen. 44 : 15). We conclude that the method was the one used elsewhere with a magic cup. The cup was filled with water and a little oil was poured upon it. The shape of the drops indicated the answer that was sought. The ascription of this art to Joseph shows that it was not objected to in Israel in the earlier period, though later it was regarded as sinful (II Kings 17: 17; 21 · 6). Its prohibition by the Deuteronomist and by the ritual code followed as a matter of course.

Another of these methods of getting supernatural knowledge or power is *sorcery.* As early as the covenant code we find the command: "Thou shalt not suffer a sorceress to live" (Ex. 22 : 17). This was probably for a double reason; she was in communion with other gods than Yahweh, and she made use of her alleged powers to injure her neighbours in person or property. Ezekiel denounces Jewish women who sew bands for all wrists and make caps for every head, to hunt lives. The purpose is evidently to inflict disease or death upon obnoxious persons, contrary to the will of Yahweh. These women are called prophetesses, from which we are authorised to conclude that they claimed supernatural knowledge, and as they are said to profane the name of Yahweh, we may suppose they claimed to receive revelations from him (Ezek. 13 : 17–23). In the time of Jeremiah sorcerers uttered false predictions (Jer. 27 : 9), and Malachi denounces them along with other evil-doers (Mal. 3 : 5). Elsewhere they are associated with Babylon (Isaiah 47 : 9 and 12), and with Jezebel, queen of Israel (II Kings 9 : 22). The similarity of ideas in Israel and outside it is indicated by the conflict of the Egyptian sorcerers with Moses, in which they duplicate some of his miracles, although they finally acknowledge his superiority (Ex. 7 : 11).

Enchantment, probably the casting of spells over a person, was also practised in Israel, but has no bearing upon the question of revelation, with which we are now concerned. Consultation of spirits, however, is illustrated by a celebrated case. The adept in this art is called possessor of an *ob*, a word of obscure meaning. The narrative of the witch of Endor makes sufficiently plain what the people believed: the necromancer had the power of invoking the spirits of the dead and received from them revelations of the future (I Sam. 28). With this art we find mention of *wizardry* (II Kings 21 : 6; 23 : 24; Isaiah 8 : 19; 19 : 3). The wizards and necromancers are said to *defile* those who consult them, sufficient evidence that they came into connection with other divinities than Yahweh (Lev. 19 : 31). From Isaiah we learn that these practitioners chirped and muttered in voices that were supposed to be those of the spirits they consulted. Down to the present day Palestinian magicians in their rites "make a sucking sound as one might chirrup to a horse."[1]

To the Deuteronomist's list of magic arts we should add consultation of the teraphim. The passage from Ezekiel quoted above shows that these divinities were appealed to for decisions, and while the action of a heathen king would not prove anything concerning the custom in Israel, the association of the teraphim with divination in a passage already cited (I Sam. 15 : 23) is significant. Moreover, we find the teraphim mentioned in company with the ephod, which was a means of discovering the will of Yahweh (Judges 17 : 5; Hosea 3 : 4; Judges 18 : 14). In one of our latest documents it is declared: "The teraphim have spoken vanity, and the diviners have seen a lie" (Zech. 10 : 2); and the account of Josiah's reforms groups the teraphim with necromancers and soothsayers (II Kings 23 : 24). That the teraphim were images of some kind seems clear from the story of David's flight and Michal's stratagem (I Sam. 19 : 13 *ff.*).

The desire to know the will of the divinity is sufficiently

[1] Bliss, *Religions of Palestine*, p. 273.

evidenced by this list of proscribed arts. It was only in the later period that they were proscribed in Israel, and in contrast with them three methods of ascertaining the divine decision were regarded as legitimate. These were dreams, Urim, and appeal to a prophet. It was only when these failed him that Saul appealed to the necromancer.[1] Of these three the Urim or, more fully, Urim and Thummim early fell out of use. It seems to have been one form of the sacred lot. A passage preserved to us by the Greek translation of I Samuel (14 : 41) indicates that after appropriate ceremonies the divinity was asked to give a negative or positive answer to the question put by the inquirer or to distinguish between two alternatives. Since there was a third possibility, that is, that the answer might be refused, the lot must have been arranged for three possible answers. The simplest hypothesis is that the Urim and Thummim were two disks, white on one side and black on the other. If both fell with the white side uppermost the answer would be affirmative; if with the black side uppermost, negative; while if one showed the white and the other the black the answer was withheld. The management of the oracle was in the hands of the priests, and even the latest code provides for depositing the sacred implements in the ephod of the high priest. In an early poem they are associated with the Levitical guild (Deut. 33 : 8), as already noted. David had the sacred lot at his command because Abiathar brought the ephod with him when he escaped from the massacre at Nob.

Dreams are regarded as means of revelation in all early religions, and they are frequently presented in this light in the Old Testament. From Abraham down to Nebuchadrezzar men prominent in the narrative are recipients of dreams. The practice of sleeping in a sanctuary in order to receive a revelation is perhaps indicated (as we have already noted) in the story of Jacob at Bethel and also in that of Solomon at Gibeon. When we are told that Saul sought an

[1] I Sam. 28 : 6. The historicity of the account is open to objection, but its value as a statement of popular belief is indubitable.

answer from Yahweh but received none by dreams we naturally think that he sought them by incubation, that is, sleeping in the sanctuary. The dreamers of dreams are associated with the prophets in several passages, and, in fact, the prophets seem often to have received their revelations in dreams. It is only in the time of Jeremiah that the dream begins to lose its reputation: "The prophet that has a dream let him tell his dream, but he that has my word let him speak my word faithfully; what is the straw to the wheat? says Yahweh" (Jer. 23:25, 28). The superiority of Moses to the other prophets is indicated by the declaration that Yahweh speaks to the others in dreams and visions, but with Moses face to face (Num. 12 : 6–8).

While Yahweh may reveal himself to any man by a dream (even to a non-Israelite), certain men are thought to be so nearly in touch with the divinity that they receive frequent revelations both by dreams and by waking visions. Such men are seers or prophets. In the earlier time the two classes seem to have been quite distinct. Two words designate the seer, which we might translate *seer* and *gazer*. The account of Saul's meeting with Samuel tells us of the seer (I Sam. 9). The young man is in perplexity concerning the lost asses of his father and is advised by his servant that in the neighbouring village there is a man of God, and all that he says comes to pass. The seer by his supernatural knowledge is able to tell about lost articles. He is a local practitioner who assists people in such matters. The pains taken by Saul's servant to give assurance that the man is honourable indicates that some of the professors of the art were not above suspicion. The narrative shows that Samuel predicted the events of the coming day, not to satisfy Saul's curiosity, but to give him assurance of the genuineness of his message concerning the kingship.

The distinction between seer, gazer, and prophet was lost sight of in the period of the monarchy. Isaiah mentions seers and gazers in the same breath (Isaiah 30 : 10); Gad, an official at David's court, is called a gazer and also a prophet (II Sam. 24 : 11). Prophets and gazers occur together in II Kings (17 : 13) and in Isaiah (Isaiah 29 : 10). Amos is called a gazer, perhaps contemptuously, by Amaziah, who warns him not to play the prophet at the royal sanctuary (Amos 7 : 12). Micah, however, classes the gazers with diviners and regards them as inferior to the prophets (Micah 3 : 7). These references show that the people at large did not distinguish between prophets, seers, and gazers. All three classes doubtless arrogated the title "man of God" and claimed supernatural illumination. In fact, however, the prophets are of different origin from the others. This is made clear by the passage which describes the band of prophets at Geba, the home of Saul (I Sam. 10 : 10). Here we find them in a company, marching in procession headed by lyre, drum, fife, and harp. They are engaging in some enthusiastic exercise, probably the dance, and so powerful is the contagion of this enthusiasm that Saul, to the surprise of his neighbours, is overcome by the same impulse and joins with them. In the parallel account we read that Saul threw off his clothes and lay naked all day and all night (I Sam. 19 : 18–24). The phenomena are strikingly like those presented by the devotees of the Great Mother in Asia Minor and by the dervishes of the present day. The motive was and is to enjoy the ecstasy of communion with the divinity. The enthusiastic exercises induce a state of exaltation in which the spirit seems rapt out of itself, or, in another conception of it, in which the divinity seems to come down and take possession of the worshipper. The Hebrews applied the word *prophesy* to the extravagant action of an insane man, as of Saul under the influence of a supposed spirit of evil (I Sam. 18 : 10). The young prophet sent by Elisha to anoint Jehu is called by the officers a crazy fellow, and Jehu at first affects to make light of his "babble" (II Kings 9 : 11). At a later date the temple police are advised to arrest irresponsible men like Jeremiah who rave and play the prophet (Jer. 29 : 26).

The primary purpose of the prophets, then, was not to secure revelations for the benefit of others but to get into close relation with the divinity for their own enjoyment. Yet it could hardly be that they would not obtain great influence among the people because of their being men of God. And since they were zealous for Yahweh they often exerted a considerable influence on the popular religion and also on political movements. It is not accidental that they come into view at two crises of Israel's history: in the time of Saul, when the Philistine encroachment was most galling, and in the time of Ahab, when the Phœnician Baal invaded the territory of Yahweh. Individual prophets appear in our narrative as political agitators. Nathan took an active part in seating Solomon on the throne (I Kings 1 : 11*f.*). Ahijah the Shilonite encouraged Jeroboam to revolt against Solomon (I Kings 11 : 29–39). Jehu ben Hanani threatened Baasha with the extermination of his house (I Kings 16 : 1–4). Elisha actively fomented the conspiracy of Jehu, and according to tradition even suggested assassination as the way to a change of dynasty in Damascus (II Kings 8 : 7–13). In the view of later times Samuel was the originator of the kingship and unmade kings as easily as he made them. Since Yahweh is the god of the social order, it is inevitable that his servants should concern themselves with affairs of state.

The prophet, being a man of God, was in the eyes of the people a worker of miracles. Moses is a conspicuous example. But others are almost as remarkable. Thus Samuel appeals to Yahweh and receives an answer in the thunder (I Sam. 12 : 18). The lives of Elijah and Elisha seem to have been written to show the superhuman power of the two men. The widow's cruse of oil (I Kings 17 : 13–16), the parting of the waters of the Jordan (II Kings 2 : 8), the healing of the waters of Jericho (2 : 19*f.*) are so many evidences of the popular belief, as are the shocking anecdotes of the two bears (2 : 23–25) and of the destruction of two companies of soldiers by fire from heaven (1 : 10–12). The power of Elijah to withhold the rain is not doubted, and although the contest at Carmel is intended to decide whether Baal or Yahweh is the true God for Israel, there is also the question whether Elijah or the Baal prophets can bring the rain. The extreme expression of the popular belief is the legend that Elijah was carried off by a fiery chariot to heaven. To appreciate this we must remind ourselves that in this period there was no thought that the saints live in heaven. The only parallel to the case of Elijah is that of Enoch—a survival from the mythological stage of belief.

The belief of the people in the divine protection accorded the man of God accounts for the deference with which the prophets were treated by those in authority and for the boldness of the prophets themselves in the presence of kings. Ehud, by pretending to have a message from God, obtained a private audience from Eglon (Judges 3 : 20). The young prophet who wished to disguise himself from Ahab commanded a man to strike him, and the refusal was punished by a lion (I Kings 20 : 36). Gehazi was punished by leprosy for misusing Elisha's name (II Kings 5 : 27). The sceptic who doubted the word of this prophet died the next day (7 : 20). It is no wonder, therefore, that the elders of Bethlehem trembled at the coming of Samuel (I Sam. 16 : 4). In the popular view, and no doubt in the view of the prophets themselves, disobedience to a man of God is disobedience to God himself, and what this means is clear: "Has Yahweh as great delight in burnt-offering and sacrifice as in obeying the voice of Yahweh? Behold to obey is better than sacrifice, and to hearken than the fat of rams" (I Sam. 15 : 22). The conviction that Yahweh speaks through the prophet accounts for the boldness with which Nathan denounced David for his adultery, and Elijah pronounced judgment on the tyranny of Ahab.

Tradition draws no clear line of distinction between priest, seer, and prophet. The annotator of the narrative concerning Saul and Samuel supposes seer to be simply the archaic term for prophet. The life of Moses shows him acting both as priest and prophet, and Samuel is presented in the threefold aspect as priest, seer, and prophet. In the course of time the seer became less prominent and there came a differentiation between priest and prophet. Where a priest became a prophet, as in the case of Jeremiah and Ezekiel, the priestly function dropped into a subordinate place. The result was to make the priest simply a minister of the sanctuary, charged with the proper performance of the ritual, whose *tora* (instruction) was strictly limited to matters of ritual cleanness, while the prophet became the preacher, the critic of the existing order, and therefore often in sharp opposition to the priesthood. Evidence that the prophets had actually appropriated the work of the seer is given by the word *vision,* used to designate the written words of the prophet. Thus the title of Isaiah's book is "The Vision of Isaiah."

This word *vision,* descriptive of the experience of the man of God, is from the same root with the word which I have translated *gazer*. It is not applied ordinarily to dreams. The idea which it expresses is that the world is full of things which are invisible to the ordinary eye but which may be seen by the man who has some special power. Thus there was an angel standing in the road by which Balaam must go, but he was not seen by the prophet. The riding animal had the keener sight. Only when Yahweh opened Balaam's eyes did he see what confronted him. Yahweh, therefore, is said to "uncover the eye" of the prophet. Balaam describes himself as one who sees the vision of the Almighty, lying prostrate but having the eye uncovered (Num. 24 : 4). When Elisha's servant is terrified by the approach of the Syrian army the prophet prays that his eyes may be opened, whereupon the servant sees the mountain full of chariots and horses of fire (II Kings 6 : 15–17). It is this supernatural quickening of the eye which makes the prophet, the seer, or the gazer. Neither the prophet himself nor the men to whom he described his visions had any doubt of the reality of the supersensible objects presented to his spiritual eye.

Similarly the ear may be quickened to hear what is not audible to the ordinary sense. What is thus heard is usually the words of a superhuman being, Yahweh or his angel. Balaam claims that he hears the words of God and knows the knowledge of the Most High (Num. 24 : 16). When Yahweh makes a revelation to Samuel he uncovers his ear (I Sam. 9 : 15); and a number of parallels might be cited. But audition is less common than vision. As time went on the word *vision* designated the word of the prophet, as we have seen. In the apocalyptic literature the vision is a purely literary device. Since the prophet is the organ by which Yahweh makes his will known to men, it is natural for him to think of his words as something placed in his mouth by the divinity (Jer. 1 : 9). Ezekiel is even more materialistic; he sees Yahweh hand him a book which he takes and eats (Ezek. 2 : 8 to 3 : 3). The psychological fact which gives rise to these descriptions seems to be the strong inner impulse to deliver a certain message which comes to the prophet without conscious and deliberate reasoning of his own. The conviction of the truth objectifies itself to him as a command of God ordering him to speak. Jeremiah tells us how contrary his message was to his natural feelings and how, in consequence, he resolved that he would not speak any more. But the inner torment became so great that he was compelled to deliver the message (Jer. 20 : 9; *cf.* 6 : 11).

Although the more marked phenomena of Hebrew prophetism are such as are elsewhere attributed to possession by a divinity, the Old Testament nowhere says that Yahweh enters into a man. What is done in cases of extraordinary manifestations is done by the spirit of Yahweh. This spirit clothes itself with the hero (Judges 6 : 34) or comes upon him (Judges 11 : 29; Num. 24 : 2). The writers seem to have formulated no distinct theory concerning this spirit. In some cases it seems to be an influence sent by Yahweh, like the spirit of jealousy or of suspicion mentioned in some passages (Num. 5 : 14; II Kings 19 : 7). It is materialistically conceived and it can be transferred from one man to another. Elisha asks for a double portion of it (the portion of the first-born son) as though it were to be divided among Elijah's heirs (II Kings 2 : 9). Yahweh takes a part of the spirit which is on Moses and puts it upon the elders of Israel (Num. 11 : 17). But in some passages the spirit seems to be a distinct personality. Micaiah sees in vision how the spirit responds to Yahweh's inquiry for a method of beguiling Ahab to his death, by offering to be a lying spirit in the mouth of his prophets (I Kings 22 : 21 *f.*).

The importance of the spirit as the organ of revelation is attested by a number of passages. The poet who speaks for David at the close of the great king's life claims that it was the spirit of Yahweh that spoke through him and that Yahweh's word was on his tongue (II Sam. 23 : 2). Joel supposes that in the Messianic time the spirit will be imparted to all the members of the theocratic community, giving dreams and visions—that is, revelations—to young and old (Joel 3 : 1). In Deutero-Isaiah we read: "This is my covenant with them, says Yahweh: My spirit which is upon thee, and my words which I have put into thy mouth, shall not depart from thy mouth nor from the mouth of thy children nor from the mouth of thy children's children forever" (Isaiah 59 : 21). The Messianic King himself will be endued with the spirit, to qualify him for his office, and the spirit is described as the spirit of wisdom and insight, the spirit of knowledge and religion (Isaiah 11 : 2).

In the prophets whose writings have come down to us the work of the spirit is to impel men to speak to their contemporaries concerning the divine will. Through the prophet Yahweh rebukes the people for their sin and threatens them with punishment. The prophet's conviction that he was called to speak in the name of Israel's God might come in the form of a vision, as we have seen, or it might be a strong inward sense of inevitableness. In any case the subject of the experience was sure that what he experienced was not the result of his own judgment or reasoning powers. Yet it was easy to mistake the source of this conviction, and among those whom we call false prophets there were probably some who were as sincere as were their opponents whose words found their way into the canon of Scripture. That some who claimed the prophetic inspiration made use of their alleged gifts for purposes of private gain is evident. The sincerely patriotic, unselfish, and religious men were in the minority, and were opposed, even persecuted, both by members of the guild and by the secular authorities. This opposition brought out the essential nobility of their characters. Later generations did them justice and took pains to preserve some record of their utterances. For this reason their works have come down to us in one division of our Hebrew Bible.

CHAPTER VII

AMOS AND HOSEA

"In the fifteenth year of Amaziah king of Judah began Jeroboam son of Joash king of Israel to reign in Samaria and he reigned forty-one years. He restored the boundary of Israel from the Entrance of Hamath to the sea of the Arabah, according to the word of Yahweh, God of Israel, which he spoke by his servant Jonah son of Amittai, who was of Gath-hepher. For Yahweh saw the affliction of Israel that it was very bitter, for there was none fettered nor free, neither was there any helper for Israel. And Yahweh resolved that he would not blot out the name of Israel from under heaven, and he saved them by the hand of Jeroboam son of Joash" (II Kings 14 : 23–27).

This statement of the Hebrew author sufficiently sets forth the state of things when the prophetic movement took a new direction. There had been great distress in the northern kingdom under the persistent aggression of Damascus, the hereditary enemy. In the time of Jeroboam II a turn had come for the better. Damascus was occupied with a more formidable foe on its northern frontier, and this gave Israel an opportunity to recover its lost territory. Jeroboam did not hesitate to seize his advantage, and he was able to extend his frontier to the traditional boundary claimed by Israel. All the signs go to show that the people under Jeroboam's sway interpreted the success of their arms, as is, in fact, declared in the passage just quoted, as due to the direct intervention of Yahweh. Congratulating themselves that they were protected by their God, they observed the rites of the ancestral religion with zeal and confidence. But their rejoicing was premature. Even before the death of Jeroboam a change set in, and within a few years of this apparent prosperity the kingdom of Israel ceased to be. The sister kingdom prolonged its existence more than a century longer, but at length it, too, succumbed.

The question which confronts us is: Why did not the fate of the nation determine the fate of the nation's God? To the mass of the people Yahweh was a national God, more powerful, perhaps, than Chemosh of Moab, but in other respects like him. When Moab perished Chemosh ceased to be more than a name. But as Israel shrank in importance, Yahweh grew, and when his worshippers could no longer call themselves a nation he became to his worshippers, and later to all the civilised world, the God of the whole earth; and his religion made its way to people to whom Israel had been unknown even by name. As historical students, we must try to apprehend the process by which the God of Israel thus freed himself from the national bonds by which he had been held, and became the God above all Gods, the Creator and Ruler of the universe. This process was due in large measure to the men whose writings have come down to us in the books of the prophets. These writings are, to be sure, fragments only, and what makes them more difficult to understand is that they have undergone extensive revision by editors who were not always in sympathy with the original authors. The progress of criticism, however, has enabled us to trace an outline of the development with some confidence.

The first thing we discover is that the prophets build upon foundations already laid. This is inevitable. However convinced the reformer may be that a radical change is needed, no revolution ever makes a clean sweep of existing institutions. Moreover, man's inextinguishable idealism convinces him that the former days were better than these. The most powerful argument which the preacher can bring in favour of his message is that what is needed is a return to the better manners of the fathers. This explains the attitude of the prophets toward tradition. They did adopt certain ideas which were current in their time, but they made use of them in a manner that was new and startling to their contemporaries. The people, as we have seen, were familiar with the idea that Yahweh was the God of Israel and that Israel was his people. The prophets assume this. They assume also the corollary—that Yahweh reveals his will to his people. Religion is knowledge and fear of Yahweh, and the knowledge must come from him in the first place, being made plain to chosen instruments who proclaim it to their fellows.

It was probably at the great autumn festival, when the crowds had gathered with sacrifices at the sanctuary at Bethel to eat and drink and rejoice before Yahweh, that "suddenly there appeared a man who checked the joyous celebration by the earnestness of his mien. It was a plain shepherd from the borders of the wilderness. Into the gay music of the revellers with their drums and harps he injected a discordant note, for he chanted the dirge which the mourners were accustomed to sing as they followed the corpse to the tomb. Through all the shouting of the crowd he heard the death-rattle: 'The virgin Israel has fallen, no more to rise,' was the burden of his song."[1] The priest in charge of the temple had no good opinion of the strolling prophets who thus disturbed the festivities, and he gave this one a warning: "Go, Seer, flee into the land of Judah and there earn thy bread, and there play the prophet. At Bethel you cannot prophesy any more, for it is a court sanctuary." As in duty bound the officer reported the incident to his monarch, and Amos was compelled to keep silence. His reply to the priest, however, has become classic: "I am no prophet nor prophet's apprentice, but a plain herdsman and a cutter of sycamore fruit. And Yahweh took me from following the flock and said to me: 'Go, prophesy to my people Israel'" (Amos 7 : 14 *f.*). It is plain that Amos wished to dissociate himself from the professional prophets

[1] Wellhausen, *Israelitische und Jüdische Geschichte*, p. 105.

of the guilds. Yet even in his denial he finds no word to designate his activity except "prophesy." He means that he was overborne by the will of Yahweh just as those prophets claimed to be. The irresistible nature of this impulse is indicated by his declaration: "When the lion roars who will not fear? When Yahweh speaks who can help prophesying?" (3 : 8.)

With reference to Yahweh's election of Israel Amos gives no uncertain sound: Yahweh had brought the people out of Egypt, had led them in the wilderness forty years, and had destroyed the Amorites before them (2 : 9 *f.*). "You only of all the nations have I known," says Yahweh (3 : 2); though later a broader view is intimated (9 : 7). Canaan is Yahweh's land, and other lands are unclean (7 : 17; *cf.* Hosea 9 : 3–5). As God of the land he gives or withholds the rain and sends blasting and mildew (4 : 6–9). It is evidence of his grace that he sends prophets and nazirites (2 : 11). In all this Amos stands on the same ground with the people at large. But on the basis of these received beliefs he builds up a very different theory. The people rejoiced at the outward prosperity which they enjoyed as evidence of Yahweh's being altogether favourable. Victories at Lo-debar and Karnaim were fresh in their minds and were taken to be the earnest of more to follow (Amos 6 : 13). They, on their part, were sure that they were gratifying Yahweh by their lavish sacrifices. Was not the covenant an agreement that he would help them against their enemies if he received the firstlings, the first-fruits, and the observance of the great festivals?

Amos answers by a flat contradiction, and by the unheard-of declaration that Yahweh does not require sacrifice but righteousness between man and man. In the material prosperity on which the people laid so much stress the prophet saw only the social evils which prosperity had fostered. The sacrifices are to him not only something indifferent, they are even contemptible: "Come to Bethel and transgress! To Gilgal and multiply transgression! Bring your sacrifices in the morning and your tithes the third day! Offer your thanksgiving sacrifice of leavened bread, and proclaim free-will offerings—this pleases you, O house of Israel!" (4 : 4 *f.*) The intimation is that all this is mere will-worship, recreation and dissipation for the people, but of no value to Yahweh. And, thinking his irony might not be understood, the prophet tells in plain words what Yahweh means: "I hate, I despise your feasts, and I take no delight in your solemn assemblies; though you offer me your burnt-offerings and sacrifices I will not accept them, neither will I regard the peace-offerings of your fed beasts" (5 : 21). And, as if this were not enough, Amos goes the length of denying that the cultus was observed in the wilderness, the time when, according to common consent, the relations of Yahweh and his people were at their best: "Was it sacrifices and offerings that you brought me in the wilderness forty years, O house of Israel?" It is evident that a strong negative is implied in the question.[1]

Instead of being gratified by the lavish offerings, Yahweh is indignant at the sins of his people and is about to destroy them—such is the conviction of Amos. What rouses his indignation is the social condition of Israel. Yahweh is the protector of the poor and will avenge their wrongs. In a sense this was not new. By tradition, Yahweh, the tribal God, was brother and friend of every member of the clan. But Amos gave the principle a broader construction. Yahweh is the God of righteousness and requires right conduct even from men outside Israel: "For three crimes of Damascus or for four I will not turn back, because they have threshed Gilead with threshing instruments of iron; and I will send a fire into the house of Hazael and it shall devour the palaces of Benhadad" (1 : 3–5). In like terms Amos threatens Ammon and Moab, and then turns to Israel: "Thus says Yahweh: For three crimes of Israel, or for four, I will not turn back; because they have sold the righteous

[1] The intent of the verse (5 : 25) is plain, though the context is obscure and probably interpolated.

for silver and the needy for a pair of shoes; they trample the head of the poor and tread down the meek; a man and his father go to the woman to pollute my name; they lay themselves down beside every altar on clothes taken in pledge, and in the house of their God they drink the wine of such as have been fined" (2 : 6–8). The accusation is that the lavish feasts at the sanctuaries are based upon oppression and extortion. Those who should administer justice turn it to wormwood (5 : 7), they take bribes (5 : 12), and hate the man who rebukes them (5 : 10). The sins of Israel are such as to astonish the nations; Philistines and Egyptians are invited to witness the tumults in Samaria and the oppressions in the midst of it (3 : 9 *f.*). The fault is with the chief men: "Woe to the secure in Samaria, the distinguished men of the chief of the nations, who think the evil day far away, yet bring it near by injustice and violence" (6 : 1–3). The women are as bad as the men, urging their husbands on to further oppression that they may have wherewith to indulge their appetite for drink (4 : 1).

That punishment must follow is the firm conviction of the prophet. What strikes him is the unreason of those who think otherwise—as though the evil day which they think far off would not necessarily follow the violence in which they indulge. To neglect this sequence of cause and effect is as unreasonable as to plough the sea with oxen, or to attempt the cliffs of the chamois on horseback (6 : 12). Warnings had in fact been given them. Twice had Yahweh set out to execute his vengeance; once with locusts, once with fire. Now this third time the plumb-line is applied to the wall and reveals its tottering condition: "The high places of Isaac shall be destroyed, and the sanctuaries of Israel laid waste, and I will stand against the house of Jeroboam with the sword" (7 : 1–9). It was this culmination of the discourse at Bethel which roused the anger of the priest. No other direct denunciation of the royal house is recorded, but there are plenty of declarations concerning the nation: "As the shepherd rescues out of the mouth of the lion two legs or the piece of an ear, so shall the sons of Israel be rescued who sit in Samaria in the corner of a couch and on the cushions of a bed" (3 : 12). There is here no thought of a remnant; what is sarcastically said to be rescued is not worth calling a remnant. The two shank bones or the piece of the ear are only evidence that the sheep has indeed been destroyed (*cf.* Ex. 22 : 12).

In his final vision Amos sees Yahweh himself standing in his temple at Bethel and shaking the building on the heads of the worshippers, with the declaration: "I will slay the last of them with the sword; not one of them shall flee away and not one of them shall escape. Though they dig into Sheol, thence shall my hand take them; and though they climb into heaven, thence will I bring them down; though they be hid in the top of Carmel I will search and take them out thence; and though they be hid from my sight in the bottom of the sea, thence will I command the serpent and it shall bite them; and though they go into captivity before their enemies, thence will I command the sword and it shall slay them; and I will set my eyes upon them for evil and not for good" (9 : 1–4).[1] It would be difficult to be more explicit. The message of Amos was one of destruction, complete and irremediable.

It does not seem hazardous to assert that Amos was an acute observer of the movements of the nations of western Asia. The great world-power, whose capital was Nineveh, was showing renewed activity about this time. Amos, to be sure, does not distinctly say that he anticipates an invasion by the Assyrian army. But he could not have been ignorant of the fact that Damascus was already hard pressed by this formidable foe, and it was easy to conclude that Israel would come next in the sequence. Amos, indeed, thinks less of the instrument than of him who wields it. To him the overshadowing thought was that Yahweh was

[1] I have quoted the whole passage because it makes plain, if anything can, that the conclusion of the book which speaks of a relenting on the part of Yahweh cannot be by Amos.

making use of this instrument for the punishment of all those nations which had been guilty of man's inhumanity to man. That Yahweh should make use of a foreign nation to punish his own people was something which the ordinary Israelite could hardly understand. This, however, was in fact the first step in the promotion of the God of Israel to his transcendent position as the ruler of the whole world. When the events of the Exile emphasised the message of the prophets the common people began to apprehend this sublime conception.

In the history of Christian theology undue emphasis has been placed on the predictive element in the Old Testament. From our present more historical point of view we see that this element was in the minds of the prophets themselves of subordinate importance. They did not suppose they were drawing up a scheme of the world's history. Their minds were occupied with the fate of their own people. They claimed, indeed, to be in such relations to Yahweh that they could interpret his will to men who were blind to the signs of the times. These signs of the times proved to them that unless Israel should turn from its evil ways, it would surely be destroyed. Their concern was with the nation and not with the individual. Where they denounce certain classes of the community, they have the sins of individuals in mind, of course, for sin is a personal matter, but the denunciation is motived by the thought that the sins of these classes are bringing the nation to ruin. Amos, at any rate, gave no thought to the fate of individuals, whether in this world or in the next, except so far as the individual was a part of the community.

Since the evils against which the prophets declaimed are social evils, these preachers are often called social reformers, as though they aimed to reconstruct society in such a way as to secure the greatest good of the greatest number. No doubt they desired social regeneration, but the form in which they clothed this ideal was not that of the modern social reformer. What they sought was the fulfilment of the will of Yahweh. In other words, they were religious idealists. Doubtless in the last analysis they were moved by sympathy with their afflicted fellow men, but this sympathy was wholly dominated by their religious faith. The sympathy was objectified in Yahweh before it was brought to bear upon men. They defined the oppression and violence which they saw not as social wrong but as sin, transgression of the will of the Almighty.

What Amos knew and what he thought everybody ought to know was that this will of the Almighty is ethical in its demands. When he exhorts: "Seek Yahweh and live!" he makes it clear that he has no ritual service in mind, for he adds: "Seek not Bethel, enter not into Gilgal, and pass not to Beersheba; for Gilgal shall surely go into captivity and Bethel shall come to nought. Seek Yahweh and live; lest he break out like fire in the house of Jacob, and there be none to quench it in Bethel. Seek good and not evil, and so Yahweh, God of Israel, will be with you as you say. Hate the evil and love the good, and establish justice in the gate" (5:4*f.* and 14*f.*). The verses might be called a compendium of Amos's principles. The demand which he was never weary of making is reiterated again in the same chapter: "Let justice flow on like a river, and righteousness like a perennial stream" (5 : 24). The very fact that Israel stood in special relations to Yahweh made it more imperative that Israel should meet these demands: "You only have I known of all the nations of the earth; therefore will I visit upon you all your guilt" (3 : 2).

It will be evident that Amos was no theologian. He nowhere speculates on the nature of Yahweh and his relation to the world. Whether he conceded any reality to the gods of the nations is not revealed by any utterance of his. He is not even consistent with himself; for, although he concedes that Israel has been brought up from Egypt by Yahweh ("you only have I known" he makes Yahweh say), yet he holds also that it is Yahweh who brought the Philistines from Caphtor and the Arameans from Kir (9 : 7). If religious thinkers in Babylon or in Egypt had developed a speculative monotheism Amos was guiltless of any knowledge of their systems. His monotheism, if such it was, was a practical monotheism. Enough for him that Yahweh, God of Israel, was powerful enough to punish his people for their sins, and that he would use the nations of the earth for this purpose. His power extends beyond the boundaries of Israel, and his ethical will is enforced upon other peoples. The cruelty of the Syrians in war, the barbarity of the Moabites who burned the bones of the King of Edom to lime, are certain to be punished by the same Yahweh who stands up to judge the oppressors in Israel. Yahweh, the God of Israel, is, within these limits, the living and active guardian of the moral order of the world. Commonplace as this seems to us, it was something new and startling in Israel.

Hosea, the younger contemporary of Amos, is a contrast to him in almost every respect. Amos is the stern moralist, sitting in judgment on his people, pronouncing them guilty, and almost rejoicing to see that justice is to be done. Hosea, though obliged to assent to the correctness of the verdict, yet suffers in sympathy with the condemned, and feels all the pain and shame that are to fall upon them as if they were his own. The point of departure for his preaching is given by the idea we have already alluded to—the idea that the prophet is in such close relations with Yahweh that his actions as well as his words are revelations of the divine will. Even the experiences which come to him without active effort on his own part may give him intimations of the higher will. Hosea had a wife who made shipwreck of their married life. Reflecting on this experience the prophet saw in it something divinely ordained to teach him the heart of Yahweh toward Israel. Yahweh is the husband, Israel the wife, and the wife is unfaithful.

To Amos the unfaithfulness of Israel is the unfaithfulness of a servant. Yahweh commands righteousness between man and man; Israel, instead of obeying the command, disobeys, and then seeks to make the dereliction good by flattering the master with another kind of service, devoting itself to the cultus, as though sacrifice and offering could be a substitute for obedience. Hosea says the unfaithfulness is the unfaithfulness of a wife. The ritual is not mere will-worship—the substitution of something else in place of obedience. It is the choice of another object of affection—the wife's preference of another to her rightful lord. This other is Baal who has usurped the place of Yahweh. Hence the wrath of Yahweh is jealousy, the most intense of the passions. The defection is, indeed, judged from the ethical standard, as truly as by Amos: "Yahweh has an indictment against his people," says Hosea; "there is no fidelity and no kindness, and no knowledge of Yahweh in the land; there is nought but breaking faith and killing and stealing and committing adultery" (4 : 1 *f.*). As in Amos, prosperity has led to luxury and excess. "When the fruits were abundant, altars were multiplied; when the land was prospered the people set up pillars at the sanctuaries" (10 : 1).

As in Amos also, the forefathers were acceptable, but they had quickly turned away. "When Israel was a child I loved him and called my son out of Egypt; but the more I called the more they went from me; they sacrificed to the Baals and burned incense to the images. Yet it was I who taught Ephraim to walk, who took them by the arms" (11 : 1–3). This choice of the Baals is the crowning sin. It is whoredom, as the prophet does not hesitate to say. Israel herself declares: "I will go after my lovers who give me my bread and my wine, my wool and my flax, my oil and my drink" (2 : 7). Hosea has the idea, which, as we have seen, is historically justified that the popular religion is of Canaanitish origin. The divinity worshipped at the local sanctuaries, though called by the name of Yahweh, was, in fact, the Baal of the early inhabitants. The oracles at the sacred trees, the sacrifices, the prostitution of the devotees, were so many evidences of Canaanitish religion. It is for this reason that Hosea denounces the priests so often. Where Amos condemns the nobles, the great landed proprietors, because of their oppression and injustice, Hosea breaks out against the priests. To him the people are perishing for lack of the knowledge which the priests ought to impart: "Since you have rejected knowledge I will reject you, that you be no longer priest to me; and since you put the *tora* of your God out of your mind I will put your children out of my mind. The more powerful they [the priests] become the more they sin against me; they exchange their glory for shame; they feed on the sin of my people and delight in their guilt" (4 : 6*f.*). To understand the accusation we must remember that the word *tora,* often translated law, means the instruction of the priest, given by means of the oracle. Cases of dispute, as we saw in the time of Moses, were brought to the priests for decision, and also cases where a trespass had been committed in sacred things. The imputation is that the priests manipulate the oracle for their personal profit, and that they even encourage the people to sin in order that they may impose penalties upon them, exacting fines which accrue to the sanctuary. The prophet has also in mind the lavish festivals by which the priests attract the people to the sanctuaries, these festivals becoming scenes of debauchery. In one passage he does not hesitate to accuse the priests of sins of violence: "Their bands are like highway robbers, they murder on the road to Shechem" (6 : 9).

Amos nowhere objects to the images of Yahweh, though, doubtless, he included them in his condemnation of the whole worship. Hosea is more specific. The golden bulls at Bethel and Dan had long enjoyed the prestige given by use and wont. They had been the objects of worship for two hundred years. If forbidden by early documents the prohibition had not been taken seriously. Hosea makes his position clear by saying that Yahweh has cast off the calf of Samaria, by which he means the one at Bethel, the chief sacred object in the northern kingdom (8 : 5). In another passage he says that the inhabitants of Samaria shall be in terror for the calf of Bethel, and that it shall be carried away as a gift to the great king (10 : 5*f.*). It seems clear, therefore, that the first effective opposition to the images of Yahweh dates from Hosea.

Amos and Hosea agree in rejecting the popular religion, and they agree further in stating their positive programme. What Yahweh desires is not sacrifice, but kindness, love of man for his fellow man (6 : 6). Yahweh is a God of justice, and from the house of Jehu he will require the blood shed at Jezreel (1 : 4). The declaration is the more remarkable in that the blood shed at Jezreel was shed in obedience to the prophetic champion of the rights of Yahweh. It does not seem extravagant to conclude that the prophets have discovered the vanity of political remedies for moral evils. The frequent changes of dynasty in this period instead of bringing about a better state of things had rather aggravated the corruption of the people, of which indeed it was the fruit and evidence. It is sometimes said that Hosea rejected the kingship and desired a return to the old tribal organisation; but this is far from evident. He does, indeed, believe that the existing rulers are not the men to save the people. "They make kings but not of my will; they set up princes but not of my knowledge" (8 : 4). What the prophet attempts to set forth is the vanity of political devices. Whether a king after God's own heart would be able to help he does not say. The actually existing monarchy is of no avail: "Where is now thy king that shall save thee? And thy rulers that they may vindicate thee? Concerning whom thou saidst: 'Give me a King and princes!' I gave thee a king in my wrath, and I take him away in my fury" (13 : 10*f.*). Distrust of political devices extends, as we should expect, to the current diplomacy: "Ephraim is like a silly dove without understanding; now they call to Egypt, now they go to Assyria" (7 : 11). "When Ephraim saw his sickness and Israel his wound, then went Ephraim to Assyria and sent to the great king; but he is not able to cure you, neither will he heal you of your wound" (5 : 13). The very nations to whom they appeal will be the instruments of their destruction: "They shall not dwell in Yahweh's land; Ephraim shall return to Egypt and in Assyria shall he eat unclean food" (9 : 3).

This recapitulation of the main points of Hosea's teaching gives little idea of the passion which filled his soul. The situation as he regarded it was indeed desperate, and he was in a heat of indignation and grief. The invasion of the land seems to him so imminent that he urges the blowing of the alarm at once (5 : 8–10). The greatness of the love which Yahweh has had for his people is the measure of the wrath, now that his wooing has been rejected. Yet there is a struggle as his love still tries to assert itself: "How shall I give thee up, Ephraim? How shall I cast thee off, Israel? How shall I make thee as Admah? How shall I set thee as Zeboim? My heart revolts within me, my compassion is kindled. Yet shall I not execute the fierceness of my anger? Shall I not destroy Ephraim? I am God and not man, the holy one in the midst of thee, and I must come in wrath" (11 : 8*f.*). The ordinary translation reverses the meaning of this passage; the conflict in the heart of Yahweh results in the determination to go on with the work of punishment. The allusion to his holiness, the quality which separates God from man and which reacts against human sin, is the pledge that he will execute justice however much his love may plead for the offender. If we were in doubt the following passage would check any illusion: "Therefore am I unto them like a lion; as a leopard will I watch by the way; I will meet them like a bear robbed of her whelps, and will rend the enclosure of their heart; there will I devour them like a lion, like a wild beast tear them in pieces" (13 : 7*f.*). The culmination of this chapter, which is, in fact, the culmination of Hosea's preaching, is in the same tone: "Shall I ransom them from the power of Sheol? shall I redeem them from death? Rather, bring on thy plagues, O Death! Hither with thy torments, O Sheol! Repentance shall be hid from my eyes" (13 : 14).

Such passages seem to leave no room for hope, and in view of them we cannot suppose those sections of the book of

Hosea which predict a restoration to be genuine utterances of the prophet.[1] An utterance which seems at first blush to express the repentance of the people is introduced only to show their incurable levity: "In their affliction they will seek me and say: 'Come let us return unto Yahweh, for he has torn and he will heal; he has smitten and he will bind us up'" (6 : 1). The answer of Yahweh is: "What shall I do to thee, Ephraim? What shall I do to thee, Israel? Your piety is like the morning mist, like the dew which soon melts away. Therefore have I smitten them by the prophets, have slain them by the words of my mouth" (6 : 4). The immediate context gives a renewed declaration of the people's wickedness, and makes it clear that the prophet had no confidence in any professions of repentance. Whether an individual here and there was impressed by the preaching of the prophet does not appear. These preachers, as we have seen, were thinking of the nation as a whole.

Our study should make clear to us the contribution made by Hosea to religious thinking. To him Yahweh is not simply the God who requires justice between man and man; he is the God who seeks the love of his people, a love that will manifest itself in the doing of his will. It was because the love was rejected that he was compelled to punish, though his own heart was torn by the necessity. What will become of him when his people is destroyed is a question not raised by the prophet. Doubtless the faith which was so deeply convinced of his love, his power, and his justice was content to leave the future with him. It does not even appear that Hosea was a monotheist in our sense of the word; the bitterness with which he declaims against the Baals indicates that he had some sort of belief in their real existence, and his declaration that other lands than Yahweh's are unclean shows that in his view other divinities had power there. Yet the vividness with which Hosea conceived the relation of Yahweh to Israel as a marriage prepared the way for monotheism,

[1] The concluding exhortation of the book (14 : 2–10) must be judged like the conclusion of Amos.

for it impressed upon the people the thought that Yahweh tolerates no rival in the affections of his people. Both Jewish and Christian thinkers have given prominent expression to this conception of Hosea.

CHAPTER VIII

ISAIAH

WITH the fall of Samaria in 721 northern Israel ceased to play a part in history, and the mission of the Hebrew race was intrusted to Judah. With reference to religion we may say that the centre of interest had shifted to Judah before the fall of Samaria, for Isaiah, one of the most influential of the prophets, began his career about 740. Before studying him we may briefly notice his contemporary, Micah, fragments of whose discourses are embedded in the book which bears his name. We might suppose Micah to be the man who transplanted the prophetic movement from Israel to Judah, for he seems to have been a disciple of Amos. Like Amos, he was a simple-hearted countryman who was revolted by the corruptions of city life. His conception of his office is like that of the older prophet—he regards himself as a plain-spoken warner, "full of might by the spirit of Yahweh, to declare unto Jacob his transgression and to Israel his sin" (Micah 3 : 8). As the transgression of Israel was concentrated at Samaria, so the sin of Judah was concentrated at Jerusalem (1 : 5). The phenomenon is too familiar to need comment; in the great cities vice makes itself more odiously visible than in the smaller towns and villages. In the cities the rich and the devotees of pleasure congregate, and there they find those who minister to their profligacy. This is what impressed the preacher who was accustomed to the simple life of the country.

The details given by Micah are much like what we read in Amos. The nobles are covetous and oppressive; they devise iniquity on their beds and when the morning comes they put their plans into effect; they covet fields and seize them, houses and take them; so they oppress a man and his house, a man and his inheritance (2 : 1 *f.*). They do not hesitate to evict the women of their people from their homes, and they sell the children into slavery because of debt (2 : 9). They plunder travellers on the highway, and when they are rebuked by the prophet they bid him hold his peace. Yet they are the ones who ought to know better: "Is it not for you, chiefs of Jacob, is it not for you to know justice? Yet they hate the good and love the evil, tear the skin from men's bodies and the flesh from their bones" (3 : 1 *f.*). While they silence the true prophets, they encourage the false who drivel of wine and strong drink (2 : 11). Prophets, seers, and soothsayers, all are in the same condemnation, and the same shame will overtake them all. Their venality is too evident: "If one does not give them to eat, against him they declare war" (3 : 5). Deceiving the people and pandering to their vices, they lead them on to their destruction. Because of this false teaching Zion is built up in blood, and Jerusalem in iniquity. Yet the evil-doers are confident that Yahweh is in the midst of them and that no evil will come upon them (3 : 11). The sequel is plainly evident to the prophet, and is announced in words that were remembered long after his time: "Therefore Zion shall be ploughed as a field for your sake, and Jerusalem shall be ruins, and the temple mount overgrown with bushes" (3 : 12; *cf.* the reference in Jer. 26 : 18). The close parallel with Amos must be evident—justice will be done though the heavens fall.

In Isaiah we find a man of more genial temper and a larger outlook. His general position, however, is the same taken by his predecessors, and we have no difficulty in supposing that he was acquainted with the words of Amos and Hosea. With Hosea he shared the belief that the life of the prophet is shaped by his calling. He says that he and the children God has given him are signs and portents in Israel. He named one of his sons Shear-jashub, and another Maher-shalal-hash-baz in order to emphasise his message. At one time he went naked and barefoot for three years, so as to impress upon his people the impending fate of Egypt (20 : 1–6). Perhaps if we had the full record of his life we should have more instances of such symbolic actions, but these are enough to show his conception of the prophet's office and work, or rather of the complete identification of the prophet's person and his work. Yet there is little of the enthusiastic visionary in Isaiah, and the impression made by his words is that of a wise and sane counsellor, preaching righteousness to the people, and even confronting the monarch in the calm consciousness of a man who is sure that he has the right on his side.

The vision by which Isaiah was determined to undertake the work of a prophet (related in chapter 6) is one of the most impressive in the Old Testament, and it reveals as clearly as any part of the book what was the guiding principle of his life. He saw Yahweh, he says, sitting on a lofty throne in the temple. We can hardly doubt that in the mind of Isaiah the Jerusalem temple was the dwelling-place of Israel's God. Amos and Hosea seem not to have given the same importance to any of the sanctuaries of the northern kingdom. In one instance, indeed, Amos sees Yahweh standing in or over the temple at Bethel, but this is only in order to throw the building down and thus destroy the worshippers. To these earlier prophets Bethel was no more than Gilgal or any of the others—Yahweh was not in them. But to Isaiah the temple of Jerusalem did not stand on the same level with the other sanctuaries of the land; Yahweh had his dwelling there as he had not in other places of worship. This attitude toward the temple became influential in the later development of religious belief.

In this temple Yahweh had his throne, where he was visible to the spiritual eye and in human form, though of supernal brightness. He was attended by the seraphim, mythological figures which are nowhere else mentioned in the Old Testament. Possibly they were originally the personification of the lightnings. Elsewhere we read of the cherubim as attendants of the throne, or the host of heaven takes this office (I Kings 22 : 19). If once serpentine in form (the word *saraph* is used to denote the fiery serpents which infest the desert), they have now become partly humanised, possessing hands and feet, though also furnished with wings. Their office is to proclaim the uniqueness of Yahweh, his apartness from earthly things. This sanctity is proclaimed as a warning, such as Moses received at the bush. To approach the divinity without undergoing some cleansing process is dangerous. Isaiah realises this, for he feels that he is undone: "I am a man of unclean lips and I dwell in the midst of a people of unclean lips," is his cry. The conception of holiness seems on the way from the physical to the ethical, for the uncleanness of the lips must refer to sinful utterance. A coal from the altar removes the defilement, for fire, especially sacred fire, is one of the most potent means of purification. In connection with the proclamation of Yahweh's sanctity the seraphim affirm that the whole earth is full of his glory. As the sun shines from one part of heaven to the other, so Yahweh enlightens his whole creation. This universalism is beyond anything we have yet found in Israel.

Isaiah's readiness to volunteer in response to the divine call for a messenger probably indicates that he had been meditating on the need of the hour, and had debated the question whether he was not the man to carry the warning to his people. The form of the command is, however, strange: "Go and tell this people: 'Hear on, but understand not; gaze on, but perceive not!' Make the mind of this people stupid and make their ears dull, besmear their eyes too, lest they see with their eyes, and hear with their ears and understand with their heart, and their health be restored" (6 : 9 *f.*). To us the strangeness is in the conception that the message is sent not to heal but to aggravate the disease, not to convert but to harden the hearers. Yet such a conception is not foreign to the Old Testament writers. Since whatever comes to pass is the work of Yahweh, the obstinacy with which the message of the preacher is so often confronted, and which seems to result from the preaching, must be the result intended by the divinity. The Pentateuchal writer had no difficulty with the thought that Yahweh hardened the heart of Pharaoh. Isaiah himself speaks of Yahweh as a stone of stumbling, a trap, and a snare to both houses of Israel (8 : 14). Isaiah, in other words, dealt with the hard facts of life, and in his observation Yahweh did often seem to inflict what we call judicial blindness by the means which would seem calculated to induce repentance. In another passage the prophet tells the people: "Yahweh has poured on you the spirit of deep sleep, and has closed your eyes and covered your heads" (29 : 10).

Holding this fixed idea of the divine power, these earlier prophets conceived that their work was to proclaim the will of Yahweh as a protest rather than as a means of grace. This we have found to be the case with Amos, with Hosea, and with Micah. At a later time Jeremiah declared that the earlier prophets had spoken of war and of pestilence and of calamity, and he intimated that any message of different tenor had the presumption against it. It is quite conceivable therefore that Isaiah saw from the beginning the uselessness of any attempt to bring his people into a better frame of mind. As the text now stands, it shows quite clearly that he regarded himself as the predictor of evil. He asks how long his commission is to run, and receives for answer: "Until the cities be waste without inhabitant, and houses be without men, and the land becomes utterly waste, and Yahweh removes men far away, and the forsaken places be many in the midst of the land; even if there be a tenth in it, it in turn shall be consumed as a terebinth and an oak whose stump alone remains when they have been felled" (6 : 11 *f.*).[1] And this sombre passage

[1] Later editors, who were familiar with the thought that a remnant would be preserved, added to the text the clause: "The holy seed is the stump." But it must be evident that this contradicts the main idea of the passage.

does not stand alone, for at the end of the parable of the vineyard Isaiah says: "Therefore the wrath of Yahweh burns against his people, and he stretches his hand against it, and he smites it till the mountains shake, and the corpses lie like mud on the streets; yet his wrath is not turned away, and his hand is still stretched out" (5 : 25). And this last sentence recurs again and again as though to impress the thought that repeated chastisements had had no effect (*cf.* 9 : 11, 16, 20, and 10 : 4).

Early in his career, then, the prophet, like Amos and Hosea, saw only the threatened destruction of the people of Yahweh by Yahweh himself. This is not to say that he held to this expectation through life. The young man sometimes applies his theories with more rigid consistency than the man who has had larger observation of life and character. The indignation of the revolutionist burns hottest in youth. Isaiah's early message is accounted for by his lofty view of the character of Yahweh. His favourite name for Yahweh is: "The Holy One of Israel." And with him holiness is no longer a physical attribute. Proof is found not only in the scene described above but in the express declaration that Yahweh of Hosts is exalted by justice and the Holy God shows himself holy by righteousness.[1] One who has this high idea of God's ethical perfection may judge a sinful world severely and expect it to be destroyed. It is probable, however, that in Isaiah's case the early severity was moderated in later years. Especially when the investment of Jerusalem by the Assyrians threatened to destroy the temple, Yahweh's own dwelling, he reflected on the blow that would thereby be struck at religion, and his faith affirmed that the sacred building would not be delivered over to the enemy.

The chief utterances of the prophet, however, echo the old refrain of the sins of Israel. Calling heaven and earth to witness, Yahweh protests: "Sons have I nourished and

[1] The authenticity of the verse is questioned by some scholars, but I think without sufficient reason (5 : 16).

brought up, but they have rebelled against me. The ox knows his owner and the ass his master's crib; Israel does not know, my people does not consider" (1 : 2*f.*). And the bill of particulars follows. First of all, Yahweh does not require sacrifice: "What is the multitude of your sacrifices to me, says Yahweh; I have had enough of the burnt-offerings of rams, and the fat of fed beasts, and I delight not in the blood of bullocks or of lambs or of he-goats" (1 : 11*f.*). The true demand of Yahweh is for righteousness between man and man: "Wash you, make you clean, put away the evil of your doings from before my eyes; cease to do evil, learn to do well; seek justice, relieve the oppressed, judge the fatherless, take up the cause of the widow" (1 : 16*f.*). We are already familiar with such expressions of the prophetic conscience, roused by the spectacle of man's tyranny and hard-heartedness. Like Amos, Isaiah denounces the rulers as most to blame: "Yahweh stands up to judge the people; Yahweh will enter into judgment with the elders of his people, and with the rulers thereof: It is you who have eaten up the vineyard; the spoil of the poor is in your houses; what mean you that you crush my people and grind the faces of the poor? says Yahweh, Lord of Hosts" (3 : 13–15). The women of the upper classes come in for a sharp rebuke (3 : 16–26), and the priests and prophets receive castigation. These are pictured as they sit at revelry, apparently in the temple itself, and make merry over the preacher who presumes to give them lessons (28 : 9–11). Their example is infectious, for the common people also "say to the seers: See not; and to the prophets, Prophesy not unto us right things, speak unto us smooth things, prophesy deceit, turn from the way, go aside from the path, trouble us no more with Israel's Holy One" (30 : 10*f.*).

We have already noticed that the originality of Hosea consisted in his application of the relation of husband and wife to the relation between Yahweh and Israel. Isaiah takes up this figure when he says: "How is the faithful city become a harlot!" (1 : 21.) Apparently, however, he is not thinking of Baal worship, but rather, with Amos, of the ritual as so much will-worship, amusement for the people, but not acceptable to Yahweh. Isaiah has little to say of defection to other gods, but much of the false religiosity of the people; their religion is mere externality; they draw near to God with their lips while their hearts are far away; their fear of him (that is, their religion) is a commandment of men which has been taught them (29 : 13).

We cannot claim great originality for Isaiah, therefore. His ideas are those common to the prophetic school. But he puts these ideas into powerful expression. A fine example is the parable of the vineyard. We may suppose that the people had gathered at the temple for the autumn festival, satisfied that all was well between them and their God. The prophet appears as one of the revellers, singing them a song composed in the light, tripping measure appropriate to the vintage season. After thus attracting their attention he breaks out with an objurgation made terrific by its word-play: "The vineyard of Yahweh of Hosts is the house of Israel, and the men of Judah are his cherished plantation; and he looked for justice, but behold bloodshed; for righteousness, but behold an outcry" (5 : 7). What sort of fruit the vineyard has been yielding is then set forth in a series of woes. These single out first of all the great landed proprietors, who get their estates by crowding out their poorer neighbours; then come the drunken revellers, who rise up early that they may follow strong drink, who tarry late into the night that wine may inflame them. Next in the list are the scoffers, who wish the day of Yahweh to come, and with them the perverse reasoners who call good evil and evil good, making the worse appear the better reason. These are apparently the politicians who defend deception as the true method of diplomacy, and regard underhanded measures as necessary to the well-being of the state. The unjust judges, who justify the wicked for a bribe, and deprive the righteous of his standing in court, close the list, unless we join with them the scribes who write out unjust and oppressive decrees.[1] In the original form of this discourse it is probable that each woe had its appropriate punishment. Some of these have now disappeared from the text, but it is evident that they included dearth, banishment, pestilence, and a visitation which is left undefined but which is compared to a sweeping storm that ruins everything in its path.

The part which the prophets took in political movements is well illustrated by the life of Isaiah. He shows also that the political interest was primarily religious. The first occasion when he took part in public affairs was the invasion of Judah by the combined forces of Israel and Damascus, in 735. The intention was to compel Judah to join in a common movement of resistance to the Assyrians. The sentiment of the people of Judah seems rather to have favoured the invaders, if we may judge by the perturbation of Ahaz. The king saw an obvious resource in calling the Assyrians to his assistance. He was meditating this step when Isaiah intervened and attempted to dissuade him. The prophet saw that the proposed arrangement with Assyria would bring Judah into a subjection which would prove burdensome and in the long run disastrous. But the spring of his opposition was not any view of expediency; he believed that Judah should trust to Yahweh and refuse the arm of flesh. To mix in the affairs of the nations would be to give up Judah's prerogative as the people of Yahweh. The promise of the child called Immanuel was intended simply to give assurance that in the immediate future the two threatening powers would become incapable of harm, and that God's intervention would be manifest in Judah. Politically this meant that it was unnecessary to call upon Assyria, because that nation was bound to act for its own sake, and any submission on the part of Judah would be a gratuitous assumption of the foreign yoke. Politically sound as the advice was, it was evidently motived by trust in Yahweh.[2]

[1] The full number of seven woes would be made out by joining 10 : 1–3, to those in chapter 5.

[2] The boy Maher-shalal-hash-baz teaches the same lesson with Immanuel. Before he should be able to say father or mother the riches

The expectation of the prophet that Damascus and Ephraim would be reduced to impotence by the Assyrians was amply realised. It seems, however, that he expected an invasion of Judah at the same time. A vigorous passage describing the march of the invading army has been preserved to us, and may belong in this period. Whenever it was pronounced, it was not literally fulfilled. As to the fate of the northern kingdom, however, Isaiah made no mistake. Their stoutness of heart did not deceive him. Not long before the fall of Samaria the prophet pronounced the spirited denunciation of the drunkards of Ephraim which he used later as a text for his discourse against the leading men in Jerusalem (chapter 28). He agrees with Amos in describing the luxury and carelessness of the people in Samaria, on whose horizon the storm-cloud of disaster already lowered.

This chapter as it now stands introduces us to the third crisis which occurred in the life of the prophet. This is the invasion of the country by Sennacherib. There was at this time a joint movement among the Palestinian powers to throw off the Assyrian yoke. It was encouraged by Egypt, and apparently Babylon had promised to revolt at the same time. Isaiah had protested against submission to Assyria in the time of Ahaz, but he believed that Judah, having once accepted the relation of vassal, should be faithful to its obligations. To revolt would be dishonest and would bring down the wrath of Yahweh. His deep-rooted scepticism concerning political measures made him protest against the Egyptian alliance, and it was probably reinforced by a sound common sense which took an accurate measure of Egyptian pretensions. It was, perhaps, when the Egyptian alliance had been consummated that the joy of Jerusalem broke out in immoderate feasting: "What ails thee that all thy people have gone up to the housetops, thou who art full of uproar, tumultuous city, joyous town? . . . The Lord Yahweh of Hosts calls to weeping and to mourning, and to

of Damascus and the spoil of Samaria would be carried away by the king of Assyria (8 : 1–4).

baldness, and to girding of sackcloth; but behold, joy and gladness, the killing of oxen and the slaughtering of sheep, the eating of flesh and the drinking of wine!" (22 : 1, 12 *f.*) What the people hailed as a day of deliverance appeared to the prophet as a day of perplexity and discomfiture.

It is unnecessary to quote the passages in which the prophet pours scorn on the men who take the toilsome journey through the desert to seek the help of Egypt and to flee to the shelter of Pharaoh (30 : 1–6), or the powerful discourse in which he describes the alliance as a covenant with death and a compact with Sheol (28 : 15). Then, as now, the diplomatists thought finesse all-powerful; the prophet had a higher ideal. This ideal, to be sure, found negative expression for the most part, and we must be prepared to meet the demand that a fruitful and positive programme should be formulated. Had Isaiah any positive measures to recommend, or was he simply a critic of the existing order? To this we find one answer: He would have the people trust in Yahweh. Trust in Egypt is contrasted with trust in Yahweh (31 : 1–3). The classic verse in which he formulates his principle, and which might be prefixed as motto to his book, is: "By repenting and remaining quiet you would have been delivered; in quietness and pious trust you would have found your strength" (30 : 15). In the crisis of the Ephraimitic invasion he himself illustrated the true state of mind and enunciated it: "If you do not believe you will not be upheld" (7 : 9), or to attempt to reproduce the play on words: "If you do not hold fast you shall not be held fast." In the more acute crisis of Sennacherib's invasion he uttered the well-known words: "Behold I lay in Zion a stone, a tried stone, a precious foundation stone: he who believes shall not waver. And I will make justice the measuring line, and righteousness the plumb-weight" (28 : 17). The positive principle thus formulated is: "Do right and let God take care of the results."

Isaiah was at one with Amos in believing that Yahweh was able to make use of the nations as instruments of his wrath. He, in fact, describes the Assyrian as the rod in his hand (10 : 5–11).[1] But the whole impression made by Isaiah is that of a more lofty conception of God than that expressed by any of his predecessors. We meet in Amos the conception of a day of Yahweh, and the intimation is that the people at large had a traditional expectation of such a day. To them it was a day in which Yahweh would triumph over all the enemies of Israel; to Amos it was a day in which he would punish the evil-doers in Israel itself. This is the view of Isaiah also, but he brings it to finer expression: "Yahweh has a day for all that is proud and lofty, for all that is exalted and lifted up; for cedars of Lebanon and oaks of Bashan, for mountains and hills, for every high tower and every fenced wall, for all ships of Tarshish and all stately vessels. The haughtiness of man shall be bowed down, and the loftiness of mankind shall be brought low, and Yahweh alone will be exalted in that day. Men shall go into the caverns of the rocks and into the holes of the ground at the terror of Yahweh, at the splendor of his majesty when he arises to strike awe throughout the earth" (2 : 12–19). The sanctity of Yahweh is here defined for us; it is his absolute supremacy above everything earthly. That to Isaiah it is ethical as well as physical we have already seen.

Some corollaries of Isaiah's belief were perhaps needful for him and his contemporaries, though their survival in the popular mind wrought mischief in a later generation. One of these was the impregnability of Jerusalem. The prophet's inaugural vision has shown us that to his view Yahweh dwelt in the temple. And in another passage he says: "Yahweh has founded Zion and in her the afflicted of his people take refuge" (14 : 32). If this be so, the conclusion cannot be remote that the sacred place will not be given up to a heathen people. This thought was fully brought home to the prophet at the great crisis of Sennach-

[1] Unfortunately, the chapter has been worked over by a later hand, but there is no sufficient reason for denying the substance of it to Isaiah.

erib's invasion. What seems clear is that though Isaiah had been predicting disaster when the people were most confident of success, yet when the situation changed for the worse his faith rose to the assurance that the worst would not be inflicted; Yahweh would not give his sanctuary over to the enemy. The event justified the prophet. And although, as we have seen, the message which he felt called to deliver was one of denunciation, yet time may have modified the sternness of his early judgment. We cannot argue, indeed, from the name of his oldest son, Shear-jashub (A-remnant-shall-return) for it may have meant that *only* a remnant would survive the Ephraimitic war. But when we read, "I will turn my hand against thee and smelt out all thy dross; I will remove all thine alloy; I will bring back thy judges as at the first, and thy counsellors as at the beginning; thereafter thou shalt be called Citadel of Righteousness, Faithful City" (1 : 25–27), we see how distinct in at least one period was the idea of purification and restoration.

Exactly how the prophet conceived the state of the commonwealth after the purifying process should have taken effect is not clear. The only clew we have is the reference to the band of disciples whom the prophet had gathered about him and to whom he committed a record of his spoken discourses (8 : 16). This party, we may suppose, took an active interest in what went on in the political world as well as in the sphere of religion. The line was not drawn, in fact, between the secular and the religious. This little group was probably considerably strengthened after the verification of Isaiah's prediction in the time of Sennacherib. Possibly they were the active instigators of Hezekiah's reforms of the cultus of which the book of Kings makes mention. But they were not only a political party, they were also a church, a religious communion finding edification in the words of their great leader and cherishing the record of these words when he himself was no longer with them.

Among the reforms attributed to Hezekiah there is one

which seems historically attested. This is the destruction of the brazen serpent which was an object of worship in the temple from the earliest times. The legend which attributes this idol to Moses shows not only its venerable antiquity but possibly also that it was regarded as an image of Yahweh. Isaiah's reaction against images was first roused, we may suppose, by the foreign gods brought to Jerusalem by Ahaz when the Assyrian alliance was formed. Opposition to the alliance with Egypt would intensify the feeling. In describing the state of Judah he affirms that the land was full not only of soothsayers like the Philistines, but also of silver and golden images (2 : 8, 18). The impotence of these alleged divinities was clear to him, for he predicts that they will be cast to the moles and the bats. It is he, perhaps, who first stigmatised the idols as nothings (*elilim*). He declared further that the people would be ashamed of the oaks which they had loved and the gardens in which they had delighted (1 : 29). The impotence of the idols must have been made evident in connection with the fall of the northern kingdom, when the golden bulls fell into the hand of the Assyrians, and also at the invasion of Sennacherib when the country sanctuaries were plundered by the invader. All this tended to increase the prestige of the temple and to strengthen the hands of those who desired an imageless worship.

Reviewing what can be known of the life of Isaiah, it does not seem hard to account for the influence which he exerted—first on his own generation, more distinctly on those that followed. He alone among the prophets of Judah seems to have correctly forecast the failure of Pekah and Rezon, then the fall of Samaria, next the futility of the Egyptian alliance, and, finally, the preservation of Jerusalem from sack and siege. But this influence could hardly have been his unless he had been a thoroughly religious man. In fact, all his utterances impress us as those of a man thoroughly honest, thoroughly courageous, and thoroughly devoted to the God of Israel. The fact that the majority was against him made no difference in the persistency with which he uttered the truth as he saw it. He tells us that Yahweh warned him not to be moved by popular clamour even when it based itself on religious beliefs: "Call not that sacred which this people call sacred; neither fear what they fear nor be terrified at it! Call Yahweh of Hosts sacred and let him alone be your fear and your object of reverence."[1] What made Isaiah a religious leader was the firmness with which he held on to this trust in Yahweh alone. The scoffing of priests and prophets was finally put to shame by his fidelity.

On account of the overlaying of Isaiah's words with later material it is difficult to say whether his hope in the remnant ever assumed what we may call Messianic form. Several chapters contained in his book give very definite expression to this hope, but the most of these are now conceded to be of later date. They are insertions of an exilic writer who could not bear to leave the uncompromising threats of the prophet unmodified by more hopeful expressions. The phenomenon is the same that we have met in the editing of Amos and Hosea. It is possible that the thought of a remnant involved the continuance of the Davidic dynasty and the reign of an ideal king. The coming judgment would purify the people (1 : 25), and the city would remain as a citadel of righteousness for all time, perhaps with a righteous ruler at its head. But we cannot get beyond the "perhaps" with reference to all this. It is not accidental, apparently, that Isaiah promises that the judges shall be restored as at the first and makes no mention of the king. On the basis of such silence we should conclude that the monarch, even of David's line, played no part in whatever picture the prophet made of the commonwealth of the future. A rudimentary expectation is all that we can with confidence attribute to him.

[1] The received text of the passage (8 : 12) is unintelligible and the emendation obvious.

CHAPTER IX

JEREMIAH

SINCE religion is a personal experience, the progress of Israel's religion is reflected in a series of personalities whose words have been preserved for us. The biographical form of our study is therefore inevitable. As we have taken up in succession Amos, Hosea, Micah, and Isaiah, so now we must endeavour to understand Jeremiah, in some respects the most interesting of all. There might indeed be a question whether he should be studied before we consider Deuteronomy. The most important event of the seventh century B. C. was the reform of Josiah, based on the book found in the temple, and this book was found early in the active life of Jeremiah. Chronologically, it would seem that Deuteronomy should be studied before Jeremiah. But against this is the consideration that Jeremiah belongs in the succession of which Amos was the first member, and that in a sense he completed that line. Deuteronomy introduced a new element into the religion of Israel, an element with which Jeremiah had little or no sympathy. It is best therefore to let him complete the series of prophets of the old school, reserving Deuteronomy to open a new division of the subject.

Whatever reforms were introduced into the worship at Jerusalem by Hezekiah were largely undone in the reign of Manasseh. This king, we are told, "built again the high places which his father had destroyed, reared again altars for Baal, made an Ashera as had Ahab, king of Israel, and worshipped all the host of heaven and served them. He built altars for all the host of heaven in the two courts of the temple, and made his son pass through the fire, and practised augury and used enchantments, and dealt with them that had familiar spirits and with wizards. . . . Moreover he shed innocent blood very much till he had filled Jerusalem from one end to another" (II Kings 21 : 3–6). It was the traditional religion revenging itself on innovators, coupled probably with Assyrian influence, which prompted this violent reaction. Jeremiah confirms what is said about the shedding of innocent blood, and we must suppose that the prophetic party, the one founded by Isaiah, was the object of active persecution. Religion was an affair of the state, and opposition to the king's religious measures would be punished as treason. The persecution seems to have been active enough to repress the public appearance of prophets of the reforming school, and this accounts for the fact that none of the fragments which have come down to us can be dated in the reign of Manasseh.

Clear light falls upon the history of Judah only with the call of Jeremiah. The occasion of this call seems to have been an irruption of northern barbarians into the cultivated country, such a migration as afterward overran and terrified the Roman world. The invading army at this time consisted of the people known as Scythians. From sources external to Israel we learn that this people wrought wide-spread desolation in the Assyrian empire, and that indirectly they were the cause of that empire's fall. To Jeremiah and his fellow prophets they appeared to be the instruments of Yahweh's wrath, as did the Assyrian armies to Amos and Isaiah. The activity of the prophets at such crises has been likened to the appearance of birds of ill omen in advance of the storm. One of them, Zephaniah, was a contemporary of Jeremiah. His book repeats the threats with which his predecessors have made us familiar: Yahweh is about to destroy the nations, Judah being one of the first to feel his vengeance. The name of Baal is to be blotted out from the idolatrous city. Those who worship the host of heaven on the housetops are singled out for punishment, along with those who swear by Moloch, those who leap over the threshold of the sanctuary,[1] and those who wear garments of foreign fashion (Zeph. 1 : 4–9). We may suppose these to be devotees of outlandish deities who made their religion known by their dress. The sceptics, the men who are settled on their lees, and who say that Yahweh will not do anything either good or evil, come in for their share of denunciation (1 : 12). The approaching calamity is identified with the great day of which the earlier prophets had spoken, a day of wrath and trouble and distress, of waste and desolation, of clouds and thick darkness. It will execute judgment on Jerusalem, but it will also bring vengeance on Assyria. In this we find little variation from what we have already read in Isaiah.

Jeremiah, the main subject of this chapter, shows himself as a man of very different disposition from Isaiah. He was naturally timid and received his mission with fear and trembling. Moreover, in his day things were distinctly going from bad to worse; the times were out of joint, and he saw his impotence to set them right. Deeply attached to his country, he suffered as every patriot must suffer when woes come upon his fatherland. Compelled to announce the coming calamity, he was misunderstood, taken to be a traitor, arrested, humiliated, and plotted against. His mission forbade him to marry and enjoy the comforts of home, so that he presented in his own person the fate of his people, whose God had left them to themselves. Yet it would be wrong to think of him as essentially weak. Much as he shrank from the work laid upon him and from the suffering it entailed, yet he was steadfast to the end. His confidence in his God made him like a wall of iron or a pillar of bronze, able to withstand the shocks and storms of time.

Like the other prophets, Jeremiah was conscious of a distinct crisis in his life when his mission was made clear to him. In a vision he saw Yahweh in human form, who told him that

[1] Leaping over the threshold is a custom found in various religions, and distinctly attributed to the Philistines by the Old Testament itself (I Sam. 5 : 5).

he had been set apart (consecrated) to his work even before birth. The nature of the work was indicated by the divinity's touching his mouth as though putting his words into it. Henceforth Jeremiah regarded himself as dedicated to the work of heralding God's will. His personal experiences and actions revealed that will. The girdle which he hid in a rock and which was spoiled by the damp and the dirt showed him the corruption of Judah; the yoke that he made and wore typified the coming subjection of his country to the king of Babylon; the potter's vessel which he dashed to pieces was an object-lesson for those who doubted the complete rejection of Jerusalem. In all this he was in line with the earlier prophets, to whom also life was dominated by their mission.[1]

We have already found occasion to suppose that renewed prophetic activity came with the Scythian inroads. It is probably not a mere coincidence that Jeremiah's preaching began at the time when this fierce people appeared on the horizon of Palestine. He saw in them the destined instruments of Yahweh's vengeance—not upon Assyria, but upon Judah. The approach of this dreaded foe spelled ruin for his people, and Jeremiah's description is one of the most vivid that we have in the Old Testament: "Declare in Judah, and publish in Jerusalem, and say: 'Blow the trumpet in the land, cry aloud; assemble yourselves and go up to the fortified cities; set up a standard toward Zion; flee for safety, stay not! For I will bring evil from the north and a great destruction. A lion is gone up from his thicket, and a destroyer of nations; he is on his way to make thy land desolate, that thy cities be laid waste without inhabitant.' For this gird you with sackcloth, lament and wail; for the fierce anger of Yahweh is not turned from us. It shall come to pass in that day, says Yahweh, that the heart of the king shall perish, and the heart of the princes, and the priests shall be astonished and the prophets shall wonder" (4 : 5–9). The whole chapter should be read, not only to get a picture

[1] *Cf.* chapters 13, 19, and 27.

of the invader, but to realise the intense sympathy which the prophet felt for his people. This sympathy leads him to cry out: "Ah, Lord Yahweh, thou hast surely deceived this people, saying: 'You shall have peace,' whereas the sword has reached the seat of life." He alludes, no doubt, to the word of some opposition prophet which assured the people that all was well. The genuineness of Jeremiah's grief is attested again a little later. It seems as if the vision of desolation haunts him continually: "My pain! My pain! I suffer at my very heart. I cannot hold my peace, for I hear the sound of the trumpet, the shout of war. Destruction on destruction is cried out, the whole land is laid waste" (4 : 19*f.*). And again in another passage: "For the hurt of the daughter of my people am I hurt; I mourn, dismay has taken hold of me. Is there no balm in Gilead, and no physician there? Why then is not the hurt of the daughter of my people recovered? Oh that my head were waters, and my eyes fountains of tears, that I might weep day and night for the daughter of my people! Oh that I had in the wilderness a lodging for wayfaring men, that I might leave my people and go from them, for they are all adulterers, a band of treacherous men" (8:21 and 9:2). The phrase "daughter of my people," it is scarcely necessary to say, is the poetical or rhetorical personification of the people itself. The Old Testament writers like to think of the people of a land as the daughter of the land. The comely and delicately nurtured daughter of Zion (6 : 2), for example, means the people of Jerusalem.

We can hardly wonder that Jeremiah's pessimistic message made him enemies, but we can understand that the solitary man found a peculiar bitterness in his lot in that those most nearly attached to him by ties of blood were alienated by his preaching, and went so far as to plot against his life. In the East, one's kinsmen ought to stand by him even if the community persecutes him. The sensitive Jeremiah, deprived of sympathy where he had the most right to look for it, broke out into imprecations on his own birth, prayed for vengeance on his enemies, and even reproached his God for bringing him into this unbearable situation. His faith indeed triumphed over these moments of weakness, and he took up his burden again, strengthened by the assurance that he would be sustained if he should persist, but with no definite promise beyond that.[1]

It is this very crisis of his faith which makes Jeremiah so instructive for the history of religion. His patriotism was in conflict with his conviction of God's will. The earlier prophets seem to have comforted themselves with the thought that as messengers of Yahweh they would be exempt from the fate which impended over the nation; but Jeremiah was so thoroughly one with his people that he felt himself smitten by every blow that fell upon them. The inner disharmony drove him to appeal to Yahweh himself, and thus the thought of his personal relation to his God came to more distinct consciousness. What most impresses us as we follow his career is that he lived the life of prayer. On this account, Jeremiah has been called, not without reason the discoverer of individualism in religion. One of the best expressions of his sympathy with his people is found in his discourse on the famine (chapter 14). Here he describes in affecting terms the distress which afflicts not only men but animals. The prophet expostulates with Yahweh as though he, by giving his own land over to desolation, shows himself unable to save it. The protest is made more vivid because other prophets have promised welfare. The reply is that the prophets have promised lies, that they are not sent by Yahweh but proclaim only the imaginations of their own brains. Further expostulation brings only the stern command not to intercede—though Moses and Samuel, the most influential intercessors of past times, were to appear on behalf of their people they would accomplish nothing (15 : 1).

It was doubtless a cause of perplexity to the hearers of such discourses that they were uttered after a sincere at-

[1] Notice 15 : 10–12, and in connection with it 11 : 18*f.;* 17 : 14; 18 : 18; and 20 : 14–18.

tempt had been made to meet the demands of Israel's God. For it was in Jeremiah's early period that the book of Deuteronomy had produced such a revival of religious feeling and such sweeping measures of reform. The attitude of Jeremiah with reference to this reform was distinctly one of reserve. He, indeed, accepted the idea of the covenant, so prominent in the thought of the Deuteronomist though not original with him. He almost quotes from the book when he says: "Cursed be the man who does not hear the words of this covenant which I commanded your fathers in the day that I brought them out of the land of Egypt, out of the iron furnace, saying: 'Obey my voice, and do according to all that I command you; so shall you be my people and I will be your God'" (11 : 1–5). But the continuation of the discourse shows only that the people have broken the covenant and have walked in the stubbornness of their own heart, and that the fearful punishment threatened by the book must be inflicted. There is even some indication that the prophet turned against the new code as though it contributed to a false security on the part of the people: "How do you say: 'We are wise, and the Instruction of Yahweh is with us'? Behold the false pen of the scribes has wrought falsely" (8:8). Since Deuteronomy calls itself the Book of Instruction we can hardly avoid suspecting that the prophet is here aiming at that very book. And in accord with this is his attitude toward the ritual, which, as we shall see, is very different from that of Deuteronomy.

The burden of guilt which rests upon the people has been accumulated by transgressions of the plain demands of ethics: "They are all adulterers, an assembly of treacherous men; they bend their tongue as it were a bow for falsehood; they rule not in fidelity; they go from one crime to another, and they do not know me, says Yahweh. Take heed every one of his neighbour and let no man trust his brother, for every brother deceives and every friend slanders" (9 : 2–5). The sweeping condemnation is repeated in all possible variations: "There is not one who seeks justice; if there were a man in the whole city who spoke truth Yahweh would spare it, but the search for one is vain" (5 : 1). We should, perhaps, make allowance for a little rhetorical exaggeration here, for we know that there were some men who listened to the prophet and protected him when his life was in danger. But these were the exceptions which proved the rule. The leaders, as always, are especially to blame. The common people might be excused on the ground of ignorance: "I said: 'Surely, these are the poor, they are foolish, they know not the way of Yahweh nor the instruction of their God. I will get me to the great men and will speak unto them; for they know the way of Yahweh and the justice of their God.' But these with one accord have broken the yoke and burst the bonds" (5 : 4*f.*). A crying example was the king, Jehoiakim, who with almost incredible levity showed himself insensible to the crisis which confronted his people, and Jeremiah did not hesitate to tell the truth: "Woe to him who builds his house by unrighteousness, and his chambers by injustice; who forces his fellow man to work without wages, and does not give him his pay! Art thou a king because thou viest with Ahab in building? Thy father ate and drank, to be sure, but he administered justice; he judged the cause of the oppressed and the poor and it went well with him. Is not this to know me, says Yahweh? But thy eyes and thy desire are set only on gain, to shed innocent blood, and to practise oppression and extortion" (22 : 13–17). There follows a very definite prediction that Jehoiakim will not come to his grave in peace, but that his corpse will be dragged ignominiously through the streets of Jerusalem and thrown outside the gate like that of an unclean animal.

Nobles, priests, and prophets are in the same condemnation with the king. "The priests do not say: 'Where is Yahweh?' and those who handle the *tora* do not know me; the shepherds transgress against me, and the prophets prophesy by Baal, and go after those who do not help" (2 : 8). Or again: "A wonderful and horrible thing has come to pass in the land; the prophets prophesy falsely and the priests are in league with them and my people love to have it so" (5 : 30*f.*). The motive is the same which made Micah so indignant: "From the least to the greatest they are out after gain; prophets and priests all practise lying and deceit" (6 : 13).[1]

Since Jeremiah and Hosea were men of similar temperament it was natural that the later preacher should adopt the figure of the adulterous wife used by the earlier one. The opening discourse of the book speaks of the bridal season when Judah had testified her love by following her husband into the wilderness. The law of the first-fruits prevailed in her case, for these are sacred. So she had been wholly dedicated to her Lord. But soon she had turned away, had polluted the land by prostituting herself to other gods, had been worse than the heathen who do not exchange their gods for others (2 : 10). At the sanctuaries, on the hills, and under the trees she had played the harlot with a lack of shame that revolted even the most hardened. The case was worse in that Judah had the example of the northern kingdom before her eyes. Judah was, in fact, the more guilty of the two, and there was more hope of the restitution of the older sister than of the younger (3 : 6–12). The defection was political as well as religious; alliances with Egypt and Assyria were sought, in distrust of Yahweh, and in the vain hope that foreign gods would be better protectors than he. The anger of Yahweh and the final ruin of Judah were sure to follow (2 : 18).

Making all allowances for the prophet's temperament, we must suppose that he had grounds for so serious an indictment. After the enthusiastic revival in Josiah's time a revulsion had followed. The Deuteronomic reform had been undertaken in the confidence that prosperity and peace would be thereby assured. This faith seemed at first to find confirmation in the arrest of the Scythian invasion, and in the fall of Nineveh. But the death of Josiah, the well-beloved, was inexplicable on the Deuteronomic theory. The fall of

[1] Read also the extended indictment of the prophets in 23 : 9–32.

Nineveh was found to be no deliverance, for it threw the country first into the hands of the Egyptians who were no more merciful than the Assyrians, and then into the power of the Babylonians who were apparently more ruthless. Hence the demoralisation of the people, resulting in recklessness or a frantic appeal to foreign gods. The moral levity is well illustrated by the release of the slaves when Nebuchadrezzar invaded the country, and their prompt re-enslavement when the danger seemed to be past (34 : 8–22).

We have seen that Assyrian deities were introduced into Jerusalem by Manasseh. After the death of Josiah they seem to have reappeared, perhaps on the theory that, being worshipped in Babylon, they had given that city the empire of the world. Among these Jeremiah names one, the queen of heaven, whose worship was openly practised in Jerusalem and was especially obnoxious to Yahweh: "Seest thou not what is done in the cities of Judah and in the streets of Jerusalem? The children gather wood, and the fathers kindle the fire, and the women knead the dough to make cakes for the queen of heaven, and to pour out libations to foreign gods, to provoke me to anger" (7 : 17*f.*). The rites are familiar to students of the history of religion. Cakes in the form of animals are substituted for animal offerings, and since such cakes were offered to the Babylonian Ishtar (who was also an Assyrian divinity) it is probably she who is designated queen of heaven in this passage.[1] The devotion of the people to her worship is brought to light in a later passage, where the women attribute all their misfortunes to the temporary interruption of her worship (44 : 19).

The foreign deities had been introduced into the temple of Yahweh itself. This was no new thing. It had been done possibly by Solomon, certainly by Athaliah, by Ahaz, and by Manasseh. The stricter party had always protested against it, however, and the conscience of Jeremiah was

[1] *Cf.* Schrader, *Die Keilinschriften und das Alte Testament,*[3] p. 441.

sensitive to every violation of Yahweh's exclusive right. Against rites traditionally connected with the worship of Yahweh he also protested. His indictment specifies the high places of the valley of Hinnom, where children were sacrificed (7 : 31). Since Yahweh protests, "Which I commanded not, neither came it into my mind," we must suppose that the popular belief regarded such offerings as something pleasing to him. Ezekiel plainly shows that this belief was prevalent in this period, and since child sacrifice was offered both by Ahaz and by Manasseh we must conclude, as we have already done, that it was one of the ancient features of Yahweh-worship, suppressed by Josiah but revived after his death.

This very survival testifies that the worship of Yahweh was not neglected. In fact, the prophets, all of them, show by their invective that the people were never indifferent to the ritual. Jeremiah, like the others, admits the zeal of the people, but like the others declares it to be vain. He claims, as Amos had claimed, that sacrifice and offerings had not been brought in the wilderness wandering, when, nevertheless, the relations of Yahweh and his people had been of the best. He goes so far as to assert in the teeth of Deuteronomy that these had not been commanded by Yahweh: "Thus says Yahweh, God of Israel: 'Add your burnt-offerings to your other sacrifices and eat flesh; for I spoke not to your fathers nor commanded them in the day that I brought them out of the land of Egypt concerning burnt-offerings and sacrifices; but this thing I commanded them: Hearken to my voice, and I will be your God and you shall be my people; and walk in all the way that I command you, and it shall be well with you'" (7 : 21–23). The difficulty the passage presents to those who still hold that a ritual law was given by Moses must be evident. For our present purpose it is enough to note that Jeremiah denied that any such law had been given. He held that Yahweh commanded the people to walk in the way pointed out by the prophets, and that the prophets concerned themselves with ethics and not with ritual. If the contemporaries pointed with pride to the enrichment of the temple service by new rites, such as the burning of costly perfumes, the prophet was ready to disabuse them: "To what purpose does there come to me frankincense from Sheba, and sweet cane from a far country? Your burnt-offerings are not acceptable nor your sacrifices pleasing to me" (6 : 20). In another place he asks indignantly: "Shall vows and sacred flesh take away thy wickedness? Or shalt thou escape by these?"[1]

It was pointed out in the last chapter that a strong confidence in the inviolability of the temple had arisen as the result of events in the reign of Hezekiah. Jeremiah does not hesitate to denounce such confidence: "Trust not in lying words, saying: 'The temple of Yahweh, the temple of Yahweh, the temple of Yahweh is this!' . . . Behold you trust in lying words that cannot profit. You steal, murder, commit adultery and swear falsely and burn incense to Baal and walk after other gods whom you have not known, and then you come and stand before me in this house and say: We are delivered to do all these abominations! Is this house which is called by my name a den of robbers in your eyes? Behold I have seen it, says Yahweh" (7 : 4–11). The sequel cites the case of Shiloh, where there had once been a famous sanctuary, and where now only ruins were to be seen, a proof that Yahweh would not hesitate to destroy his own dwelling. This was answer enough to those who were under the delusion that, because Yahweh had taken up his residence in the temple, he was therefore obliged to protect it, no matter what his worshippers might be or do. To protect them in their evil courses would be to make him an accomplice of their crimes.

With reference to this whole set of beliefs that Yahweh had bound himself irrevocably to Israel or to the temple, Jeremiah energetically protested that the God of Israel has liberty. This is the lesson of the potter, a lesson which has

[1] The original reading here adopted has been preserved by the Greek translator (11 : 15).

been frequently misunderstood. As Jeremiah watched the potter he saw that, when the vessel he was shaping did not please him, he did not hesitate to crush it together and begin over again. Was it not clear that if Yahweh did not find his people to his mind he could with the same sovereign freedom crush them out of existence and begin a new work? They, on their part, hugged the delusion that in some way he had committed himself to them and could not give them up. Yet this delusion he had tried to nullify by the word of the prophets, diligently preached (7 : 13, 25). He had hoped that they would repent, would cease to sow among thorns, and would break up the new ground. But now there seemed no more chance of this: "If a man put away his wife and she become another's, shall he return to her again? Would not that woman be too thoroughly polluted? And thou who hast played the harlot with many lovers, wilt thou return to me? says Yahweh." The question evidently calls for a negative answer.[1] The sinful habit has become so ingrained that it cannot be given up.

This conception of sin as a habit, something ingrained, is first distinctly brought out by Jeremiah. He had of course no thought of an original taint introduced by the transgression of Adam. But he saw his contemporaries so enslaved by evil that there was a real moral inability to turn to righteousness. In spite, therefore, of his frequent exhortations to circumcise the foreskin of the heart, the prophet had no confidence that his preaching would be effective: "To whom shall I speak and testify that they may hear? Behold their ear is uncircumcised, and they cannot hearken; the word of Yahweh is to them a reproach, they have no delight in it" (6 : 10; *cf.* 4 : 4). The prophet pictures himself as a refiner of silver, but one who works in vain because

[1] The Greek text seems again to be original. Hebrew custom seems to have regarded a divorced woman who had entered a second marriage and been again divorced as still taboo to her first husband (Jer. 3 : 1; *cf.* Deut. 24 : 4).

the ore he uses contains only baser metal. "The bellows blow fiercely; the lead is consumed of the fire; in vain does he go on refining, for the dross is not taken away; refuse silver shall men call them because Yahweh has rejected them" (6 : 29). Even more emphatic to those who first heard it must have been the text which has to us lost something of its force by repetition: "Can the Ethiopian change his skin, or the leopard his spots? Then may you do good who are habituated to evil" (13 : 23). The fact that habit fastens the chains of evil so that its victims find it morally impossible to reverse their steps is nowhere more forcibly expressed. Again we hear Yahweh asking: "Why has this people turned away in a perpetual backsliding? They hold fast to deceit and refuse to repent. They should be ashamed that they have committed abomination, only they cannot blush any more, neither do they know how to be ashamed" (8 : 5, 12). We are reminded of Lessing: "Blush at least, Lucinda, that you have lost the power of blushing!" In Jeremiah's view the girdle soiled by damp and mildew was the fit symbol of Judah in its corruption.

Jeremiah's theology was the simple faith in Yahweh held by the other prophets. Yahweh is a God of righteousness, and he requires righteousness in man. He is the living God, and the others do not profit (2 : 8). The perversity of the people is seen in their turning from him in prosperity, but in distress calling upon him to save them. The other gods are like broken cisterns, which hold no water; he is the fountain of living water which never fails. "What evil did your fathers find in me that they forsook me and went after vanity?" (2 : 5.) Whether this word *vanity* indicates the non-existence of the other divinities is not clear. For Israel there is only one Helper; that is, Yahweh. And that Yahweh has power over the other nations is assumed, as in the case of the other prophets. The prophet even sees himself commissioned to give the cup of Yahweh's wrath to Judah's neighbours as well as to herself (25 : 15–29).

From Yahweh's power and justice on one hand, and the

ingrained sinfulness of Israel on the other, follows logically the certainty that punishment must come. Like the northern kingdom, Judah is to be banished from Yahweh's presence (7 : 15). The completeness of the destruction is symbolised by the earthen pot dashed to pieces before the eyes of the people (19 : 10*f*.). Yet there is always the possibility that the people will repent. The prophet put his discourses in written form, thinking that if a compendium of his various messages could be read to the multitude they would bethink themselves (36 : 3). But an occasional gleam of hope like this makes the prevailing gloom only the more visible. At the very beginning of his mission the preacher was obsessed by the vision of complete ruin: "I beheld the earth and it was a chaos, and the heavens had no light; I beheld the mountains and they trembled, and all the hills moved to and fro; I beheld, and lo there was no man, and all the birds of heaven were fled; I beheld, and lo the fruitful field was become a wilderness, and all the cities were broken down before Yahweh, before the fierceness of his wrath" (4 : 24*f*.). The concrete details must leave no doubt in the hearers' minds: "The corpses of this people shall be food for the birds of heaven and for the wild beasts, and no one shall scare them away. I will cause joy and gladness, the joy of the bridegroom and the joy of the bride, to cease from the cities of Judah and from the streets of Jerusalem, for the land shall become a desert. In that day, says Yahweh, they shall bring out the bones of the kings of Judah and the bones of her princes, and the bones of the prophets, the bones of the priests, and the bones of the dwellers in Jerusalem out of their tombs and spread them out before the sun and the moon and the host of heaven" (7 : 33 and 8 : 1). No more fearful threat could be uttered to men who believed that the soul finds rest only when the body has been properly buried.[1]

[1] Outrage of the tombs was one of the ways by which the Assyrian kings sought to strike terror into their enemies, as is shown by the boast of Ashurbanipal, *Keilinschriftliche Bibliothek*, II, p. 193.

What would follow after the blow had actually fallen? This question finds no direct answer in the genuine words of Jeremiah. The passages which promise restoration are not from the hand of the prophet, but are inserted by later editors in the manner already familiar to us. One intimation that Jeremiah had some hope that a remnant would be spared is given, however, in his attitude toward the first group of exiles—the men carried away in 597. Those who were spared in this visitation and who remained in Jerusalem seem to have plumed themselves on the thought that they were the righteous remnant, and that the exiles were the wicked who had been punished. Jeremiah looks at the matter in another light. To him the good figs of his vision typify the exiles. Yahweh will set his eyes on them for good (chapter 24). To the same effect is the letter which the prophet sent to these same exiles (29), designed to keep them from false hopes of an early return. The prediction that the exile would last seventy years was, however, intended not so much to set a time for the return as to wean the exiles from any hope of immediate change in their lot.

It must be clear that the importance of Jeremiah in the religion of Israel arises not so much from any definite doctrine promulgated by him as from the example he gave of a man true to his convictions throughout a lifetime of trial and opposition. The steadfastness of the man excites our admiration even at this distant day. During his life his people were blind to it, but after his death, when the fulfilment of his predictions called attention forcibly not only to his message but also to his character, the conviction that he had indeed been in the counsel of the Almighty came with overwhelming force. The result was to cause his memory to be cherished, his message to be studied, and to some extent his example to be followed. True religion was here set forth in an object-lesson which none could misunderstand. Religion was seen to be a matter of the individual heart in communion with its God. When the nation perished this religion still found its dwelling-place in the heart of the humble and contrite. In teaching this lesson, Jeremiah takes one of the leading places in the history of human thought.

CHAPTER X

THE BEGINNINGS OF LEGALISM

WITH Jeremiah the old school of prophets came to an end. By the time he had completed the first five years of his ministry, a new force had appeared in the intellectual and religious life of Israel, something which was to supersede the prophets as organs of the divine will. This new force was a book, and the account of its discovery and effect is one of the most dramatic that we have in all Hebrew literature. It was in the reign of Josiah, when the royal officers were taking account of the money in the temple chest in order to apply it to the repair of the building, that the priest, Hilkiah, informed them, casually, it would seem, that he had found a book, which he called the book of Yahweh's Instruction. It has been pointed out recently that this is parallel to a story in the Egyptian inscriptions according to which a certain king, when about to rebuild a temple, found a plan of the original temple in the old foundation wall and by it was guided in his erection or restoration. There is also a statement in one of the chapters of the Book of the Dead to the effect that this chapter was found under the feet of one of the statues when the prime minister was on a tour of inspection of the temple. Other parallels are cited both from Egyptian and from Babylonian sources, so that we might suspect the story to be simply one of the floating anecdotes which are current in different regions. On the other hand, they may all testify to the custom of depositing books of importance, like other valuable objects, in the sanctuaries, a custom which may well have prevailed in Israel from an early time. The contents of the book thus found, if we are right in identifying it with Deuteronomy (in the primitive form of that book, that is), give no indication that the report of its finding in the temple is a fiction.

The important thing is that the book had a marked effect on the king when it was read to him and that the result was a thorough reform of religious practice in Judah. The country sanctuaries were violently suppressed; the temple was cleansed of everything that was contrary to the demands of the newly found document; and the people, acting through their natural leaders, took a solemn obligation to act in accordance with the demands there formulated. The reforms thus inaugurated correspond closely with the programme laid down in our book of Deuteronomy, and we can scarcely doubt that this book was the source of the influence exerted on king and people. For our present purpose it is not necessary to determine the exact limits of the original book and of the various accretions that have been made to it from time to time. The tone of all the Deuteronomic writers is homogeneous, and their religion expresses itself in like phrases throughout.

Why the programme of the prophetic party should be embodied in a book is not hard to conjecture. We have seen that Isaiah gathered a small group of disciples to whom he committed his written words as a solemn testimony. These men had hardships to endure during the reign of Manasseh and found it impossible to appear in public. Nothing would seem more natural than that they should not only cherish the written words of their master but should themselves engage in writing down their ideas of what was needed in Judah. Their consciences were revolted by the open and flagrant superstition practised and encouraged by Manasseh. In their reflections they realised the need of more definite and specific regulations than had been laid down by the earlier prophets. The prophets, to be sure, had insisted on righteousness as the supreme requirement of Yahweh. But none of them had given more than a very general definition of what was meant by righteousness. A rule of life in black and white, laying down what was commanded and what was prohibited, would be a boon to all right-minded men, they thought. Moreover, the prophets had been unpractical men in some of their requirements. They had inveighed against the traditional worship. But they could hardly have intended to do away with all ritual. Religion is inseparably connected (in the minds of men of that time at least) with external manifestations of devotion. The really pious heart desires to approach the divinity with a gift. It might well occur, therefore, to the members of the school that the position of their predecessors with reference to the ritual was extreme.

And we must remember how deeply the ritual was impressed upon popular custom. It not only went back to immemorial times; it was sanctioned by the Mosaic tradition as set forth in the earliest narratives. To take away the sacrifices and offerings, to abolish the great festivals, closely interwoven as they were with the life of the people, would be to deprive men of what they dearly prized and perhaps to shake their faith in all religion. To all this was added the practical consideration that vested rights of the priesthood were not lightly to be taken away. The members of this guild had ancient privilege on their side. To do away with all public ceremonies would certainly make enemies of this powerful class. Some of its members, we may suppose, were right-thinking men who might be won to the side of reform if only they could be protected in their prerogatives. The party of reform among the priests may have been strengthened by the reaction under Manasseh. The reforms of Hezekiah, whatever they were, gave prestige to the temple at Jerusalem; the reaction under Manasseh not only revived the country sanctuaries but introduced foreign gods, and we may suppose foreign priests, into Jerusalem. It is not a mere accident that Hilkiah, the priest, is the one who first calls attention to the new book—the desire for a positive programme had reached even the priestly class.

The book was thus a compromise between prophetic and

priestly ideals. It was put into the form of discourses from the mouth of Moses, because Moses was the first of the prophets and also the first of the priests. Codes bearing his name were already in circulation and the covenant on which Deuteronomy lays so much stress was attributed to him. The authors of Deuteronomy were, no doubt, confident that they were enforcing the demands that Moses would make were he living in their time. In some respects they were justified in thinking that their book was simply an enlarged edition of Moses' own code. Their ethical demands were in many cases based on traditions which popular belief traced to the great lawgiver himself. The Mosaic colouring doubtless helped to deepen the impression made by the reading. But something of the influence of the book must be traced to the times in which it came to light. The Scythian invasion was fresh in the minds of the people; the denunciations of the book were reinforced by the preaching of Jeremiah; there was probably a general feeling that reformation was needed in Judah. Josiah was still a young man, earnestly striving to do right, impressionable, we may suppose, and already under the influence of the prophetic party. All things considered, we see how the book made its deep impression and how it impelled to the solemn covenant which, for the time being, made it the supreme law of the state.

For the time being, I say, for it is evident that the effect was only temporary. The drastic nature of the measures taken by Josiah was sure to provoke a reaction, especially when the high hopes of temporal prosperity, held out by the book as a reward for obedience, were disappointed; when the unexpected and heart-breaking death of Josiah seemed to smite the theory of the book in the face; when the Assyrian yoke was succeeded by that of Egypt, and that again almost immediately by that of Babylon. When the ruthless Jehoiakim came to the throne, then the pendulum swung back again and all the work of the reformers seemed to be undone. Jeremiah shows that the old heathenism returned and moral degradation with it. The reform itself had disappointed its advocates by its superficiality, as Jeremiah again witnesses. But though the effort seemed to be without permanent fruit, the more remote effect was all that the promoters of the movement could have anticipated. The idea of a book as the repository of the revealed will of God became established and has been one of the most influential ideas in the history of mankind. The Deuteronomists themselves continued their activity, and the Old Testament in our hands shows marks of their influence in almost every part.

First of all we must notice that the Deuteronomistic confession of faith has been cherished by the Jews through twenty-five centuries. This confession is the well-known *Shema* which the loyal Jew repeats every morning and evening: "Hear, O Israel, Yahweh our God is one Yahweh; and thou shalt love Yahweh thy God with all thy heart and with all thy soul and with all thy strength. And these words which I command thee shall be in thy heart, and thou shalt teach them to thy children and shalt speak of them when thou sittest in the house, and when thou walkest in the way, when thou liest down and when thou risest up. And thou shalt bind them as signs upon thy hands and as frontlets between thy eyes, and thou shalt write them upon the doorposts of thy house and upon thy gates" (Deut. 6 : 4–9). These verses may be said to be the text upon which Deuteronomy is never tired of enlarging. Its points are three: the unity of God, the duty of loving him, and the manifestation of the love by obedience to the commandments written in the book.

The unity of God which is here affirmed is opposed to the popular conception which looked at the various sanctuaries as the homes of so many local divinities. These might all be called by the name Yahweh, but the devotees of any one of them did not think of him as more than the god of the place or the clan in which he was worshipped. The author wishes to put an end to this confusion of thought. He is not attempting to state a speculative monotheism; his frequent use of the phrase "other gods" would rather favour the thought that he believed in the existence of such others. He persistently asserts that Yahweh is the greatest of all gods, which again would admit that such gods have some reality. The prayer of Solomon, a thoroughly Deuteronomic document, addresses Yahweh with the declaration: "There is no god like thee either in heaven above or on the earth beneath" (I Kings 8 : 23). Later readers were no doubt able to construe such expressions in terms of an absolute monotheism, but it is doubtful whether the writers so intended them. Yahweh is One, and he is the only God who should receive worship in Israel, and this just because he is greatest of all and most powerful of all.

Some writers of this group attempted to reconcile Yahweh's supremacy with the fact that other gods had such a powerful hold on the minds of the gentiles, by assuming that Yahweh himself had so ordained it. Thus the author of the Song of Moses, now forming a part of the book of Deuteronomy, says: "When the Most High gave the nations their portion, when he gave the children of men their lots, he set the bounds of the peoples according to the number of the sons of God; but Yahweh's own portion is his people; Jacob is the lot of his inheritance."[1] Here we see Yahweh as the supreme ruler, having under him the inferior divinities, the sons of God as they are called elsewhere (Gen. 6 : 1). Yahweh has himself arranged that the nations should worship these inferior divinities in order that Israel may have the prerogative of devotion to him. In another passage these inferior divinities are regarded as identical with the sun and moon and constellations, which the author knew to be objects of worship among the nations (Deut. 4 : 19).

The deduction which the author makes from his strict belief in the unity of Yahweh is one strange to his contemporaries. This is that the one Yahweh has but one sanctuary in which he should be worshipped. The practical measure which he has most at heart is the abolition of all

[1] Deut. 32 : 8*f*. The text of the current Hebrew has suffered, and the emendation is now generally accepted.

sanctuaries outside of Jerusalem and the concentration of all worship at the capital. The reason why sacrifices should be brought at this one place is, of course, that Yahweh has his dwelling there. There is here, however, some confusion of thought. Yahweh dwells in the temple, since that is the place to seek him; even the dwellers in foreign lands should turn toward the temple when they pray. Yet Yahweh dwells in heaven and hears them thence. In the prayer which is offered when the tithe is brought, the worshipper says: "Look down from heaven thy dwelling-place and bless thy people Israel and the land that thou hast given us" (Deut. 26 : 15). Yet the sacrifices are distinctly declared to be brought *before Yahweh* (14 : 23; 15 : 20). Both beliefs were held—that Yahweh dwells in heaven, and that he dwells in the temple—with no consciousness that they were inconsistent. Probably the throne in heaven was conceived to be just above the temple, and not very remote from it. An attempt to combine the two ideas is made when it is said that Yahweh has made his name dwell in the temple (I Kings 8 : 29; *cf.* 5 : 9; 9 : 3, also Deut. 12 : 5 and 21). At a later time we read that heaven is Yahweh's throne, and earth is his footstool, which may be another attempt to secure his presence both in the temple and in the heavenly dwelling. What the Deuteronomist has most at heart is to convince his readers that Yahweh is a God near at hand, and not a God afar off: "What nation has a god so near it as Yahweh our God is near us?" (4 : 7.)

Obedience to the law now laid down is motived not only by the greatness and power of Yahweh but also by his moral character. His leading attributes are justice and fidelity. He does not regard faces nor take bribes; he secures the rights of the orphan and the widow; he loves the client, giving him bread and clothing (10 : 17*f.*). He keeps covenant and loving-kindness with them that love him and keep his commandments, to a thousand generations, but repays them that hate him by destroying them (7 : 10*f.*). He is merciful even to sinners if they repent: "Yahweh thy God is a merciful God; he will not fail thee nor destroy thee, nor forget the covenant with thy fathers which he swore unto them" (4 : 31). This idea of the covenant goes back to early times, as we have seen. The Deuteronomists dwell upon it with almost wearisome iteration. The covenant by which Yahweh and Israel were bound to each other was entered into with the forefathers. It was an act of free grace on the part of Yahweh: "Say not in thy heart after Yahweh thy God has driven them (the Canaanites) out before thee: For my righteousness Yahweh has brought me into this land, whereas for the wickedness of these nations Yahweh drives them out before thee. Not for thy righteousness or for the uprightness of thy heart dost thou go in to possess the land, but for the wickedness of these nations Yahweh thy God drives them out before thee, to establish the word which he swore to thy fathers" (9 : 4*f.*). The proof that Israel was not chosen for its righteousness is found in the record of the wilderness wandering which is rehearsed to show their constant disobedience (9 : 7–20). And in like manner the choice of them had not been made because of their greatness, for they were few in number (7 : 7). The reader is shut up to the conclusion that the election of Israel was an act of Yahweh's mere good pleasure.

This election brings Israel into such relations with Yahweh that it is properly called his own possession, a phrase which frequently recurs (7 : 6; 14 : 2; 26 : 18; *cf.* Ex. 19 : 5). The relationship may also be defined as that of father and son: "You are sons of Yahweh your God" (14 : 1). Hosea had already said that Yahweh had called his son out of Egypt, but the Deuteronomist makes the conception more individual: each Israelite may call himself a son of Yahweh. The conception may have been a current one, however, for in an older source the Moabites are called sons and daughters of Chemosh (Num. 21 : 29). The originality of the Deuteronomist consists in his making all these ideas bear on the question of obedience to the law which he promulgates. Sons should obey a father; a sacred people should show their separateness from other nations by conformity to the will of their God; the people of the covenant are bound by the terms of the covenant, and this means obedience. Yahweh, on his part, has been faithful and has a right to expect fidelity on the part of Israel. Yahweh's beneficence calls for gratitude, and gratitude is another motive to obedience.

One of the most distinct statements of the author's position is the one which comes near the close of the book: "Thou hast avouched Yahweh this day to be thy God, and that thou wouldst walk in his ways, and keep his commandments and his ordinances and his statutes, and wouldst hearken to his voice; and Yahweh has avouched thee this day to be a people for his own possession as he has promised thee, and that thou shouldst keep all his commandments; and to make thee high above all peoples that he has made in praise and in name and in honour" (26 : 17–19). The ethical character of the will thus emphasised is brought out by our author's treatment of the Decalogue. The idea of a decalogue as the basis of the covenant is as old as the Yahwist. But the covenant of the Yahwist is a plain case of bargain with the Divinity. Yahweh agrees to go with the people and give them possession of Canaan if they will agree to pay him the dues at the sanctuary; and the commands of this earlier decalogue are concerned with these dues—the festivals, the firstlings, and the first-fruits (Ex. 34). An enormous advance is registered therefore by the Deuteronomist when he makes the Decalogue entirely ethical. God now commands nothing in the way of sacrifice, but he enjoins the duties which man owes his fellow man, along with such reverence as is due to God himself. Even the desire of the heart is to be regulated in accordance with the law of right (Deut. 5 : 1–21). The supremacy of ethical above ritual requirements is indicated further by making this Decalogue the covenant proposed by Yahweh himself at Horeb and accepted by the people with fear and trembling. In thus distinguishing it, the author shows himself the heir of the best prophetic tradition.

Heir of the best prophetic tradition we may also call him in the emphasis he lays on the social programme of the prophets. He constantly urges the claims of the poor and the oppressed. The wage-earner, whether Israelite or foreigner, is to receive his pay promptly at the close of each day (24 : 15); the gleanings of field, olive-yard, and vineyard are to be left for the client, the orphan, and the widow (24 : 19 *f.*); the festivals at the sanctuary are to be occasions for helping slaves and the dependent classes, among which we find the Levites (16 : 11, 14). This mention of the Levites is noteworthy, for it shows that the priestly class as a whole was needy, dependent on the charity of the well-to-do (12 : 18; 14 : 27; 18 : 1–4). The Israelites are to remember that they had been slaves in Egypt and to sympathise with the slave accordingly (16 : 12; 24 : 22). Yahweh loves the client and gives him food and raiment; love for the client therefore becomes a part of religion (10 : 18). The Sabbath is to be observed in order that the slave may have a time of rest from his toil (5 : 14). The runaway slave is not to be returned to his master; the hungry man has a right to eat from field and vineyard; the millstone, an indispensable implement in every household, must not be taken as pledge for a loan; the garment of the widow must not be taken in any case; the cloak of the poor man, if taken, must be returned to him at sunset that he may have covering for the night; every seven years there is to be a remission of debt for all poor debtors (15 : 1–3). The earnestness of the author in insisting on this last command indicates perhaps that he was not very confident of its practicability, and in fact some of these regulations are impossible of enforcement. None the less they testify to the writer's moral sense. Injustice is an abomination to Yahweh—in the matter of weights and measures (25 : 13–15), for example, and in the matter of bribery (16 : 18–20).

It must be borne in mind that these humanitarian regulations are intended for Israel alone. A very different standard is set up for the relations between Israelites and gentiles.

Usury may be exacted of the foreigner but not of the fellow Israelite (23 : 20*f.*). The year of release is for one and not for the other (15 : 3). The "stranger within thy gates," so often commended to the mercy of the reader, does not mean any foreigner who happens to be in the country, but the client who has come into definite relations of dependence to some citizen, and who is therefore himself on the way to full citizenship. Other foreigners are still regarded as enemies. The reason is not far to seek; the crying sin of Israel in the past had been worship of other gods than Yahweh, and temptation had come from those foreigners who were most closely in contact with Israel, that is, the Canaanites. Hence the sharp contrast between the treatment of Israelites (including the clients) and the treatment of Canaanites. These latter are to be exterminated without mercy. In the belief of the author all the calamities of the past had come from yielding to the seductions of these idolaters.

There was a measure of truth in this charge. The original worship of Yahweh had been simple, even austere. The worship which the people had adopted in Canaan was ornate, sensual, licentious. On this ground the Rechabites thought that fidelity to Yahweh required avoidance of all Canaanitish customs. The mass of the people, however, saw in Yahweh a Baal, and their worship differed little from the orgies of the early inhabitants. From the ethical point of view the reaction of the Deuteronomist is quite intelligible, most clearly directed at the old sanctuaries of the land: "You shall surely destroy all the sacred places in which the nations that you dispossess serve their gods, upon the mountains and upon the hills and under every green tree; you shall pull down their altars, and break in pieces their pillars, and burn their asheras with fire; you shall hew down the graven images of their gods and destroy their names out of that place" (12 : 2*f.*). Since pillars and asheras were the regular accompaniment of the altars of Yahweh, and since even the graven images often represented him, there can be no doubt that the author was aiming at all the sanctuaries in which, as he supposed, Canaanitish influences were discernible even though they were ostensibly dedicated to the God of Israel.

The earnestness revealed by these prohibitions reminds us of the zeal of the Puritans against statues and relics of the saints. But in the mind of the Israelite reformer the extermination of idolatry meant also the extermination of idolaters. All the Canaanites (he ordains) are to be put under the old Semitic *ban* (herem). By this everything in the enemy's city was to be utterly destroyed, as is set forth in the story of Achan. With enemies outside of Canaan terms may be made; if they surrender they shall be made tributary; if they refuse and are conquered the men may be slain and the women and children may be made slaves: "But from the cities of these peoples which Yahweh thy God gives thee for an inheritance thou shalt save alive none that breathes, but thou shalt utterly destroy them. . . . That they may not teach you to do after the abominations which they have done unto their gods; so would you sin against Yahweh your God" (20 : 16–18). Logically, all covenants with the ancient inhabitants are prohibited. It is to us some consolation to think that the author is setting forth an ideal no longer attainable, for in his day there were no Canaanites to be exterminated, amalgamation with the Israelites being an accomplished fact.

Israelites who yielded to the temptation to polytheism were to be treated with the same severity. A rumour that any Israelite city was worshipping other gods than Yahweh was to be promptly investigated, and if it was found to be true, the guilty city was to be destroyed, the whole population put to the sword, the cattle slaughtered, even things without life were to be burned as a holocaust to Yahweh (13 : 13–17). The old ritual idea of taboo is here in evidence; whatever has been dedicated to another god becomes a source of defilement to Israel, and even to touch it will bring one into a state of pollution and expose him to the wrath of Yahweh. Drastic action was to be taken against individuals who seduce men from their allegiance to Yahweh, especially false prophets, soothsayers, and all who were addicted to magic arts. The faithful Israelite was to spare neither brother, wife, nor friend if any of them became a source of temptation (13 : 7–12). Men must not even inquire how the Canaanites worship their gods lest they be led to adopt their customs (12 : 29*f.*). The traditional marks of mourning are forbidden because they are connected with the worship of the manes (14 : 1). The exchange of garments between men and women, the planting of different seeds together, ploughing with a mixed team, and wearing of garments made of wool and linen combined are all under the ban, doubtless because all were in some way associated with other divinities. Even the silver and gold which have been in contact with idols are an abomination, and he who takes them will fall under the curse of Yahweh (7 : 25).

The number and minuteness of these specifications justifies us in making Deuteronomy introduce the first stage of legalism. The authors who wrought out this system had the not uncommon idea that a complete rule of life can be written down for men's guidance. They supposed that they had, in fact, written down such a rule, and that it represented the divine will. The word *command* and its derivatives occur no less than sixty times in the book of Deuteronomy alone, and the phrase "commandments and ordinances," or in the fuller form, "commandments, statutes, and judgments," is a mark of Deuteronomic authorship wherever found. By a writer of this school, David is made to charge Solomon in these words: "Observe thou that which Yahweh, thy God, commits to thee, by walking in his ways, and keeping his commandments, his judgments, and his testimonies, according to what is written in the Tora of Moses" (I Kings 2 : 3). The idea is clear: Yahweh has laid down a path in which a man must walk, and the first inquiry of the righteous man should be: What doth Yahweh require? The hearer or reader should impress the words of the book on his heart and soul, bind them on his hand, write them between his eyes and on the door-post of his house, teach them to his children, talk of them constantly, meditate on them day and night (Deut. 11 : 18–20). The reason is the intrinsic excellence of the law, for in the view of the writers no nation ever had righteous statutes like this Tora (4 : 8). For this reason it can never be surpassed, and men are solemnly forbidden either to add to it or to take away from it (4 : 2).

It is in this insistence on its own completeness and on the regulation of the whole life by its precepts that Deuteronomy differs from the earlier documents which seem to belong in the same class. The Decalogue of J specifies the terms of the covenant which are binding on Israel; the Covenant code provides a law for certain cases which might arise. But neither Decalogue nor Covenant code attempted to regulate the whole life of the individual. Deuteronomy marks a new stage of thought by its attempt to do just this—to lay down in black and white a complete rule of life for the Israelite. That, in fact, it codifies existing social custom we have already seen. On the side of ritual it draws upon priestly tradition. In some cases it adopts superstitions which were contrary to its own principles, but which were too strongly intrenched in popular belief to be done away. Thus it requires the sacrifice of a heifer to placate the ghost of a slain man (21 : 1–9). It does not call the rite a sacrifice, and it attempts to make it innocuous by placing it under the supervision of the priests, but its original nature is only thinly disguised.

Although the authors suppose their code to be complete and final, they do not mean to supersede the prophets, the divinely inspired teachers of Israel. They represent Moses as the ideal prophet and put in his mouth a promise that there shall be a succession of similar teachers (18 : 15–22). Yet these prophets of the future are to be subordinate to the law now promulgated, for even if they seem to have supernatural sanction for their preaching they are not to be listened to in case their doctrine differs from that of the book. It did not occur to the writer that by this regulation he made the prophet superfluous and opened the way to the scribe, the interpreter of the written document. No more did he see that his emphasis of the Jerusalem sanctuary would put enormous power into the hands of the hierarchy, the guild which had the temple already in possession.

The fundamental character of the Deuteronomic requirement of a single sanctuary must be evident. What is of equal importance is that the sacrifices are now first legitimated in an ostensibly prophetic document. The earlier prophets had denounced burnt offerings and sacrifices, tithes, and free-will offerings as indifferent or even abhorrent to Yahweh. But the Deuteronomist enjoins them as equally important with justice and mercy. Tradition was undoubtedly on his side. The earlier narratives had pointed out that the sanctuaries were places of worship for the patriarchs, and that they had sacrificed there. The earlier codes also had enjoined that all Israelites should appear before Yahweh three times in the year, and that they should not come empty-handed. The eating and drinking and rejoicing before Yahweh which had scandalised Amos and Isaiah, and which Hosea had identified with spiritual adultery, is now made a part of the law of Yahweh. It is, to be sure, purified from some of its more notorious abuses, and its concentration at the central sanctuary made it more amenable to police supervision. Further, the ritual requirement is combined with the ethical, and the attempt is made to use the sacrifices for humanitarian purposes. The tithe is no longer simply a tribute to Yahweh; it is to be given to the poor and needy, they being in some sense his clients. Every third year it is to be wholly used in this way, while on those occasions when it is brought to the sanctuary it is to be shared liberally with the dependent classes (14 : 28 *f.*). This combination of ritual and ethical requirements was of practical importance, for, as we have seen, the comparative failure of the older prophets is explained by the fact that they made no allowance for the human longing for ritual. The adoption of the ritual by the Deuteronomists and its concentration at Jerusalem created, we may say, a church which was able to survive the destruction of the national life.

The doctrine of rewards and punishments which underlies the book and which comes frequently into distinct expression is a deduction from the preaching of the earlier prophets. That preaching had constantly threatened national disaster as the consequence of national disobedience. Deuteronomy formulates the theory mechanically, we may say, and has no hesitation in giving details. The frequent phrase, "that thy days may be long in the land," is only one example. More explicit is the promise that the rain on which the productivity of the land depends will be sent in case the law is obeyed, and withheld if other gods are worshipped (11 : 13–16). The fullest statement of the theory is found in the list of blessings in the twenty-eighth chapter, which is followed by an even more elaborate catalogue of curses. It is possible that a precedent existed for the series of curses in some ancient custom performed at Mount Gerizim (11 : 29; 27 : 11–26; *cf.* Joshua 8 : 30–35). The full force of these curses came home to the people who endured the calamities of siege and exile in the time of Nebuchadrezzar, and the sense of sin so prominent in postexilic Judaism arose from combining the words of Deuteronomy with the disasters which came so soon after its promulgation.

It was of importance for the later development of religion that the earlier history of Israel was rewritten, or at least re-edited, under Deuteronomic influence. According to the view of the Deuteronomic editors all the calamities of the people in the past had come from their lack of conformity to the Deuteronomic standard. The almost rhythmical succession of victory and disaster in the book of Judges is made to teach this lesson. Oppression by the enemy regularly follows apostasy from Yahweh, while repentance is as regularly followed by deliverance (Judges 2 : 10–19). In the books of Kings we are repeatedly informed that the people sacrificed at the high places even after the temple was built, and the prophets who are introduced in those books to rebuke the people or the rulers enforce the thought that this defection from Yahweh is the cause of their calamities. The whole story, from the time of Joshua down, is made the dark picture of religious declension relieved by a few bright spots.

To point the contrast the history of the conquest was rewritten to show that Joshua was a worthy successor of Moses, and strictly true to the Deuteronomic programme. What actually took place at the conquest we know from the fragment preserved in the first chapter of Judges. Israelites and Canaanites amalgamated, and it was not until the time of Solomon that the Israelite element became predominant. But the Deuteronomist, to whom everything Canaanitish is an abomination, makes Joshua exterminate the earlier inhabitants, saving alive nothing that breathed. The only exception was made by the Gibeonites and their allies, and they obtained their treaty by fraud. The neglect of the Israelite leaders to take counsel of Yahweh in this case is censured, with the implication that the covenant would not have been allowed had he been consulted. The conclusion of the account is the unhistorical statement that Joshua reduced his new allies to slavery.[1]

The number of hands that must have been employed in this reconstruction of the history shows the extent of the influence which Deuteronomy exerted in the exilic and post-exilic period. Henceforth Israel was the people of a book.

[1] Joshua 9 : 15 and 26*f*. On the extermination of the Canaanites, *cf*. 10 : 40; 11 : 17; 6 : 17–24; 7 : 12–26.

CHAPTER XI

EZEKIEL

In the death of the state of Judah it might seem to the onlooker that the battle for a purer Yahweh religion had been lost. But while the disintegration in Palestine was for the time complete, there was a spot far in the East where the ideas to which the prophets had given expression were cherished. This was the district in Babylonia where the exiles, carried away in 597, were settled. These exiles seem to have had some sort of civil organisation of their own. They were permitted to build houses, to plant gardens, and to consult each other concerning their common interests. At first their cohesion was secured by the hope of an early return, a hope which was fostered by prophets of their own as well as by messages from Jerusalem. When this hope was rudely shattered by the fall of their beloved city they were still united by the bond of religion. Their faith in Yahweh was, at least in the case of the more earnest, strengthened by the fact that the words of the prophets had been fulfilled.

The most drastic expression of Yahweh's threats was, as we have seen, that contained in the book of Deuteronomy. For the future of Judaism it was an important fact that by the fulfilment of these threats this book was more firmly fixed in the regard of the exiles. Other thoughts expressed in it were calculated to appeal to them. The strange customs of the people among whom they found themselves living would justify Deuteronomy's condemnation of all heathenism. Not less important was the assertion that Yahweh had made Israel his own by a deliberate act of choice. His truth and righteousness, emphasised by the calamity which had fallen, gave ground for believing that he would not refuse to hear the prayer of the penitent who should turn to him with all their heart. The soil was thus prepared by Deuteronomy for the establishment of a new type of religion, and the man to cultivate the soil was not lacking.

This man was Ezekiel, to us one of the least sympathetic of the Old Testament characters. We Occidentals of the twentieth century find it difficult to understand his exaggerated visions, his fits of silence, and his grotesque actions. Yet he was only the complete example of a man possessed by the prophetic ideal. His visions differ from those of the other prophets only in their pitiless distinctness of detail; his actions only carry out to logical sequence the belief that the prophet's actions are a part of his message. The point in which he differed from his predecessors is due to the influence of Deuteronomy. What he receives from Yahweh is a book (Ezek. 2 : 8 to 3 : 3). In a sense we may call him the first of the scribes, the exponent of a written revelation. And since he was of priestly birth and training, it is clear that the ritual element in Deuteronomy is the one that most distinctly appealed to him. The priestly ideal, embodied in the word sanctity, was already emphasised by the Deuteronomist. Ezekiel reveals his own point of view when he protests his own scrupulosity in the matter of ritual cleanliness (4 : 14). From this point of view we must interpret his work.

Ezekiel most distinctly influenced his people by his plans for the future. But before these could be fully appreciated the prophet had a destructive work to do. This was to rid the exiles of many cherished notions. The prophetic ideal had never really impressed the great mass of the people. By Ezekiel it was so firmly held that he demanded a complete break with the past. Not that he had ceased to be an Israelite; the God whom he worshipped was the ancestral God, Yahweh, who in the most literal sense had taken up his dwelling at the centre of the earth—in Jerusalem: "In the midst of the nations I have set her [Jerusalem] and round about her are the lands" (5 : 5)—such is the declaration of Yahweh himself. Temporarily the temple was abandoned, because it had been too much polluted for Yahweh to remain there; but it was his chosen dwelling-place, and he would surely return thither.[1] In the first period of his preaching the prophet uttered the most sweeping condemnations of Israel's past; if the people continued to walk in the ways in which the fathers had walked they were sure to perish.

The prophet's attitude toward foreign nations is that of the narrowest patriot. This might be supposed to come from the bitterness which the misfortunes of Judah had produced. But this would be an incomplete statement. Ezekiel desired not so much to see vengeance wreaked upon the oppressor as to see his God vindicated from the aspersions which the heathen were casting upon him. The fall of Jerusalem seemed to prove that Yahweh was too weak to protect his own city and his own temple. Ezekiel knew that he was the omnipotent one, and that the future must prove this to the heathen themselves. Yahweh himself declares that the result of his judgments will be to make them know that he is Yahweh (22 : 16 and elsewhere). Justice requires the fall of Jerusalem, but it requires also the punishment of the gentiles.

Ezekiel gives a detailed description of the vision which convinced him of his prophetic mission, and in it we discover the influence of ancient Israelite tradition. What he saw was a mighty cloud interfused with fire, in which as it drew nearer he discovered four living creatures, each with four faces and four wings. Beneath them were four wheels, and in the middle space an altar-fire. Above was a throne, and

[1] It is probably not without significance that Ezekiel nowhere uses the Deuteronomic phrase concerning Yahweh's making his name dwell in the temple. He thought too realistically to be satisfied with such a statement.

on it a human form of supernal brightness, which he discovered to be Yahweh himself. The whole is called by the prophet the glory of Yahweh (1 : 28). The thunder-cloud, in which the earliest Israelite belief saw the chariot of Yahweh, seems to furnish the basis for this vision. The composite figures which appear in it are the cherubim which guarded the ark in the temple of Solomon. The altar-fire is that of the temple itself. The originality of the prophet is to be found not in the details of the vision but in the use which he makes of them. The cherubim are transformed into supporters of the throne; the altar is made movable that it may accompany Yahweh in his wanderings. The wheels are to show that Yahweh is not bound to a single spot, but can move freely to all quarters of the earth. Since the temple is to be destroyed Yahweh is about to leave it and take up his residence in the mountain of the gods in the far north, whence he will visit his faithful exiles at intervals until the temple is rebuilt, when he will return there as of old.

The celestial vision so fills Ezekiel's heart that he never reflects on the heathen divinities, and never inquires whether they have any reality. His only allusion to them is in passages which tell of Israel's idolatry. Here they are called "abominations," or "sticks."[1] Yahweh, however, is conceived of as highly anthropomorphic. In fact, he shows human passion in a marked degree in the very thing which Ezekiel has most at heart, that is, his anger at the sins of his people and his determination to vindicate his own reputation. Trespass on the sanctity of Yahweh is not only disobedience to the divine law; it is insult to the divine majesty. This is what arouses the anger of the divinity both against Israel and against the other nations. The detailed statement may be cited: "On the day that I chose Israel and swore to the offspring of the house of Jacob, and made myself known to them in the land of Egypt, saying: I am Yahweh your God—on that day I swore to them that I would bring them out of the land of Egypt to a land flowing with milk and honey,

[1] *Gillulim;* the meaning of the word is not quite certain.

the glory of all lands. I said to them: Cast away every one the abomination of his eyes; defile not yourselves with the idols of the land of Egypt; I am Yahweh your God. But they rebelled against me and would not hear me; they did not cast away the abominations of their eyes, nor forsake the idols of Egypt. Then I resolved to pour out my fury upon them and accomplish my anger upon them in the land of Egypt; but I dealt with them for my name's sake, lest it should be profaned in the eyes of the nations in the midst of which they were, and in whose sight I had made known to them my purpose to bring them forth from the land of Egypt. I brought them forth from the land of Egypt and brought them into the wilderness" (20 : 5–10). The passage goes on to show that the same thing had been repeated, first in the wilderness, but also in the land of Canaan. In every case the people had been unfaithful and had served other gods. In each particular case of unfaithfulness, also, Yahweh had been moved to destroy them, but had reflected for his name's sake and had spared them.

From this chapter we see that Ezekiel condemned the whole past history of Israel. In fact, as has been said by another, it was he who taught the people to misunderstand this history. To the earlier prophets the wilderness wandering was a time of harmony between God and the people (Hosea 11 : 1–3; Jer. 2 : 2*f.*), and the defection had begun only after the entrance into Canaan. But in the view of Ezekiel idolatry had begun in Egypt, and Yahweh would have been justified in destroying the people at the very beginning. This is undoubtedly the result of his reflection on the sinfulness of his contemporaries, for he finds no terms strong enough to describe the state of things in the Jerusalem of his own day. His vision takes him to the sinful city, and he sets forth in detail what he sees there. The parable of the adulterous wife, first used by Hosea, is adopted by Ezekiel and carried out in detail, and the parable is repeated in such form as to indict the two sister nations (16 and 23). The figure of the vine, used by the older prophets, is also taken up by him, but given a new turn: "Of what use is the wood of the vine, the wild stock of the forest? Is even a peg got from it to hang things on?" (15 : 2.)

The crying sin of Judah, as of Israel, is the worship of other gods, and this the prophet supposes to have been carried on at all the sanctuaries of the land: "I brought them into the land which I had sworn to give them, and wherever they saw a high hill or a leafy tree there they offered sacrifice, there they presented their offensive oblations, there they proffered their sweet savours and there they poured forth their libations" (20 : 28). This was not only treason to Yahweh; it was also direct disobedience to his commands. The view of Deuteronomy, according to which a specific law was promulgated in the wilderness, is adopted to the full: "I gave them my statutes and taught them my ordinances which if a man do he shall live in them; I gave my Sabbaths also to be a sign between me and them that they might know that it was I, Yahweh, who sanctified them. But the house of Israel rebelled against me in the wilderness, my statutes they did not keep, they rejected my ordinances which if a man do he shall live in them, and they sorely profaned my Sabbaths" (20 : 11–13).

This last phrase—"they profaned my Sabbaths"—shows the distinctly priestly point of view. Sin is defilement, and the object of the commandments is to prevent pollution of that which is sacred to Yahweh. The land which he has chosen for himself should be kept clean from all that he objected to. The indictment charges that Israel defiled this land—committed sacrilege, that is. The acme of guilt was reached when the very temple was profaned by idolatry. The vision, in which the prophet sees the image which causes jealousy in the temple court, sees the women weeping for Tammuz (a Babylonian god) in the sacred enclosure, sees the elders of Judah burning incense to their fetishes in a chamber of the building, sees also the worshippers of the sun turning their backs on Yahweh (chapter 8), is intended to make the reader realise the extent of the profanation. The prophet does not hesitate to say that Judah is worse than Sodom (16 : 48, 51 *ff.*). The conclusion is that the time of forbearance is past and that the catastrophe is at hand (chapter 9). What is ritually unclean must be cast out of Yahweh's land. After the blow has fallen the prophet, looking back upon it, makes Yahweh say: "In my sight their ways were like the most abominable ceremonial impurity; thereupon I poured my fury on them for the blood they had shed in my land, and because they had defiled it with their idols; according to their ways and deeds I judged them" (36 : 17–19).

It would be a mistake to suppose that Ezekiel is indifferent to ethics. The specifications in the indictment make his position clear. He is in line with the best prophetic tradition, and in this he follows the lead of Deuteronomy, when he denounces bloodshed, oppression of the client, the fatherless, and the widow, incest, bribery, usury, and fraud (22 : 1–12). A specific instance is his condemnation of Zedekiah's perjury (17 : 16). But in the same breath with these crimes we find enumerated what we regard as ritual offences—eating with the blood, despising the sacred things, and profaning the Sabbaths. The priestly habit of mind, it is evident, classes all transgressions as defilement; all sin is invasion of the sanctity of Yahweh.[1] The implications of this view are more extensive than we at first realise. The unconscious violations of taboo are as dangerous as witting transgressions. The effect is evident in the later Levitical documents. What Ezekiel calls the justice of Yahweh is the almost mechanical reaction of his sanctity against that which is unclean.

In the application of this justice to the individual this prophet goes beyond any that we have yet met. In his day the problem of the individual was brought to the front. After the introduction of Deuteronomy there was a clearly marked line of division between the righteous, those who

[1] The prevailing view of sin in the Babylonian religion seems to be the same.

adhered to the book and strove to obey it, and the sinners who disobeyed. But in the calamities which befell the state the righteous suffered with the wicked. Jeremiah had wrestled with the problem whether this was consonant with the justice of Yahweh, but Ezekiel was compelled to confront it even more directly. His solution was the assertion that Yahweh deals with every individual in exact accordance with his deserts. And he meant that this justice was meted out in the present life—the idea of a retribution beyond the grave had not yet arisen in Israel. The boldness with which the prophet announces the programme of the divine administration arouses our wonder: "The soul that sins shall die; the son shall not bear the consequences of the father's iniquity, and the father shall not bear the consequences of the son's iniquity. The righteousness of the righteous shall be put down to his account, and the wickedness of the wicked to his account" (18 : 20). The popular doctrine was other: "The fathers have eaten sour grapes, and the children's teeth are set on edge." Tradition was embodied in this saying, as we see in the earlier documents and in later ones also. The solidarity of the family made the children suffer for the father; and, on the other hand, the merits of the father might induce Yahweh to spare the son who had offended—it was for David's sake that Solomon was dealt with so mildly. Ezekiel breaks with this tradition and the pains he takes to set forth his theory shows his consciousness of its novelty. He declares that, so far from the fathers being able to help their children in the coming calamity, even Noah, Daniel, and Job would not be able to deliver their children from punishment (14 : 14). Pictorially the same thing is said when the angel is told to mark the few righteous men in Jerusalem before the slaughter of the rest (9 : 4).

The bearing of this thought upon the prophet's activity among his compatriots must be evident. He did not believe that the punishment would cease with the fall of Jerusalem. Upon the exiles there would be further visitation. It was his mission by all means to save some; hence his exhortation: "Turn from your evil ways, O house of Israel; why will you die?" (33 : 11.) And Yahweh swears by his own life that he does not desire the death of the wicked but rather that he should turn from his way and live (18 : 32). The appeal to the individual which results makes Ezekiel the first pastor in history. He watched for souls as one that must give account. This is well brought out in his comparison of himself to the watchman on the city wall: "As for thee, O son of man, I have made thee a watchman to the house of Israel; when thou hearest a word from my mouth thou shalt warn them. When I say to the wicked: thou shalt surely die—then if thou speak not to the wicked to warn him to turn from his way, he shall die for his guilt, but I will hold thee responsible. But if thou warn the wicked to turn from his way and he turn not, he shall die for his guilt, but thou hast delivered thyself" (33 : 1–9).

In thus preaching, Ezekiel takes no account of the sinful habit of which Jeremiah had so clear an idea. To him righteousness consists in a number of single acts, and in like manner wickedness consists in single acts, in the one case of obedience, in the other of disobedience. At any single moment a man may change his course of life, the righteous may become wicked, and the wicked may become righteous by an effort of the will. The part which each will have in the chastisement that is to come will be determined by the actions in which he is engaged at the time (*cf.* 33 : 12 and 17). This is a mechanical theory, but probably it was what the contemporaries of the prophet needed.[1] Their temptation was to despair because of their belief that the sins of the past lay heavy upon them: "Our transgressions and our sins are upon us and we are rotting away in them" (33 : 10). Encouragement could come only from the thought that each man had it in his power to turn and do right. Ezekiel was

[1] "He states the doctrine of free-will in that crude and exaggerated form which is inevitable with ideas that are still new." (Addis, *Hebrew Religion*, p. 224.)

not altogether consistent in carrying out his theory, for after the fall of Jerusalem he saw that those who escaped were not such as he had classed among the righteous. He accounts for the fact by supposing that Yahweh had spared these to show the exiles what kind of men the Jerusalemites were, object-lessons to convince them that the punishment was deserved (14 : 21–23).

The faithful who respond to the preaching will become the seed of a new commonwealth, in which Israel's true ideal will be reached. Such is the message which followed the fall of Jerusalem. The end is to be accomplished by an act of God, but the prophet is to co-operate. This is the meaning of the vision of dry bones. The bones come together by divine power, but they do so when the word is uttered by the human voice. A restoration is necessary for the vindication of Yahweh himself. He could not leave the heathen to believe that he had not been strong enough to protect his own. The banishment of Israel caused the gentiles to scoff: "These are the people of Yahweh, yet were forced out of his land! Then I took pity on my sacred name which the house of Israel had [thus] caused to be profaned among the gentiles whither they went. Say to the house of Israel: Not for your sakes do I act, but for my sacred name which you have profaned among the nations to whom you are come. I will make sacred my name which is become profane among the nations, and the nations shall learn that I am Yahweh when through you I manifest my sanctity in their sight. I will take you from all lands and bring you into your own land; I will sprinkle pure water upon you and you shall be clean from all your impurities; from all your idols I will cleanse you; I will take the heart of stone out of your bosom and give you a heart of flesh; my own spirit I will put within you; I will cause you to follow my statutes and to observe my ordinances; you shall dwell in the land which I gave your fathers; you shall be my people and I will be your God" (36 : 20–28). This detailed statement may be paralleled from several other discourses. The root idea is that of sanctity as we have already defined it—that mysterious attribute which separates Yahweh from the world of common things—his divinity. This will be made known by his action on behalf of Israel, so that all the world shall see his power. This, we may say, is the external aspect of the restoration. The internal is the renewal of the covenant by an act of free grace. Israel will be chosen anew and regenerated by such an influence as will make them obedient to Yahweh. The complaint of the earlier prophets had been that the people were too stupid to understand the ways of God. This is what is meant by the heart of stone, for the heart is to the Hebrew thinker the seat of the intellect. This will all be changed; the new Israel will understand and will desire to obey the commandments which give life. This ideal will be reached and applied not to Judah alone but also to the exiled northern kingdom; even Sodom will not be shut out, for it also is a part of Yahweh's domain (16 : 53).

The nations, however, are not to share in the new kingdom. They must be punished in order to vindicate the reputation of Yahweh and because of their attitude toward Israel. To prevent aggressions such as Israel had too often suffered from in the past, also, they must receive an exemplary lesson: "Of all the malignant neighbours of Israel, not one shall be any longer to them a pricking brier or a piercing thorn; they shall learn that I am Yahweh" (28 : 24). Specific denunciation of these neighbours—Ammon, Moab, Edom, Tyre, Sidon, and Egypt—are therefore included in Ezekiel's book. Their humiliation will both vindicate Yahweh's power and secure Israel in undisturbed possession of its land for all the future. But the most signal vindication of Yahweh, and at the same time the best pledge of future security, will come through the destruction of Gog. In the earlier time the prophets had described the invasion of Palestine by a cruel and relentless enemy. Isaiah had seen that the oppressor of Israel, though acting as Yahweh's instrument, would have to be punished for the arrogance with which it had carried out its mission. When this anticipation had been fulfilled by the downfall of Assyria new foes had come upon the scene. We have read how Jeremiah was shaken to the inmost soul by the Scythian irruption. What would happen if Israel were restored to its own land and a new invasion should come upon them from those obscure northern regions which had vomited forth these barbarian hordes? To answer this question Ezekiel shows us the foes again brought on his land by Yahweh, this time not to ravage it but to meet their doom. By an act of God and without human intervention they will be exterminated, and with them all danger for the future will disappear. The nations will thus finally be convinced that Israel went into captivity for their sins, and the true glory of Yahweh will be revealed (39 : 21 *f.*).

To our prophet the crowning event of the world's history will be the return of Yahweh to his temple, which will take place after the restoration of the people to their own land. The importance of the event may be measured by the particularity with which the restored temple is described, and the care taken to regulate all that belongs to it. The description which fills the last nine chapters of the book is called a vision, but it bears all the marks of an elaborately thought-out plan. It shows us the logical development (in material form) of the priestly ideal. According to this ideal Israel existed in order to guard the residence of Yahweh so carefully that his sanctity will not be invaded. As the intrusion of things repulsive to him had been the cause of Israel's misfortunes in the past, so in the future Israel's welfare and the peace of the world will result from this effective guardianship of the sanctuary from pollution. To suppose that this end would not be secured would be to suppose that the restoration would fail of its object.

In the good time to come the centre of the land will be the temple. It will be erected on a very high mountain and by its form, as well as by its situation, it will declare the inviolability of Yahweh. Jerusalem, being situated at the centre of the earth, is the appropriate place for the sanctuary, and it will be guarded by Yahweh's own people dwelling about it. The transjordanic territory is to be abandoned and all Israel is to dwell in Canaan, properly so called. The Dead Sea is to be made sweet by the waters flowing from the temple spring and all the land will enjoy abundant fruitfulness. The tribes will be settled, seven to the north and five to the south of the temple in such order as to break up the old jealousies. The temple is to be separated from the city of Jerusalem, that there may be less danger of defilement and is to be further protected by a sacred tract of land in which the priests dwell.

The temple itself is planned after the scheme of the one destroyed by Nebuchadrezzar, even the ornaments of palm-trees and cherubim being retained. Two courts, however, are to surround it, to secure more thorough separation from common things. The service is to be in the hands of the old priestly family of Zadok (appointed by David and confirmed by Solomon), to whom the Levites are to be subordinate. This is in deliberate contradiction with earlier practice, as Ezekiel himself tells us. Before the exile the menial work of the sanctuary had been performed by slaves given to the temple by the kings. These were foreigners uncircumcised in flesh and in heart as the prophet complains. The new temple is to have in their place the Levites, that is, priests of the old country sanctuaries. By the destruction of the sanctuaries in the days of Josiah these had been deprived of their means of support, and, although the Deuteronomist ordained that they should have a place in the Jerusalem temple, they had not been able to make good their claim in face of the Zadokites who were already in possession. They had become hangers-on of the sacred place, thankful to get a morsel of bread by performing menial service. This arrangement, which was apparently in effect before the fall of Jerusalem, is now distinctly legitimated by Ezekiel. Its advantage was that it provided consecrated persons for all the offices and definitely allowed the exclusion of laymen from the sacred precincts. Even the prince is not to enter the inner court, but is to stand in the east gate when his sacrifice is offered (46 : 2).

The commonwealth will have little need of a secular ruler, and the prince is altogether secondary to the priesthood. The early experience of Judah with the monarchy had not been such as to encourage hope in a king. The few references to a new David show that Ezekiel did not care to make him prominent, and the prince of whom he speaks is to be only the collector of taxes for the temple service, not for himself or his household (45 : 13–17; 46 : 16–18). The prosperity of the people depends upon the priests, and exact regulations are laid down by which they must preserve their ritual cleanliness. Doubtless these regulations concerning clothing, marriage, and the observance of mourning are drawn from tradition, but we may suppose that the codification was intended to give them new importance. The chief duty of the priests is, of course, to offer sacrifice, though the work of instructing the people in matters sacred and profane is still theirs (44 : 23*f.*).

Not only is the personnel of the temple thus exactly regulated; the services are brought into a system with special reference to this same matter of pollution and its avoidance. In the old days the primary purpose of sacrifice had been to gratify Yahweh by a gift, or else to enter into communion with him. The festivals were occasions for eating and drinking and rejoicing before Yahweh. This old joyous ritual is now replaced by a series of rites designed to preserve the purity of people, land, and sanctuary. It was traditional custom, no doubt, to apply sacrificial blood to a person or thing which had become ceremonially defiled, in order to remove the taboo. Ezekiel makes use of this same means to consecrate the building and its utensils, and provides that the consecration shall be renewed at stated intervals. His thought is that in a world full of unclean things the temple may contract defilement in spite of the most scrupulous care. The whole sanctuary is to be reconsecrated twice a year

(45 : 18–20). This is expressly said to be on account of any one who has erred or is dull of understanding, and it is in accordance with the view later carried through in the Law, namely, that wilful transgression must be punished, but that unwitting trespass causes defilement and must be purged away. And since defilement is contagious, even the sanctuary and its utensils may become polluted through the ignorance of the worshipper. The sacrifices which are performed in order to secure the purifying blood are called sin-offerings. But the purpose of all the sacrifices is now supposed to be purification, as we see from a passage which in our version says that the prince shall provide the sin-offering, and the meal-offering, and the burnt offering, and the peace-offering "to make atonement" for the house of Israel (45 : 17). It would probably better represent the original idea to render "to purify the house of Israel," since the idea of atonement in the theological sense does not seem to be found in the Old Testament, at least not in connection with the sacrifices.

By this programme the ritual side of religion triumphed. Ezekiel completes the process begun by Deuteronomy, and the result is to reverse the teachings of the prophets. Amos declared Yahweh's scorn for offerings, sacrifices, and the festivals; Isaiah is equally emphatic in his condemnation; Jeremiah denied that Yahweh had given a law concerning ritual. Ezekiel, with sublime indifference to these declarations, makes ritual Yahweh's first concern. Ecclesiasticism has triumphed and will increasingly dominate Jewish thought.

CHAPTER XII

LEGALISM TRIUMPHANT

By putting religion into legal form Ezekiel protected it from a disintegrating syncretism. On the other hand, legalism is always in danger of degenerating into formalism. It is easy for us to exaggerate this danger and to underrate the advantages of a rigid code. The imageless worship of Yahweh was more elevated than the idolatry to which the whole gentile world was addicted. Humanly speaking, it could not have been preserved pure unless it had been guarded by ritual barriers. The terrible earnestness with which the prophet sought to exclude everything unclean from the sanctuary communicated itself to the Jewish community. The fact that the exiles were shut out from participation in civil affairs made them all the more devoted to matters of religion.

The rebuilding of the temple at Jerusalem in the time of Darius was doubtless inspired by the Messianic hope. The disappointment which followed seemed to indicate that not enough care had been taken to separate the clean from the unclean. Those who clung to their faith in Yahweh as the only God could imagine no other reason for his delay to reveal himself. Hence came the anxious inquiry for ritual tradition, and a persistent effort to put that tradition into written form. Ritual is, from the nature of the case, capable of indefinite expansion. Deuteronomy, as we have seen, had comparatively few priestly regulations; Ezekiel added to the number; the guild of scribes who came after him carried on the process. Apparently the exiles who lived at a distance from the temple were more zealous in this work than were the inhabitants of Jerusalem. The very fact that the ritual could not be carried out by those in exile made it easier for them to develop its theory. Evidence of their state of mind is given by the Talmud, which formulates the most elaborate rules for ceremonies though these have not been observed for eighteen centuries. The underlying thought is, of course, that when the kingdom comes everything necessary for a complete service must have been provided for.

For two centuries or more after Ezekiel the industry of the scribes spent itself in the collection of ritual traditions. The result was the elaborate code contained in the middle books of the Pentateuch. It is now almost impossible to disentangle the many strands which have here been interwoven. Some of the material is doubtless ancient, representing customs in vogue at Israelite sanctuaries before the Deuteronomic reform. But whatever its source, all of it has been brought under Ezekiel's point of view. One body of laws has, in fact, been supposed to be the work of Ezekiel, though the evidence is not convincing. This is the so-called Holiness code, which avows its design to protect the sanctity of Yahweh. Its watchword is: "Be ye holy, for I am holy" (Lev. 19 : 2). We have already discovered the inadequacy of this translation. It would be more in accordance with the author's idea to read: "Be ye separate from all that is profane because I am thus separate." This code (Lev. 17–26) occupies a position intermediate between Ezekiel and the fully developed priestly system. The author uses many of Ezekiel's phrases and may be called a disciple of the prophet. If we may judge from the concluding exhortation of his book, he himself lived in exile, for this section regards dispersion among the gentiles as the supreme misfortune, and it shows the hope of the exiles by the promise that if they repent Yahweh will remember his covenant with the fathers and again be their God.

The scrupulosity of this writer is shown by his inclusion in his code of many things not mentioned in Deuteronomy.

He reveals the power of the antique way of thinking, according to which all the more unusual processes of life are under the control of supernatural powers. These powers are no longer regarded as gods, yet they have a real existence, and must be conciliated or warded off. Diseases are inflicted not directly by Yahweh but by the demons. These demons are taboo to the worshipper of Yahweh; hence the person afflicted by the disease is unclean, and must be shut out of the community. For uncleanness is contagious, and the presence of the sick man in the camp (which here doubtless stands for the sacred city) is a source of danger. The code therefore attempts to guard the community by shutting the leper out of its bounds, and by providing an elaborate rite of purification before he can be readmitted to the sanctuary.

I have used the leper as an illustration because the law concerning him shows most clearly the point of view of this whole school. The regulations concerning the leper seem to belong to one of the later strata of the Pentateuch, but other cases of defilement are treated in the Holiness code. Most surprising to us are the laws concerning the sexual life, especially concerning childbirth. Parallels from other religions show that there was a wide-spread belief that the birth of a child is under the influence of a demon (originally a divinity) of reproduction. The child and mother are therefore unclean after the birth, and there must be an elaborate purification after the forty or eighty days of separation. It would be a mistake to suppose that the Hebrew writers regard the sexual life as sinful in our sense of the word. There is no trace of asceticism in the Old Testament. Marriage is incumbent on all, and the birth of a son is a sign of the grace of Yahweh. The treatment of the young mother as unclean is therefore a survival from early beliefs or usages.

From the same point of view we must judge the elaborate prohibitions of marriage within certain degrees of kinship. These are uttered in conscious opposition to foreign religious practice. The text intimates as much: "After the doings of the land of Egypt wherein you have dwelt you shall not do, and after the doings of the land of Canaan whither I bring you you shall not do, neither shall you walk in their statutes" (Lev. 18 : 3). This sentence prefaces the prohibitions of which I have spoken. The inference is plain—that in these countries marriages within the kin were allowed or encouraged from alleged religious motives. Ezekiel says plainly that sexual license was common in Jerusalem before the fall of the city (Ezek. 22 : 10*f.*). Probably the worship of a foreign or old Canaanite god of fruitfulness was responsible for these abuses, and the reason for the prohibitions of our code is the acute reaction of the religion of Yahweh against foreign custom. This accounts for the mention of child sacrifice in connection with these sexual offences; it was regarded as Canaanitish in origin. The author takes pains to emphasise his view at the close of the chapter, when he says that the land is defiled by all these things (Lev. 18 : 24–30).

As in the case of Ezekiel, all sins are judged from the ritual point of view. Hence the incongruous grouping together of such things as cutting one's hair or beard, tattooing the person, eating with the blood in one class, and prostituting one's daughter, oppression of the client, and the use of false weights and measures in the other. And in the same paragraph we find positive commands to observe the Sabbath, to show reverence to old age, to love the client as one's self (Lev. 19 : 26–36). From Deuteronomy are repeated the prohibitions of sowing two kinds of seed in one field and of wearing cloth in which two kinds of thread are woven together (19 : 19). We are not able to point out in every case the exact heathen superstition against which the prohibition is directed, but the probability is that such a superstition existed. There is evidence, for example, that in some cases heathen diviners wore a garment in which wool and cotton were woven together.[1] The scrupulosity of the Holiness code is manifest when it makes the touch of an unclean animal a source of defilement (Lev. 11 : 43).

[1] Goldziher, *Zeitschr. d. alttest. Wissenschaft*, XX, pp. 36*f.*

Since Yahweh has separated the people from all mankind to be his consecrated ones, the obligation to purity rests upon every Israelite. But there are degrees of purity, and the priests who come into the immediate presence of the divinity must exercise more care than the layman who stands at a greater distance. Hence the legislation for the priests, which follows the precedent set by Ezekiel. Bodily blemishes shut a man out from active service, though not from sharing the sacred food (Lev. 21 : 16–18). Mourning rites defile the mourner, as we have seen. The demand of bereaved nature, however, is too insistent to be altogether ignored. Hence the concession, according to which the priest may express his grief for father, mother, son, daughter, brother, or unmarried sister (vss. 1–4). Even for these there must be no shaving of the head or making marks in the flesh, these acts being connected with the worship of the manes. The high priest now appears distinctly as the culmination of the sacred caste, in whom therefore separation from the common must be most complete. He must not rend his clothes, must not approach any corpse, and must not observe any of the conventional signs of grief even for his father or his mother (21 : 10–15). The code seems to prohibit his leaving the sanctuary at all, lest his sanctity be contaminated (vs. 12), but in practice this was not enforced. The severity of the law is seen in the enactment that any Israelite who approaches the sacred things in a state of defilement shall be cut off from his people (22 : 3).

The way in which ancient custom is adopted in this legislation is illustrated by the treatment of a newly-planted vineyard or orchard. For three years the fruit must be regarded as unclean; the fourth year it is all consecrated to Yahweh; after this it becomes the property of the owner. The evident reason for the law is that originally the first three years, or perhaps the first four years, were sacred to the local Baal, that is, it was taboo to man. In this legislation the taboo is recognised as uncleanness, and the special act of consecration to Yahweh in the fourth year is designed to remove the taboo and make the fruit safe for men to enjoy (19 : 23–25). Among the Bedawin at the present day, the first milk yielded by a domestic animal is regarded as sacred.

We saw that Ezekiel practically abolished the old joyous festivals and substituted an exactly regulated series of observances under the strict supervision of the priests. The Priestcode in like manner codifies the regulations concerning festivals and sacrifices. Four stages of ritual are traceable in the order, Deuteronomy, Ezekiel, Holiness code, and Priestcode proper. To the last stage we may now give some attention. It is distinguished by the thorough way in which it transfers the ideal church from the future, where Ezekiel located it, to the past. Ezekiel saw a sanctuary in the middle of the land surrounded by a priestly people which would guard it from pollution. Yahweh will here take up his abode and will be served constantly by a duly consecrated body of priests and Levites. Here the sacrificial service will secure the constant presence and blessing of the divinity. The priestly writer believes that this ideal had once been realised. This was during the wilderness wandering. The theory is in flat contradiction to Ezekiel, for this prophet traced Israel's defection back to the time of the exodus. But there was another tradition according to which Israel had been faithful in the earliest period, and the defection had come only after the entrance into Canaan. Upon this tradition the priestly author bases his scheme. According to his account, the revelation made to Moses on the Mount was a command to make a sanctuary so that Yahweh might dwell in the midst of his people from that time on. The earlier narrative gave some sort of countenance to this idea by its mention of the tent of tryst. But there is a vast difference between the simple oracle tent, of which Joshua was the sole minister and guardian, and the elaborate tabernacle whose dimensions and materials are now so exactly described to us, and to which some thousands of Levites are attached as its servants.

Moses' forty days on the Mount were occupied with study of the plan for this elaborate and costly structure. The plan was simply that familiar to us. There are the two chambers; the Most Sacred, in which Yahweh himself dwells; and the Sacred antechamber with a lamp-stand and a table for the bread of the presence. Around the whole is a court fenced off by curtains in which is the great altar for the sacrifices and the laver for priestly ablutions. The whole is the shadow of Solomon's temple thrown by the imagination of the writer upon the background of the desert. To make such a structure plausible, at least to a certain extent, its dimensions are reduced, and the materials are such as might be appropriate for a portable sanctuary. At the same time, concessions to historic probability are not very marked. Gold, silver, precious stones, leather, and brocade are lavished, as though the resources of an empire were at the disposition of the wandering clans in the barren south country. The ideal which has mastered the writer is that Israel as it came out of Egypt was already the fully fledged nation of Solomon's time—a people thoroughly unified—organised under Moses, the theocratic ruler—mustering six hundred thousand fighting men and devoted to the ecclesiastical ideal of postexilic Judaism.

Yahweh has brought Israel from Egypt that he may dwell in the midst of them, and this is actually accomplished when, after the completion of the tabernacle, the cloud descends and rests upon it, or fills it (Num. 9 : 15–23). This cloud is the same in which Yahweh descended upon Mount Sinai, and, like Ezekiel's chariot, it is made of flame. For this reason Moses' face shone when he had been in the Presence (Ex. 34 : 30–35). The special place of Yahweh's presence was the lid of the ark, which now receives the name *kapporeth,* rendered in our version "mercy-seat," but which probably means "place of purification," because the purifying blood is sprinkled there on the great Day of Atonement. The ark, an implement taken over from the earlier narratives, is now overlaid with gold and provided with the golden lid just mentioned. Here Yahweh promises that he will meet with Moses and commune with him (Ex. 25 : 22; Lev. 1 : 1; Num. 7 : 89).

The sanctuary thus constructed becomes the central object of the camp. Aaron and his sons guard the entrance, and the Levites camp about it "lest wrath come upon the congregation" (Num. 1 : 52 *f.*). Ezekiel's distinction between priests and Levites is thoroughly carried out. The priests, however, are Aaron and his sons, instead of the sons of Zadok. The exigencies of the case required an ancestor of the clan who was of older date than Zadok, and Aaron, already known to tradition, was the only one available. The gradation in the priesthood is carried one step farther than in Ezekiel, for Aaron as high priest is sharply marked off from his sons by his greater sanctity. In him the sacredness of the whole order is concentrated, and this is so powerful that his intervention with the incense calms Yahweh's anger (Num. 17 : 11–15). His importance is indicated again by the declaration that if he falls short of what is required the wrath of Yahweh will fall upon the whole congregation (Lev. 10 : 6).

The material nature of the sanctity on which stress is here laid is shown by the treatment of the implements of the service. Their sacredness is so great and so deadly that, if they are not carefully wrapped up by the priests before they are seen by the Levites, whose duty it is to carry them on the journey, they will kill even these consecrated persons (Num. 4 : 15; *cf.* vss. 18 *f.*). In accordance with this is the sanctity of the whole camp from which all unclean persons must be rigorously shut out "lest they defile the camp" (Num. 5 : 1–4). The sanctity of the divine name is such that the blasphemer must be put to death (Lev. 24 : 10–23). The danger of trespass is set before us in the story of Nadab and Abihu, who are slain by fire proceeding from Yahweh because they offered incense with strange fire (Lev. 10 : 1–7). In what their offence consisted is not made clear to us, and it is possible that the story is based on the attempt of some irregular priests to arrogate to themselves a part in the service. The author's main idea is that any infringement of the sacred Law, any deviation from the exact ritual, will be punished by an act of God.

The importance of sanctity is expressed again in the elaborate rites by which the tent and altar are made ready for the residence of Yahweh (Lev. 8 : 10 *ff.*) and in the account of the consecration of the priests. Here the most elaborate precautions are taken to remove every trace of defilement. The priests are washed, anointed, invested with the sacred garments; a sacrifice is offered on their behalf, blood from the altar and oil are sprinkled on the priests and on their garments. Only after this has been done are they fit to approach the altar and present the food of Yahweh. No less than twenty-four acts are performed in this rite of consecration (Ex. 29). The lamina or gold plate which the high priest wears bears the appropriate inscription "Sacred to Yahweh," and it is expressly declared that by wearing it Aaron takes away the guilt of the sacred things which the people consecrate (Ex. 28 : 36–38). The meaning is that the sacred character of the high priest counteracts any defect in the gifts of the people. The danger incident to the priest's office is indicated by the statement that if they do not wash their hands and feet before approaching the altar they will die (Ex. 30 : 21).

The exact regulation of the sacrificial service is the logical sequence of the consecration of sanctuary and priests. The daily burnt offering is the condition of Yahweh's dwelling among his people (Ex. 29 : 38 and 45 *f.*). In the thought of later Judaism the suspension of this recurring expression of loyalty to Yahweh was the most painful feature of the desecration of the temple by Antiochus. The whole sacrificial ritual is defined as to its material, the method of slaying the animal, the disposition to be made of the blood and flesh. The four kinds of sacrifice—burnt offering, peace-offering, sin-offering, and guilt-offering—are described (Lev. 1–7).

Exact measurements are given for the meal-offering and the libation (Num. 15 : 1–12). The number of victims to be brought on Sabbaths and festivals is specified (Num. 28). To one of these authors we owe the exact regulation of the Passover (Ex. 12 : 1–20). Nowhere is any reflection indulged in as to the meaning of this elaborate ritual—priestly tradition gave it sanction and that was enough. Some of it, as I have said, was very old, and the original point of view sometimes comes to the surface, as where the animal is said to be burned as a fire offering of fragrant odour to Yahweh (Lev. 3 : 11), or where even more distinctly, not to say crassly, it is said to be the food of Yahweh (Num. 28 : 2; *cf.* Ezek. 44 : 7).

Characteristic of the postexilic point of view is the prominence now given to the sin-offering and the guilt-offering. These two classes are rarely mentioned in the earlier literature. In Ezekiel they become important because of his theory of sin, a theory which was fully developed by the priestly writers. According to this view sin is anything that offends the sanctity of Yahweh. The Law attempts to define what these things are, but in making the attempt it has become so elaborate that one may often be in doubt whether he is a transgressor or not. One may easily sin in ignorance, by coming in contact with an unclean animal or with a person suffering some sexual defilement. Unwitting sin is, however, dangerous to the person affected and to the whole community, for the sanctity of Yahweh reacts against every defilement. To provide against this danger is the aim of the priestly writers. In their theory transgression of the Law by a person who knows what he is doing must be punished by death or excommunication. "That soul shall be cut off from the congregation" is their declaration, leaving it uncertain whether he will be visited by an act of God, or put to death by the civil authority, or excommunicated. In practice excommunication was the method taken, and this accomplished the end sought, which was the purification of the congregation from contagion. The stringency of the Law is shown by the number of offences on which this penalty is to be inflicted.

What really troubled the pious observer of the Law was unwitting violation of the commandment. Such "sins" could not be punished by the community, but they were sure to bring down the wrath of Yahweh. To meet this danger the purifications were ordained, and the purifications were effected by the sin-offering and the guilt-offering. Thus a man who discovered that he had unwittingly contracted defilement, or who even suspected that he had, could always find relief by bringing one of these offerings. Whatever atonement they effected extended only to this class of offences. The limits of witting and unwitting, however, are so drawn as to make the latter class as large as possible, and this is an intelligible concession to human weakness. The law of the guilt-offering says: "If any one commit a trespass against Yahweh, and deal falsely with his neighbour in a matter of deposit or of bargain or of concealing a theft, or of taking advantage of his neighbour, or have found that which was lost and have dealt falsely therein, or have sworn to a lie . . . then he shall restore that which he took wrongfully adding a fifth of its value . . . and shall bring his guilt-offering to Yahweh."[1] It is clear if this definition be allowed that a wide variety of offences might pass for unwitting, and so claim the benefit of the law of purification.

I have just spoken of "whatever atonement" these sacrifices effected. It is fair to notice here that in the sin-offering and guilt-offering there is no idea of expiation in the sense in which the word is ordinarily understood—that is, the victim was not a substitute giving his life for the life of the guilty man. The emphasis laid upon the blood, which is often interpreted as favouring the theory of substitution, is due to quite another consideration. By ancient tradition blood is sacred, either because it is the blood of an animal dedicated to the divinity, and so partakes of his sanctity, or else because this mysterious fluid, containing the life of

[1] Lev. 5 : 20–26 in the Hebrew (6 : 1–7 English).

the animal, has in it intrinsically something supernatural. From the most ancient times the blood had been the portion of the sacrifice which was too sacred to be appropriated by man and which must be carefully presented to the divinity. The gift was grateful to him and made the offerer acceptable. But there was more in it than this: the blood might be applied to anything defiled or common and the object was thereby consecrated. This is seen in the consecration of the priests to which allusion has been made. By its blood the sin-offering effects a removal of pollution. If a substitutionary atonement were aimed at we should expect the flesh of the victim to become taboo, being laden with the sin of the offender transferred to it. But we are distinctly told that the flesh of the sin-offering is most sacred (Lev. 6 : 18–22 and 7 : 1). The priests are strictly commanded to eat this flesh in the sanctuary (6 : 19; 7 : 5 *f.*). An exception is indeed made in certain cases where the offering is brought on behalf of the priests themselves. Here it is ordered that the flesh shall be burned outside the camp, probably because it was felt to be unbecoming for the priests to profit by their own imperfections. The whole treatment of the subject shows that the authors were not interested in any theological theory; they did not ask themselves why the sacrifices took away the guilt. Enough for them that the blood is a powerful cleanser. Moses *unsins* the altar by sprinkling the blood of Aaron's sin-offering on it (Lev. 8 : 15). The reason why the blood was not in ordinary cases sprinkled on the supposed guilty person was apparently twofold; for one thing, the blood was too powerful—if sprinkled on the person it would make him unfit for the ordinary duties of life; and, on the other hand, the writers of these regulations were more interested in keeping the sanctuary clean than in purifying the persons who brought the sacrifice. The sacredness of the sacrifice was such that the offerer was sufficiently cleansed by laying his hands on the head of the animal, whereas the altar, which possibly had been defiled by the very neglect which was now made good, needed the application of the blood to keep it fit for the service. What is certain is that the death of the victim is nowhere treated as a punishment, and there is no intimation that the victim takes the place of the guilty man.

The idea of purification reaches its climax in the ritual of the great day which we call the Day of Atonement (Lev. 16). The underlying thought is that the sanctity of the dwelling may have been impaired by the uncleanness to which the people were so liable. This sanctity is so great that no one must enter the inner chamber except the high priest, and he can enter only on this one day in the year. On this occasion he must take special precautions, offering a sin-offering and a burnt offering for himself and then putting on vestments kept for this occasion. The bells on the skirt of his robe notify the divinity of his approach, lest, coming unannounced, he provoke the divine anger. In entering the Presence he is to carry a censer with burning incense so that the cloud will prevent his looking directly at the object of his reverence, for this would be fatal. After purifying himself and his household by this first sin-offering he is to cast lots on two goats, one of which is thus assigned to Yahweh and the other to Azazel. The one for Yahweh is a sin-offering for the people. This one is slain and the blood is brought into the inner sanctuary and sprinkled both on the cover of the ark and all about this most sacred room in order to cleanse it from the impurities of the children of Israel. In the same way the high priest is to "unsin" the altar by sprinkling the blood upon it (16 : 15–18).

The account makes plain the purpose of the sin-offering. The sanctuary in the course of the year may have been defiled by some of those unwitting sins to which every man is liable; therefore there must be a special purification reaching even within the veil. This is effected by sprinkling the blood of this sin-offering in the most sacred place and also upon the altar. The further ceremony is without parallel in Hebrew religion, unless the bird set free at the cleansing of the leper be an exception. It consists in loading the other goat (scapegoat, we call it traditionally) with the sins or rather with the impurities of the people and sending it thus laden into the wilderness. According to Hebrew tradition, though this is not directly asserted in our text, the goat was taken to the edge of a precipice and thrown down from it. Since the goat is distinctly said to be for Azazel, and since in postbiblical documents Azazel is known to be one of the demons, it seems clear that we have here one of the ancient sacrifices to these uncanny beings elsewhere so sternly repressed. The rite is a cathartic one, like many which we meet in other religions. In these rites sin or disease or impurity is transferred to an object, animate or inanimate, and then thrown away or driven out of the community.

The use of two goats in this ceremony shows plainly enough the twofold aspect of the idea of purification: the removal of uncleanness and the communication of sanctity. This double-faced idea underlies the whole Levitical system. The rite of circumcision is both removal of impurity and consecration to the divinity. Its importance is indicated by the penalty of death or excommunication imposed for neglect of the rite. The Sabbath is a sacred day, and any profanation of it is punished in the same way (Ex. 35 : 1–3). This is brought out by an anecdote in which Yahweh himself decrees the death of a man for the comparatively trifling act of gathering sticks on that day (Num. 15 : 32–36). The blasphemer of the sacred name is punished in the same way, and it is apparent from the anecdote which enforces this lesson that it is wrong to mingle the sacred Jewish blood with that of gentiles, for the offender in this case was son of an Israelite mother and an Egyptian father (Lev. 24 : 10–23). The rite of cleansing the leper, which is curiously parallel to the consecration of the priest, shows this twofold aspect. It takes pains to remove the taboo of the disease, and at the same time it dedicates the convalescent to the service of Yahweh. The mechanical nature of the idea of defilement is attested by the treatment of a house infected with mould or mildew. It is pronounced leprous and submitted to the judgment of the priest just like the human leper.

Other enactments of this literature might be adduced, but these are sufficient to show the motive of the authors. The very punctiliousness of their demands shows the earnestness of their conviction. To them Israel was no longer a nation among the nations; it was a church whose first, and one might say whose only, duty was to keep itself unspotted from the world. While the temple stood and the rites were duly performed, and while the Jews kept themselves free from demonic influences, all would be well. Not only the prosperity of the scattered Jewish communities but the well-being of the world at large depended on the observance of the Law. The danger of formalism which resulted from this emphasis of the *opus operatum* is obvious. The authors of the code would reply to our objection: "Formalism or no formalism, we are bound to obey the divine ordinances, and this is, in fact, our life." Men of a more sophisticated age may easily underestimate the amount of serious religious purpose which finds satisfaction in the strict observance of such a ritualistic system.

It is easy to misunderstand also the zeal of the authors for the prerogatives of the priesthood. If the service of the temple was to be worthily performed the ministers of the sanctuary must have an adequate support. It was not altogether because the priestly writers were themselves priests (we do not know that they were) that they made such extravagant demands for tithes and contributions. If the prosperity of the race depends on the hierarchy, it is a small thing for the laymen to provide an adequate support for its members. Deuteronomy has shown us that in the early period the members of the priestly caste were reckoned among the poor of the land, dependent upon the charity of the faithful. Ezekiel sanctioned the exclusion of all laymen from the sanctuary, and at the same time provided that all the offices should be in the hands of consecrated persons. The Priestcode assumes that Ezekiel's arrangement was in effect from the Mosaic age, and takes care that the whole priestly clan shall be duly supported. First of all, forty-eight cities, including the most important places in the country, are set apart for the tribe of Levi—something quite contradictory to the declarations of earlier authors (some of them priestly even), according to which Levi was not to receive any territory (Num. 18 : 21–24). Then they are to have a tithe of the gross produce of the land. Of this the priests are to have a tithe. Considerable portions of the offerings also go to the priests, and this is doubtless in accordance with ancient usage. The subject is of subordinate interest to the student of religion, illustrating as it does only the tendency of a hierarchy to claim more and more for itself in the way of emoluments and in the way of dignity. The climax was reached in the Greek period, when the high priest became the civil as well as the ecclesiastical head of the community, and when the titles of king and high priest were given to the same person.

The separatism, the scrupulosity, and the externalism of the Pharisees developed from the ideas embodied in the Priestcode. Fortunately for the history of religion, the Priestcode was only one part of the literature of Israel in this period. Within the rigid frame provided by the Law there was room for a more spiritual and vital piety than that of the ritualists. The best evidence is found in the documents which we have still to study.

CHAPTER XIII

THE DOGMATIC BIAS

We have seen how thoroughly Ezekiel taught his people to misunderstand their own history. We have seen also how members of the Deuteronomic school rewrote the earlier narrative to make it teach Deuteronomic lessons. The priestly writers could not do otherwise than carry on this process. The greatest treasure of Israel was its literature. But the lesson taught by this literature must be made plainer if it was to edify a generation dominated by priestly ideals. These ideals were thoroughly theocratic; the wilderness period was a time of gracious obedience, because Yahweh directly controlled his people by the mouth of Moses. The record of Israel's later history was a record of defection, partly because the monarchy was a human institution, not divinely ordained and not divinely guided. Hence the view of the later strata of the books of Samuel, according to which the demand for a king was a proof of the depravity of the people, and a rejection of Yahweh himself. In this same strand of the narrative Samuel is presented as the theocratic ruler, a second Moses, who has only to pray to Yahweh in order to secure a miraculous deliverance from the Philistines (I Sam. 7 : 3–14). That this is not history needs no demonstration.

It is not always easy to distinguish between the Deuteronomic redaction and that of the priestly writers. In fact, the point of view of the two schools was so similar that it was easy for the later to expand the text of the earlier. The prayer of Solomon, for example, is Deuteronomic in tone, but it has evidently been retouched by a hand which we may properly regard as that of a priestly writer. Without attempting to point this out in detail we may notice the distinctly priestly document which underlies the book of Genesis and the earlier chapters of Exodus. We have already noticed those narrative portions of these books which belong respectively to the Yahwistic and to the Elohistic writer. When these narratives are dissected out we have left what evidently was a single document, mostly genealogical in nature, which belongs to the priestly school. It was apparently composed as an introduction to the laws contained in Leviticus. It was designed also to replace the patriarchal stories of J and E, which from the later point of view were scarcely edifying. For an introduction to the Law it was sufficient to give an outline which would lead the reader rapidly from Adam to Abraham, and from Abraham to Moses, without dwelling upon these unedifying details.

This author whom we will call P, resembles his predecessor E in that he prefers the name Elohim for God. His theology, however, is less anthropomorphic than that of either of his forerunners. This comes into view at once when we compare his account of the creation (Gen. 1 : 1 to 2 : 4*a*) with that of J. He makes God transcendent, working by his spirit and word alone. The divinity no longer fashions man of clay, and he does not find it necessary to experiment with the animals before deciding to make woman as man's fit associate. We hear nothing of Yahweh's walking in the garden, or of his cross-questioning Adam about his conduct. The local colour has disappeared; there is no serpent; no cherubim guard the paradise. The mythology has been discarded, and we have something which approaches a scientific cosmology. A trace of anthropomorphism survives indeed in the statement that man is made in the image of the Creator, and a faint echo of the Babylonian myth is heard in the word *tehom,* used for the primeval waters, for this is evidently the Tiamat of Mesopotamian cosmology. But these faint survivals show how thoroughly the mythological stage of thought has been left behind.

It is possible that the succession of works of creation in this account has been borrowed from Babylonian sources, for Babylonian science was in high repute throughout the empire of Xerxes. But if so the arrangement has been subordinated to Jewish conceptions, for the compression of these successive acts into the six days of the creative week is plainly dictated by the Jewish reverence for the Sabbath. The reason for the sanctity of the day is now seen to be that God himself rested on that day and consecrated it as a sacred day. The correspondence of things on earth and of things in heaven requires that the day be observed in both. Later Jewish authors carry this idea of correspondence so far as to require the angels to observe all the Jewish festivals, and some of them are insistent in their demand that the calendar be so arranged that the earthly festivals shall be observed at the proper time, since otherwise the discordance would interfere with the divine purpose.

The priestly writer bridges over the period between Adam and the deluge by a genealogy in which he records the age of each patriarch at the birth of his eldest son. The interest of this table is plainly chronological and the explanation is not far to seek. In the postexilic period, when the new era was ardently hoped for, it was supposed that the duration of the present world could be calculated and the time of the consummation of all things could thus be foreseen. The world was to exist four or six or seven thousand years, or as many periods, which could be discovered by the study of history. Which of the schemes underlay this author's figures he does not tell us. Possibly he drew upon Babylonian tradition, for his ten antediluvian patriarchs are shadows of the ten kings which Babylonian mythology assigned to the primeval age.

The ordered and schematic arrangement of this author's creation story made him, in a sense, the first of the evolutionists, and his theory of development comes to view in his treatment of the institutions of Israel. The Sabbath was introduced at the beginning; at the deluge the prohibition of blood as food was imposed; at the birth of Isaac circumcision was commanded; and at the exodus the observance of the Passover. A certain amount of dependence on tradition dictated this order in the narrative, for circumcision antedated Moses, and the Yahwist had already brought the Passover into connection with the exodus, his view being also adopted by the Deuteronomist. The priestly writer by accenting these institutions marked off four periods of the world's history, beginning respectively with Adam, Noah, Abraham, and Moses. The Greeks also had a scheme of four ages, as we know, but it is not necessary to suppose that the Hebrew thinker was influenced by Greek thought.

It is not accidental that Sabbath and circumcision are singled out as having special significance. These were the two institutions which the Jews could observe in the dispersion and which, therefore, most distinctly served the purpose of a test for the faithful observer of the Law. Our author thinks them obligatory not on the Jews alone. In reference to the Sabbath, at any rate, he felt authorised to say: "We Jews are the only people who are faithful to the divine ordering." How, in fact, the observance of a day of rest was introduced into Israel is still unknown. The preexilic references to it seem to indicate that it was a lunar festival. In Babylonia the seventh, fourteenth, and twenty-first days of each month were regarded as days of ill omen on which, therefore, it was safer not to undertake any work. It is difficult, however, to see how this monthly scheme could be dissociated from the phases of the moon so as to give rise to the Hebrew series of seventh-day observances independent of the lunar months. But the importance of the number seven in Hebrew thought is evident from the documents in our hands. It might well be that the idea of consecrating one day in seven by abstaining from labour arose without direct connection with the moon. The thought would be the same which we find in the so-called sabbatical year, one year in seven, in which the land was allowed to lie fallow as a tribute to Yahweh, the Lord of the soil.

The difference between the Deuteronomic and the priestly point of view is shown by the treatment of the Sabbath in their respective decalogues. The Deuteronomist, with his characteristic humanitarianism, insists upon the day of rest as a boon to the slave and the hireling: "Thou shalt remember that thou wast a slave in the land of Egypt and Yahweh thy God brought thee out thence by a mighty hand and by an outstretched arm; therefore Yahweh thy God commands thee to keep the sabbath" (Deut. 5 : 15). The priestly writer in adopting the Decalogue changes the reason for the observance of the Sabbath and inserts his preconceived notion that it was consecrated by Yahweh himself: "For in six days Yahweh made heaven and earth, the sea and all that in them is, and rested the seventh day; wherefore Yahweh blessed the sabbath and hallowed it" (Ex. 20 : 11). The difference is enormous—the humanitarian institution has become something imposed by divine command and binding for that reason. As a sacred thing it marks Israel off from the rest of the world: "You shall keep my sabbaths, for this is a sign between me and you throughout your generations, that you may know that it is I, Yahweh, who consecrate you" (Ex. 31 : 13). The full stringency of the command comes out in the same connection, where it is distinctly ordered that the disobedient shall be put to death: "You shall keep the sabbath, for it is a sacred thing to you; every one who profanes it shall surely be put to death; whosoever does any work therein shall be cut off from his people" (Ex. 31 : 14). That we may be in no doubt as to the severity of the commandment we are told of a man who was found gathering sticks on the sacred day and was brought to Moses for judgment. The sentence of death was given by a direct revelation from Yahweh (Num. 15 : 32–36).

Emphasis on the Sabbath is, for the reasons already indicated, a mark of postexilic authorship. In the book of

Jeremiah we read a passage which is quite out of harmony with the rest of that prophet's discourses. It exhorts the kings and the people in the words: "Take heed to yourselves and bear no burden on the sabbath, nor bring it in by the gates of Jerusalem, neither carry forth a burden out of your houses on the sabbath, neither do any work but hallow the sabbath as I commanded your fathers" (Jer. 17 : 21). There follows a specific promise that if the Sabbath is observed the kingdom and temple will stand forever. The view of this writer is that profanation of the Sabbath was the reason why Jerusalem was destroyed, something which is nowhere else affirmed by the prophets until we come to Ezekiel. Postexilic also is the identification of "keeping the Sabbath" with "holding fast the covenant" which we find in another writer (Isaiah 56 : 6). The contrast between this theory and that of the earlier prophets, according to which the Sabbath, like the other ritual observances, is a matter of indifference to Yahweh or even displeasing to him needs only to be mentioned.

As to circumcision, we know that it was an ancient tribal mark common to a number of peoples, among them the group allied by blood with Israel. It became the distinguishing badge of the Jew when he lived in the midst of people who did not practise it. The pre-exilic writers lay no stress upon it, but in Ezekiel's view uncircumcision is uncleanness. The priestly writer regards it as the sign of the covenant and, as we have seen, threatens death for its neglect. The Talmud goes further and declares that if it had not been for circumcision the world would not have been created. Jewish authorities add that the higher order of angels were created with the distinguishing Jewish mark upon them.

According to the document now before us the permission to eat flesh given to Noah and his sons was accompanied by the prohibition of blood. We may suppose the author moved by ancient custom in this case also. According to early ideas the blood is sacred and consequently belongs to the divinity. So late as the time of Ezekiel the prohibition of its enjoyment by man was supposed to be because it was the food of God and was brought to him on the altar (Ezek. 44 : 7). That this belief existed to a late period is indicated by the pains taken by the Psalmist to contradict the popular impression (Psalm 50 : 13). The priestly author could not give this reason to Noah because he thought that sacrifice was not commanded until the time of Moses; but, all the same, blood was to him an uncanny thing which no one ought to eat. The divine command given to Noah should naturally bind all of Noah's descendants. In this case, therefore, as in the matter of the Sabbath, the Jews regarded themselves as the only people who were faithful to the divine order of things.

The scheme of the priestly writer included a gradual revelation of Israel's religion. It also included a gradual narrowing of Yahweh's interest from mankind at large down to Israel. The early history of the world is divided into ten periods each marked by the title: "This is the genealogy." The series ends with the genealogy of the sons of Jacob (Gen. 37 : 2). But whatever evolution there was stopped with Moses, for he received the final and complete revelation of the will of Yahweh. In the wilderness the ecclesiastical commonwealth was organised in the form which it must have throughout all future generations. The new epoch is marked by the revelation of the name of Yahweh —this had been stated by the Elohist also. The census of Israel is taken twice in the wilderness, as if to assure us that the nation as it existed in the time of Solomon was born full-grown at the exodus. The colossal miracle by which three million people were sustained in the desert forty years does not disturb our author, since it is the convincing evidence of Israel's election.

As the organisation of this priestly commonwealth in the wilderness was effected by direct divine activity, so was the settlement of the tribes in Canaan. This land was the land of Yahweh, promised by him to the patriarchs, and kept in view at the exodus (Gen. 17 : 1–8; Ex. 2 : 24). The conquest had been narrated by a Deuteronomic author in such a way that the priestly writer did not need to revise it to any extent, but the division of the country among the tribes must be brought into the scheme by relating the direct divine command given to Moses before his death (Num. 34). The second half of the book of Joshua narrates how the command was carried out. The allotment was accompanied by a provision that the land should be inalienable. The family which receives title at the conquest retains it for ever. If there be a deficiency of male heirs daughters may inherit, but on condition that they marry kinsmen, so that in any case the land shall not pass out of the tribe to which it was first given. The sabbatic system is now made to secure this end, there being a general reversion of land to the original owners at the end of seven sabbatic periods (Lev. 25). The author is not a socialist, desiring to prevent a monopoly of landed property; he is a religious idealist endeavouring to secure the perpetuity of the allotment made originally by the direction of Yahweh himself. It is, of course, obvious that no one but an Israelite will ever be able to obtain foothold in Palestine, and that consequently the sanctity of Yahweh's territory will always be preserved.

What customs of war are logically implied in the exclusive sanctity of Israel is set before us in the anecdote of the slaughter of the Midianites (Num. 31). This tribe having seduced the Israelites to idolatry, Moses sends an expedition against them. The warriors think it enough to slay the adult males and bring the women and children to the camp of Israel. But Moses and Eleazar instruct them that all the males, of whatever age, and all the women, except virgins, must also be slain. These, therefore, are executed in cold blood. The soldiers, being ritually unclean by reason of their contact with the dead, are shut out of the camp seven days and are then sprinkled with the holy water kept for purification. The booty is purified by fire and water and divided into halves, one for the men who took part in the expedition, the other for the rest of the people. From each portion, before its distribution to individuals, a contribution is made to the sanctuary, and in addition to this, which is intended to be a fixed tax (as a precedent), the warriors insist on giving a thank-offering. There seems to be no historic basis for the story; it only embodies the author's idea of the way in which the Israel of the future will deal with the heathen.

Since the history of the Judges and the history of the Kings had been worked over by a Deuteronomic hand the priestly school did not find it necessary to re-edit these books. But one of its members, dissatisfied with the record, made a new compendium of the history, containing what he thought best for people to know. Probably he intended his work, which is preserved to us in the books of Chronicles together with Ezra and Nehemiah, to take the place of the other narrative books. For the period between the creation and the accession of David he contents himself with a genealogical outline. He assumes apparently that the Law is in the hands of his readers and that this is enough for this earlier period. He has little use for the Judges, and he probably regarded Saul as an apostate. In fact, he ascribes this unhappy king's death to the vengeance of Yahweh because of the visit to a necromancer (I Chron. 10 : 13). His interest becomes keen when he writes of David. His David, however, is not the David of the earlier narrative—the man who shows many human weaknesses. Whatever throws a shadow on the great king is carefully excluded from the narrative. What is shown us is a great churchman, devoted to the service of the sanctuary. The account of the bringing up of the ark, taken from the earlier narrative, is changed in details so as to make David conform to the Mosaic Law. The Levites, who are conspicuous by their absence from the earlier story, now appear as the legitimate carriers of the sacred object. And being thus brought into the story, the author makes use of them to show David's care for the ritual; for it is at his command that the Levites arrange the companies of singers and of doorkeepers (I Chron. 15 : 16–24). We are assured that even before this time David and Samuel had set the Levites in their office as doorkeepers for the tabernacle, and that they lodged about the house of God (9 : 22 and 27). This house of God is the Mosaic sanctuary, which the author supposes to have been at Gibeon in this period. Only on this hypothesis could he understand Solomon's going thither to sacrifice. At this sanctuary, we are told, David organised the guilds of Levitical singers "until Solomon should build the house of Yahweh" (6 : 16–32; *cf.* 15 : 11). Further, in conjunction with Zadok, David divided the priests into twenty-four courses, and made twenty-four courses of singers for the sake of symmetry (24 and 25). Obed-edom, originally a foreigner, is now made a Levite, progenitor of a family of temple servants. Thus the correctness of the service is assured from the time of David on.

The work of David, however, is only preliminary, for in the view of postexilic Judaism the most important event in the history of the world was the building of the temple. This could not be ascribed to David, because all the world knew that it was the work of Solomon. Our author, however, gives David as much of the credit as was possible. According to him David made all the preparations, gathered all the materials, and even received the plan from Yahweh himself (28 : 11). The extravagance of the provision is indicated by the figures given—a hundred thousand talents of gold and a million talents of silver, besides uncalculated amounts of timber, stone, bronze, and iron (22 : 4 and 14). All that was left for Solomon to do was to carry out the plans of David, and to conform to the Law of Moses (II Chron. 8 : 12–14).

Since the temple is the place of Yahweh's residence, and the only legitimate place of worship, the rebellion of Jeroboam and the northern tribes was apostasy from Yahweh. Having this conviction, the Chronicler leaves the northern kingdom out of his history. The crowning sin was that Jeroboam expelled the true priests from their office. Accordingly, the priests and Levites and all true believers are said to have emigrated from the northern kingdom (II Chron. 11 : 13–16; 13 : 4 *ff*.), and citizens of that kingdom are under the wrath of Yahweh (25 : 6–10). We are not concerned here with the historicity of any of these statements, but with the author's point of view. His belief is that Judah has the favour of Yahweh as long as the temple service is carried on according to the Law of Moses, supplemented by the regulations of David. A good king makes it his first concern to see that the Law is observed. Thus Jehoshaphat orders the Levites to go through the kingdom and instruct the people in the book of the Law (II Chron. 17 : 7–10). At the coronation of Jehoash the princes allow none but priests and Levites to enter the temple (23 : 3–7). Hezekiah exhorts the priests and Levites to consecrate themselves and to reconsecrate the temple (29 : 4 *f*.); he re-establishes the courses of priests and Levites and gives order for their proper support (31 : 2–6). Josiah stations the priests in their offices and arranges the Levites according to the writing of David and the decree of Solomon (35 : 3 *f*. and 15). The presence of the Levitical singers with the army of Jehoshaphat is enough to secure a great victory over the Ethiopians (20 : 21–24). On the other hand, Uzziah's leprosy (the fact was known from the earlier narrative) is now accounted for as a punishment for an act of sacrilege; the king is said to have intruded into the temple and to have had the presumption to offer incense, thus trespassing on the prerogative of the high priest (26 : 16–20).

Prophets and Deuteronomists had conspired to establish the view that the Exile was a punishment on Judah for its disobedience to Yahweh. The Chronicler adopts this view, and gives it the proper ritualistic colouring. To him the specific sin which called for exile was the neglect of the sabbatic years. Seventy years of exile are called for, to give the land the rest of which it had been deprived during the four hundred and ninety years which had preceded (36 : 21). The author believes that all Judah was carried away, so that the land was destitute of inhabitants until the return under Joshua and Zerubbabel. Since the family of David was not then restored to the throne the care of Yahweh for the temple was indicated by his moving gentile kings to rebuild it and to provide for the worship. Hence we learn of the decrees of Cyrus and his successors. Cyrus recognises Yahweh as God of heaven who has given him his power (Ezra 1 : 1–3); Darius encourages the work of rebuilding and provides for the sacrifices (6 : 6–12); Artaxerxes goes beyond either of them and authorizes Ezra to enforce the Mosaic Law, exempts the temple servants from taxation, and provides lavishly from the public revenues for the carrying on of the service (7 : 17–26). The performance of the ritual is the most important thing in the world, overshadowing the restoration of Israel's nationality. If the service cannot be provided for by a king of David's line, the next best thing is to have a gentile king attend to it. Hence the evident satisfaction with which these various decrees are reproduced (we cannot tell from what source) in the narrative.

A considerable part of the book (Chronicles, Ezra, and Nehemiah) is taken up by genealogies, and this fact is explicable when we remember the priestly point of view. By divine command the temple service is in the hands of the priests and Levites. These must be of genuine Levitical blood. The community which lives about the temple in like manner must be genuinely Israelitic, for it was the descendants of Jacob whom Yahweh had chosen to be his people. The line was, therefore, sharply drawn in the postexilic community between the people of the land who were suspected of Canaanitish admixture and those who could show their purity of blood. These last alone were (in theory, at least) admitted to membership in the new community. The book of Ezra shows us the rigid logic of the purists, who demanded the divorce of foreign wives even when they had borne children to their husbands. So drastic a measure can hardly have been carried through, but the demand shows the standard set by the legalists, of whom Ezra is the type. The most important man in the community is now the scribe, to whom the written law is everything, and obedience to it is the whole duty of man. To enforce this lesson is the purpose of the literature we have been considering.

CHAPTER XIV

THE MESSIANIC HOPE

THE history of the Jews in the Persian period is very imperfectly known. In the early part of it Zerubbabel, apparently a descendant of David, was civil governor in Jerusalem, and the little community under his rule rebuilt the temple. The city had lost its earlier importance and the district subject to it was insignificant in size. The people were discouraged, the city walls were not restored, and the temple itself was a sorry structure compared to the one erected by Solomon. It was nearly a century after the Persian conquest of Babylon before the fortunes of the sacred city began to revive, and the impetus then came from outside of Palestine—an energetic Jew arrived from the court of the great king armed with authority from his master and animated by patriotic zeal for the city of his fathers. Under his influence other Jews came from the East and took up their residence in Palestine. These immigrants looked upon themselves as the true Israel and distrusted the remnant in Palestine who claimed to be of the same stock. Their unyielding temper is revealed by Nehemiah's own record, which shows how antagonism existed from the time of his arrival. The introduction of the priestly law and the measures taken against foreign marriages accented the division. On one side was the party of those who came from the East with such of the "people of the land" as accepted the Law; on the other was the country party, led by one Sanballat, prefect of Samaria, which, when finally excluded from Jerusalem, built a temple on Mount Gerizim and became the sect of the Samaritans.

The postexilic community nourished its intellectual life on

the books which had come down from earlier times and read into them more hope for the future than they actually contained. It was easy to find in the stories of the patriarchs pledges for the continued favour of God. The narrative of the deliverance from Egypt afforded a parallel to the hoped-for redemption from another slavery. The experiences of the exile had strengthened the sense of sin, but this sense of sin had always beneath it the faith that repentance would be followed by pardon and restoration. The precedent was set by the narratives of the wilderness wandering which told how the rebels had actually been forgiven. Nehemiah's prayer gives an affecting picture of this state of mind. The penitent, after confessing the sins of the fathers, reminds his God that Moses had given assurance that the outcast Israelites should be gathered again if only they would turn to Yahweh (Neh. 1 : 6–9).

It was natural that much attention should be given to passages which were predictive in form. The literary device of putting such passages into the mouth of ancient worthies was not unknown even in the pre-exilic period. Thus the patriarch Jacob is made to foresee the fate of his sons. The promise of dominion to Judah had been amply verified by the kingship given to David. But the postexilic Jew found it impossible to believe that that fulfilment was final. It was more in accordance with the richness of divine grace to expect a larger verification in the time yet to come. The same is true of the utterances of Balaam. This enigmatic seer had been called to pronounce a curse on Israel, but the curse had been turned into a blessing. And the most striking part of it was the vision of a star out of Jacob and a sceptre from Israel (Num. 23 : 21; 24 : 17). Whatever might be said of the fulfilment in David, the religious reader could hardly bring himself to suppose that a word of God would exhaust its full meaning in any one age. It is true that to us, who have the trained historical sense, this seeking of a double meaning in Scripture seems to be fallacious, but there can hardly be a doubt that by just this method many fainting souls have been strengthened not only in Judaism but also in Christianity.

The books of the prophets were studied in this way and they were also supplemented by the scribes to whom the severity of the early message was often intolerable. Some hopeful features may have been discovered in the messages of these great preachers, even though the message was (as it so often was) one of denunciation. Thus, underneath the sombre accusations of Hosea there was the thought that Yahweh still loved Israel though forced to cast her off. Isaiah at some time in his career had given hints of a remnant which would survive the coming calamity. It was he who had declared that a sure corner-stone was laid in Zion. Even Jeremiah had intimated that a restoration would come after seventy years. The intention of the prophet was, as we know, to discourage the optimism of the exiles, who were looking for an early redemption; to impress upon them the need of adjusting themselves to the life in Babylon. But now the seventy years had passed and the hope of revival became vivid. In like manner Ezekiel had thought of forty years as the duration of the captivity (Ezek. 29 : 11–13). Ezekiel, in fact, was the man who gave definite form to the hope of a restoration. His programme, which we have already considered, was thoroughly supernatural—that is, it looked for an act of God to change the nature of the soil of Canaan and to change also the hearts of the people. The change in the soil had not come, but thoroughly penitent Israelites might hope that the divine grace had already operated on their hearts.

The definite lines with which Ezekiel had drawn his picture of the future commonwealth made a deep impression on his people. His scheme included three essential features of what we know from his time on as the Messianic hope. These were: the punishment of the hostile world-power, the restoration of Israel to its own land, and the dwelling of Yahweh in the midst of the new commonwealth. The headship of a prince of the house of David is included, but this was in Ezekiel's view only a minor feature. His belief in the visible presence of Yahweh in his temple made an earthly prince superfluous. The prince in his scheme becomes only the steward of the sanctuary. In saying, therefore, that Ezekiel is the father of the Messianic expectation, we must be careful to note that the expectation is Messianic in the broader sense only; it looked for the restoration of the theocratic community but did not picture it as a kingdom in which the personal Messiah would be the dominant figure.

Loyalty to the house of David would, however, be strengthened by the experiences of exile, and it is probable that the majority of the people could conceive of the restored nation in no other way than as a monarchy with a member of the legitimate dynasty on the throne. Evidence of this state of mind is given by the two little books of Haggai and Zechariah.[1] The two prophets were active in connection with the rebuilding of the temple in the reign of Darius I. Haggai shows us how the expectation of a miraculous intervention of Yahweh really prevented activity on the part of the people. They said that the time for rebuilding had not come, just because Yahweh gave no sign of returning to his people. Haggai reasoned the other way: that Yahweh would do his part when the people did theirs. They looked upon the bad harvests as discouragements; he thought them a result of their neglect of the house. "You looked for much, but it came to little, and when you brought it home I shrivelled it up. Why? says Yahweh Sabaoth: Because of my house which lies waste while each of you takes pleasure in his own house" (Hag. 1 : 9).

Under this encouragement Zerubbabel, the governor, and Joshua, the high priest, set to work and the temple was rebuilt. Haggai is confident that this event foreshadows the great restoration. "I will shake the heavens and the earth and overturn the throne of kingdoms. . . . In that day I will take thee, O Zerubbabel my servant, and will make thee

[1] Zech. 1–8 only belongs here; the rest of the book bears marks of a later date.

a signet; for I have chosen thee, says Yahweh Sabaoth" (Hag. 2 : 21–23). Since the king of Judah is the signet on Yahweh's right hand (Jer. 22 : 24), there can be no doubt that Haggai expects the restoration of the house of David to come at once, with Zerubbabel as the reigning monarch. His contemporary, Zechariah, shared this expectation. In vision this prophet sees evil banished from the land, the nations rendered impotent to harm Judah, and Zerubbabel crowned king of the new commonwealth with the high priest as his coadjutor. The exiles will return and Yahweh himself will dwell in the midst of his people (Zech. 8 : 1–8). The declaration concerning Zerubbabel (6 : 9–15) has been obscured in the current Hebrew text, but the original is still discoverable. Disappointment followed, and it is possible that the expectation brought a tragic fate to Zerubbabel, but the hope lived on.

The hope lived on, but it had to struggle with indifference and scepticism. Evidence of this is given by the little book called by the name of Malachi. The change of view which has taken place is plain when we compare this preacher with Amos and Isaiah. To them the cultus is hateful to Yahweh; to him the neglect of the ritual is the great sin of the people. He complains that the altar is defrauded of its dues and that the priests connive at this sin. The temple service is the centre of the prophet's thought; what afflicts him is that the lame and the blind are brought in sacrifice (Mal. 1 : 6–8) and that tithe and tribute are withheld (3 : 8). The reason of this neglect is scepticism, and this has arisen from Yahweh's long delay to carry out his promises. Two parties exist in Jerusalem: one is that of the unbelieving, who say: "Every one that does evil is good in the sight of Yahweh and he takes pleasure in them; where is the God of Justice?" (2 : 17.) These say: "It is vain to serve God, and what profit is it that we have kept his charge and have walked mournfully before Yahweh Sabaoth? Now we call the proud happy, yes they that work wickedness are built up, they tempt God and escape"

(3 : 13*f.*). Opposed to them is the little band of those who trust Yahweh. To these the prophet gives assurance that they are not forgotten of their God, but that their names are preserved in a book of remembrance for the coming day (3 : 16*f.*). This day is a day of judgment, for Yahweh will sit as a refiner of silver and purge the dross from his people (3 : 2). "The wicked will be as stubble and will be burned root and branch, but to those that fear the Name the sun of righteousness will rise with healing in his beams" (3 : 19*f.*; 4 : 1*f.*, E. V.).

The common expectation held by the pious throughout this period is here reproduced, but with some details that seem to be original with Malachi. The idea of a heavenly book of reckoning, in which are written the names of those who are well-pleasing to God so that they may be rewarded in the time of trial, is not met with in the earlier literature unless we take into account the brief and obscure allusion in the Pentateuch (Ex. 32 : 32*f.*). Malachi is also the first to mention the prophet Elijah as herald of the Messianic time. Elijah suggested himself as the proper person for this office, not only because he was a courageous advocate of the true religion in a time of backsliding, but because he had been taken to heaven and so had escaped the common lot of man. Having been admitted to the heavenly counsels, he would be able to announce the plan of God with authority. But it is noticeable that Malachi does not expect a human Messiah; he believes that Yahweh himself, or rather the angel who represents him, will come and regulate affairs in the Jewish community.

In the circle of those who feared God the Scriptures of the prophets were read and studied, and it is easy to see how they were supplemented by sections which gave expression to the longing for redemption. In many cases leaflets embodying this longing were circulated from hand to hand and finally added to the books of the prophets. Thus, in the book of Jeremiah, we have the complete Messianic programme set forth in language that we cannot possibly suppose to have been used by that preacher (Jer. 30 and 31). The opening section gives the theme: "I will turn again the captivity of my people Israel and Judah, says Yahweh, and I will cause them to return to the land that I gave their fathers and they shall possess it." There follows a sketch of the dismay which will overtake the nations when Yahweh breaks the yoke of oppression. Yahweh will thus be the saviour of his people and they shall have a second David, a prince of their own blood. The land will be secure and its fruits will abound, so that the virgin will rejoice in the dance. The climax is reached with the promise of a new covenant: "Not according to the covenant which I made with their fathers in the day when I took them by the hand to lead them out of the land of Egypt, which covenant of mine they broke; but this is the covenant which I will make with the house of Israel after those days, says Yahweh: I will put my Law in their inward parts and on their heart I will write it; and I will be their God and they shall be my people; and they shall no more teach every man his brother and every man his neighbour, saying: Know Yahweh!—for they shall all know me, from the least of them to the greatest of them, says Yahweh; for I will forgive their iniquity and their sin I will remember no more" (Jer. 31: 32–34).

The vitality of the Messianic hope doubtless came from this distinctly religious appeal. The sense of estrangement from their God was the hardest thing that the exiles had to bear. Their comfort was found in such assurances of forgiveness as we have here. At the same time we must remember that many of the Jews found a less spiritual consolation in the predictions of vengeance which circulated in this period. Ezekiel's treatment of Gog set the example for a number of writers who envisaged the hostile power, not as a mysterious invader from the north, but as the actually existing Babylon which had besieged Jerusalem and burned the temple. Babylon became the typical figure, the archenemy, guilty of oppression of Israel and of sacrilege committed against the God of Israel. This typical position it retained even after the rise of the Persian empire, for Cyrus did not destroy the great city; he, in fact, made it one of his capitals, and it remained the most important city of the East until after Alexander's triumph. So long as this embodiment of luxury, pride, and godlessness stood, the Jews were longing for her overthrow as the crowning proof of the divine justice; hence the bitterness of some of the prophecies which concern themselves with this event. A good example is the supplement to the book of Jeremiah (Jer. 50 and 51). Repeatedly the writer assures us that Babylon is about to be destroyed, for Yahweh is about to take vengeance for his temple. Repeatedly, also, the exiles are exhorted to flee out of the land of their captivity and return to their own land. In this narrow circle of ideas the author moves round and round without making any progress. At the end we are assured that Jeremiah sent the written leaflet to Babylon and had it read as a testimony against the city and then cast into the Euphrates. The literary device is transparent. What interests us, however, is the desire for vengeance which breathes in the lines. A similar but more finished production has been included in the book of Isaiah (Isaiah 13 and 14). Here we read how Babylon, the oppressor, is to be overthrown by Yahweh's army, mustered from the ends of the earth for this purpose, and accompanied by convulsions of nature (13:1–10). The redeemed Israelites will sing a song of triumph over the slain king of Babylon, taunting him with his ignominious fate: "Cast out from the tomb like a despised branch" (14 : 18*f.*). Few passages show so distinctly the hatred felt by the Jew for his oppressors.

In its complete form the Messianic expectation involved four things: the punishment of the foreign nations; the return of Israel to its own land; a new covenant; and the rule of a king of David's line. But not all these features are emphasised at the same time. The political colouring varies greatly. Some hearts felt an ardent longing for the supremacy of Israel over all the nations. But for the most part the religious desire for forgiveness, purification, and the presence of God is the one most distinctly expressed. The severity of Hosea was corrected by a later hand, which promised that Yahweh would heal the people's backsliding and love them freely (Hosea 14 : 4). A similar consolatory conclusion was added to the book of Amos, specifically promising the re-erection of the fallen tent of David, together with millennial plenty in the land. The original book of Isaiah was completed by a picture of paradisiacal peace and fruitfulness. How far such passages were intended to be taken literally is still obscure to us.

As we have seen, the figure of a human ruler was not constantly present in these anticipations. In many instances the thought of Yahweh's coming to rule his people, in the midst of whom he would dwell, overshadowed the earthly king. Yet in many places we meet the king of David's line who will fulfil the promises made to his great ancestor (II Sam. 7). The supplementer of Amos, in assuring us that the fallen tent of David shall be raised again, doubtless means that there will be a son of David on the throne. One writer apostrophises the decayed town of Bethlehem with the promise that it shall again give birth to a ruler of the ancient stock (Micah 5 : 1–3). Isaiah's prediction of the child to be born, whose name, Immanuel, will testify to the deliverance of Jerusalem from its besiegers, suggested a rapturous description of the Coming One, whose very name indicates that he will be a hero prince, godlike in his deeds (Isaiah 9 : 5). Another passage now embedded in Isaiah's book declares: "A king shall rule in righteousness and princes shall reign in judgment, and a man shall be a hiding-place from the wind, a covert from the tempest, as rivers of water in a dry place, as the shadow of a great rock in a weary land" (Isaiah 32 : 1 *f.*). It is by no means sure that in such passages the authors were thinking of one single superhuman, or at least heroic, figure; they probably had in mind the succession of Davidic rulers who would secure peace and prosperity for their subjects. This is true even where the prediction seems most distinctly individual, as in the celebrated passage which declares that the spirit of Yahweh will fit the king to be a just judge, a vindicator of the oppressed (Isaiah 11 : 1–8). But again it is Yahweh who will be the protecting cloud over all the dwellings in Jerusalem (Isaiah 4 : 5), making the human ruler superfluous. In the good time to come the righteous will dwell with Yahweh and will see him, their king, in his beauty: "There Yahweh will be with us in majesty, Yahweh the lawgiver, Yahweh the king" (33 : 17 and 21).

The material we have considered makes it obvious that no pains were taken to bring the expectations of the Jews into a single harmonious picture. It is probable that really religious people fixed their hope more on the personal presence of Yahweh in his temple than on any human ruler. The most distinct prediction of a human Messiah aside from the two we have considered is the one in Zechariah which describes him as meek and riding on an ass (Zech. 9 : 9). Such a personage is overshadowed by the divine majesty, under whose protection his reign is one of uninterrupted peace. But in either form—whether it pictured the reign of Yahweh or whether it looked for a son of David—the Messianic hope kept the Jews faithful to their religion and obedient to their Law.

CHAPTER XV

SPIRITUALISATION OF THE MESSIANIC HOPE

THE preceding chapter has shown the importance of the Messianic expectation in keeping alive the religion of the Jews. But this expectation was not consistent in all its parts. To make a real contribution to the religious history of mankind it needed to be unified and spiritualised. These qualities it received in the book which now forms the second half of Isaiah (Isaiah 40–66). Whether these chapters are the work of one man or whether they belong to a group of like-minded thinkers is a question of minor importance. What is clear is that the same ideas are expressed in all parts of the book, and that these ideas mark it off distinctly from the rest of the Old Testament.

In form we have here a series of poems which treat of God and his relation to the world, of Israel in its present low estate, of the problem of suffering as illustrated in the experience of the chosen people, of sin, of forgiveness, of the religious life and of the future glory. Throughout, the author speaks as a prophet, that is, as the mouthpiece of Yahweh. Yet in him the experiences of the believer find expression, whether in the joy of perfect trust or in the pain of conflict with temptation and doubt. The preacher is fully conscious of his mission to comfort the faint-hearted and to confute the unbelieving. He will not only proclaim the will of God, he will justify his ways. His unshaken confidence in the God of Israel as God of the whole earth makes him the first of universalistic theologians, but a theologian made by the heart rather than by the intellect.

His fundamental thesis is this: Yahweh is the only God,

beside him there is no other: "I am Yahweh and there is none else; beside me there is no God: That men may acknowledge both in the East and in the West, that beside me there is no other—who form light and create darkness, who make welfare and create calamity—I, Yahweh, the true God, am author of all this" (45 : 5–7). The terms used make us think that the author has in view the Persian dualism which apportions light and darkness to the two opposing chief powers. But if this be true it is also true that he more distinctly opposed the crass polytheism which was the religion of the common people of gentile race among whom the Israelites dwelt. The alleged gods of the heathen are the objects of his most biting invective. To him they are only so many manufactured articles. The smith who prepares such an image over the burning coals, instead of being strengthened by it, grows faint at his work; the carpenter who marks out the human figure on a piece of timber and fashions it into an idol does not reflect on the absurdity of the process: "Half of it he burns in the fire, and upon the coals thereof he roasts flesh; he eats the flesh and is satisfied, he warms himself also and says: Aha, I am warm, I feel the glow; and the residue he makes into a god! Makes it into an image and bows down to it! He prostrates himself before it and says: Rescue me, for thou art my god!" (44 : 16*f.*) Of course, it would be easy to show that this does less than justice to the more thoughtful of the heathen to whom the image is only the symbol of a spiritual being. But as against the religion of the common people the protest was justified, and this accentuation of the contrast between Yahweh and the idols was what Israel needed at this time. Not syncretism of all religions was the need of the hour, but the proclamation of the one God, the Creator of the world, and the Father of the human spirit.

The intensity of the author's faith comes out in his challenge to the other gods: "Let them draw near and announce to us what shall happen; relate former events, how they were foretold, that we may reflect upon them; or else declare to us the future that we may mark their issue; announce the things that are to come hereafter that we may know that you are gods; yea, do something either good or bad that we may marvel and have something to see! Behold you are nought and your work is nothingness!" (41 : 22–24.) In spite of the greatness of Babylon, her divinities are as impotent as others: "Bel bows down and Nebo stoops; their images have passed to the beasts and to the cattle" (46 : 1). The contrast is here drawn between the helpless and senseless images which are a burden to their worshippers, which have to be carried when danger threatens, these on the one hand; and on the other, Yahweh, the living, active, supporting God, who bears his people up in his arms. Such scorn of the idols became ingrained in Jewish thought and finds frequent expression in later documents.

That Yahweh is Creator of the world had been affirmed by pre-exilic writers. But the religious application of the belief had not been made. Now we learn not only that he is Creator but that the work of creation and the work of providence are one. He who sits on the vault of heaven, weighs the mountains in scales, and the hills in a balance, is the one who is still at work ruling the affairs of the nations. History is the carrying out of his purpose: "My purpose shall stand, and all my pleasure I will perform; as I have spoken I will bring to pass; as I have planned I will accomplish" (46 : 11*f.*). This implies the attribute of wisdom as well as that of power: "Who has measured the mind of Yahweh, or who as his counsellor gave him knowledge? With whom has he taken counsel that he might obtain insight, and be taught the path of right and be shown the way of understanding?" (40 : 13*f.*) The immediate practical bearing of such declarations is easily seen, for it is the author's conviction that the historical activity of Yahweh is especially concerned with Israel. It was he who had called Abraham when but one man and increased him to a great nation (51 : 2); it was he who had led Israel through the Red Sea and annihilated the pursuing host (43 : 16; 51 : 9*f.*). The present misery of Israel proves nothing against this care on the part of Yahweh, and nothing against his power, for it is he who has given his own people over to punishment, because of their sins. Proof is given by the earlier prophecies in which Yahweh made known what was coming to pass, for only the God who makes history is able to predict what history is to be: "The former events, behold, they came, and new things do I announce; before they spring into being I tell you of them" (42 : 9). "It was I who both announced and declared and there was no strange god among you; you are my witnesses, says Yahweh, and I am your redeemer from the beginning" (43 : 12*f*.).

The immediate practical interest of the author is seen in the context. His purpose is to encourage the depressed Israelites by assuring them that the power of this Creator and Governor of the universe is at the disposition of those who will avail themselves of it: "Why sayest thou Jacob, and speakest, O Israel: My fortune is hidden from Yahweh and my right is unnoticed by my God? Hast thou not perceived? Hast thou not heard? An everlasting God is Yahweh, the Creator of the ends of the earth; he faints not nor can he be wearied; his insight is unsearchable; to the weary he gives vigor and to the powerless he increases strength; youths may faint and grow weary; young warriors may stumble, but they who wait for Yahweh renew their vigor; they put forth as it were eagles' wings; they run and are never weary; they go onward and are never faint."[1] In similar passages Israel or Zion is again and again exhorted to look to Yahweh as the true source of strength, the one who is about to intervene for the redemption of his people. And this means that exiled Israel is about to return to its own land. It is for this that a voice is heard commanding to make a highway through the desert; Yahweh at the head of his people, like a shepherd leading his flock, will make his

[1] Isaiah 40 : 27–31; *cf.* 41: 8–20; 51: 17 *ff.;* 52 : 1–6. I have used Cheyne's excellent translation in the *Book of Isaiah, Printed in Colors* (1898).

triumphal march back to his chosen dwelling. Jerusalem's long period of mourning is ended; she has received the full recompense for her sins; forgiveness and restoration must follow.

Since Israel is in virtual slavery its deliverance is a real redemption, a buying back of the bondman. The frequent title which Yahweh gives himself is that of Redeemer. This word, however, has not the full meaning which Christian theology is accustomed to give it. It properly denotes the next of kin, on whom devolves the duty of avenging a man's quarrel or of ransoming him from captivity if he has fallen into the hands of the enemy.[1] Such a kinsman is Yahweh—he will bring his people out of their slavery, and he will punish their enemies. Their present state is, to be sure, low enough—it is a people spoiled and plundered, they are all snared in dungeons and hid in prison-houses; they are become a spoil and there is no rescuer; a plunder and there is none to say: Restore! (42 : 22.) "Yet now says Yahweh thy Creator, O Jacob, and thy Fashioner, O Israel: Fear not, I redeem thee; I call thee by name, mine thou art" (43 : 1). And the Redeemer is also the avenger. The oppressing power is Babylon, and she is to suffer what she has inflicted on others. Her gods will be carried away with the other spoil of the city; she herself, the tender and delicate, once a queen who boasted that she has never submitted to a master is to be humiliated like the lowest slave: "Now hear this, O voluptuous one, who sittest securely, who sayest in thy heart: I, and none other; I shall not sit in widowhood nor know the loss of children—both these shall come to thee in a moment, in the same day, loss of children and widowhood; in full measure shall they come upon thee" (47 : 8*f.*). To accomplish this purpose upon the ancient enemy Yahweh himself will intervene as a warrior, rousing himself to mighty deeds and raising the battle shout (42 : 13*f.*).

The human instrument of this vengeance is purposely left

[1] The Hebrew term is go'el, which occurs nine times in these chapters. The verb from which it is derived is found five times.

obscure. An unnamed deliverer is alluded to in one passage and his appearance is propounded as a riddle for the false gods and their worshippers: "Who was it that roused up from the east him on whose steps victory attends, that gives up peoples before him and into kings strikes terror? His sword makes them like dust, his bow like driven stubble; he pursues them, passes on in safety, the path with his feet he treads not" (41 : 2*f.*). The traditional interpretation of this passage makes it refer to Cyrus and the conquests of Persian power under his leadership, and, in fact, Cyrus is mentioned by name in two verses in close juxtaposition (44 : 28; 45 : 1). It is a question, however, whether these two references are not later insertions into our text, the product of the Jewish tradition which made heathen kings the nursing fathers of the restored temple. It is contrary to our author's habit to name specifically the persons whom he has in mind. The most that we can say is that he has the expectation of a deliverer who will accomplish all Yahweh's will upon the nations and bring back the exiles to their home. It is even possible that he had the personified Israel in mind as this instrument of Yahweh's purpose: "Behold, I have made thee a new sharp threshing instrument having teeth; thou shalt thresh the mountains and make them small, and shalt make the hills as chaff" (41 : 15).

Restoration to temporal prosperity is not so prominent in the author's thought as is the spiritual blessing which is to come in the new time. The wiping out of the load of guilt which has oppressed the people is frequently emphasised. The punishment had been deserved: "Thy first fathers sinned, and thy mediators rebelled against me, and thy princes profaned my sanctuary; so I gave up Jacob to the ban and Israel to contumely" (43 : 28). Yet in the midst of the indictment Yahweh pauses to declare: "Yet I am he who blots out thy rebellions and thy sins I remember not" (43 : 25). And punishment is not a mere mechanical process of balancing a certain amount of guilt against an equal amount of suffering; it is a purifying process, purging out the baser metal in the furnace of affliction (48 : 10). To take a New Testament passage as the expression of the writer's thought we may say that he regarded Israel as thus made a vessel of honour fit for the Master's use. Israel is an instrument for accomplishing a larger purpose than has yet appeared: "By myself have I sworn, a true word has gone out of my mouth, a word that shall not be recalled: That to me every knee shall bow, every tongue shall swear" (45 : 21–23). It is in this universalism that our author advances beyond all his predecessors. By what process is his hope to be realised?

The answer to this question is to be found in the figure which appears at intervals throughout the book and which receives the name Servant of Yahweh. He is first introduced to us as one gentle in his method, who will not quench the dimly burning wick but yet who will courageously set forth the Law so that for his instruction the far lands will wait (42 : 1–4). More fully he describes his own mission: "Hearken ye far countries unto me and listen ye distant peoples; Yahweh has called me from the womb; from my mother's lap has he celebrated my name; he made my mouth like a sharp sword, in the shadow of his hand he hid me; he made me a polished shaft, in his quiver he stored me. He said unto me: Thou art my servant, Israel, in whom I will glorify myself; so I was honored in the eyes of Yahweh and my God became my strength. But as for me, I said: I have labored in vain; to no purpose have I spent my strength; nevertheless my right is with Yahweh and my recompense is with my God. And now Yahweh says: It is too light a thing to raise up the tribes of Jacob, and to restore the preserved of Israel; so I set thee as a light of the nations, that my deliverance may reach to the ends of the earth" (49 : 1–6). In both passages we see an ideal prophet pictured, one who will carry Yahweh's message to the ends of the earth. In his case, as in the actual experience of the preacher of righteousness, the mission involves suffering on the part of the one who undertakes it: "My back I gave to the smiters, and my cheeks to them that pulled out the beard; my face I hid not from insult and spitting" (50 : 6). The culmination is found in the description of the suffering servant giving his soul even to death (52 : 13 to 53 : 12).

Opinion is still divided as to this ideal missionary, whether he is a single individual, historical (of the past or who is yet to come), or whether he is a personification of a group. There seems to be a growing consensus in favour of the latter interpretation. And the group thus personified and idealised must be Israel, not the empirical Israel in the midst of which the author lived, but the ideal Israel, the faithful few who were chosen of God to carry his message and to endure on his behalf. This would seem to be evident from such passages as the one already quoted, where the servant is directly addressed by the name Israel (49 : 3). And again: "But thou Israel my servant, Jacob whom I have chosen . . . to whom I said: My servant art thou; I have chosen and not rejected thee" (41 : 8–10). The only difficulty in the identification is made by the sharp contrast between the ideal and the actual. In the New Testament use of the word "church" we find the same double meaning. The ideal church, the bride of Christ, is without spot or wrinkle or any such thing. But the church which actually exists is made up of frail and fallible men who too often must be rebuked for their unfaithfulness and immorality. There is an Israel within Israel to which alone the description of the servant can be applied.[1]

This distinction between the ideal and the real Israel—that is, between the loyal and obedient kernel of the nation and the empirical mass, careless of its privileges—throws light on another problem. Some of the older prophets were perplexed by the fact that the innocent so often suffer with the guilty. Jeremiah had questioned Yahweh as to the justice of his action just on this ground; Ezekiel had solved

[1] Whether the figure of the Servant has not borrowed some features from an ancient mythical character, as is maintained by Gressmann and others, is not clearly made out.

the problem by ignoring some of the facts. Our author, as we have seen, believes in the purifying nature of affliction, but he goes one step further in that he sees suffering to be the way in which a missionary must walk in order to carry out his mission. In the passage which forms the culmination of the Servant poems Yahweh himself makes this plain. Here he calls attention to the Servant as one who has suffered deeply—"Marred was his appearance out of all human likeness, and his form out of semblance to the sons of men." But as marked as the suffering will be the obeisance of many: "Before him kings will be awe-struck, for that which had not been told them they see" (52 : 14).[1] At this point the gentile kings themselves take up the description. They confess that they had thought the Servant smitten of God and afflicted. Now they see that he was, indeed, afflicted but not for his own sake; the innocent suffered for the guilty: "Surely he bore our griefs and carried our sorrows" (53 : 4). The smitten Israel even goes down to death in quiet resignation to the will of God. But death is not the end; a resurrection is to follow so that the Servant shall see the fruit of his labour. Since the only resurrection of which we have had a hint up to this point is the resurrection of the nation, foretold by Ezekiel, we must suppose that this is the conception cherished by the author.

This, then, is the wonderful plan of Yahweh in the affliction of his people. He will not only punish them for their sins; he will not only purify them from their evil desires; he will bring all the world to the conviction that Israel is his Servant, suffering for others and thus carrying out his mission. The gentiles will recognise that severity toward the Servant is an evidence of grace for them. They will be moved to receive instruction at the mouth of the revived Israel, will be convinced that Yahweh is God and

[1] *Cf.* 49 : 7*f.*: "Thus saith Yahweh to him whom man despiseth, to him whom the nations abhor, to the servant of rulers: Kings shall see and arise, princes and they shall worship; because of Yahweh who is faithful, even the Holy One of Israel who has chosen thee."

none else, and so the glory of Yahweh will shine to the ends of the earth. "This is the salvation that is to go forth, the deliverance that is to endure forever" (51 : 4*f*.). The description of the suffering Servant is followed, therefore, by an invitation to the desolated Zion to triumph in the prospect of coming glory (54). The covenant to be established will include the gentiles: "Thou shalt call people whom thou knowest not, people who know not thee shall run unto thee, because of Yahweh thy God, and for Israel's Holy One, for he has glorified thee" (55 : 3–5). This thought of the mediatorial mission of Israel is the most important contribution of our author to enlightened religion.

It is only natural that the hopes here expressed should take on a transcendental colouring. The expectation that the return of Yahweh to Palestine will be accompanied by a transformation of the land is certainly as old as Ezekiel. Our author gives glowing expression to this hope. The wilderness is to become an Eden, the waste places of Zion will become like the garden of Yahweh (51 : 3). The new Jerusalem will shine with supernal brightness: "Thou afflicted, storm-tossed, unconsoled; behold, I will set thy bases in rubies, and will found thee with sapphires; I will make thy battlements of jasper, thy gates of carbuncles, and all thy borders of jewels" (54 : 11*f*.). Christian interpreters are tempted to apply the description to the heavenly Jerusalem, the abode of the blessed, but our author has in mind the earthly city, the dwelling of Yahweh, transformed by his presence: "No more will the sun serve thee for light nor for brightness will the moon illuminate thee; but Yahweh will be to thee an everlasting light, and thy God thine adornment" (60 : 19). Nations will come to this light and kings to the brightness of the rising (60 : 3). Into this sacred city "no one that is unclean or uncircumcised shall enter" (52 : 1); its people shall be all righteous, the redeemed of Yahweh, a sacred people (60 : 21; 62 : 12). The supremacy of Israel will consist in its priestly office: "You shall be called priests of Yahweh; servants of our God will they name you" (61 : 6). In this way Jerusalem will become a joy to the whole earth, for all flesh will come and worship there (62 : 3; 65 : 18; 66 : 23). In the land of Israel the wolf and the lamb will lie down together: "They shall not hurt nor destroy in all my sacred mountain, says Yahweh" (65 : 25). The life of man will be prolonged, so that he who dies at a hundred years of age will be thought to be untimely cut off (65 : 20).

Whether the various elements of this picture could be combined into one consistent whole may be doubted. What interests us especially is the author's conception of religion. This we see to be not merely national but also individual. Not only is the afflicted and storm-tossed Zion encouraged, but the depressed member of the community receives a message of cheer. The proselyte who fears that he may be shut out of the company of the faithful because of his foreign blood, and the eunuch who feels that his physical mutilation unfits him for the service of Yahweh, are singled out for encouragement (56 : 1–8). Those who hunger and thirst for righteousness receive their message: "On high as the Holy One do I abide, and with him who is crushed and lowly in spirit, to revive the spirit of the lowly, and to revive the heart of those who are crushed" (57 : 15). And the essence of religion is seen to be faith: "They that wait for Yahweh shall not be ashamed" (40 : 31; 49 : 23). "Whoso walks in darkness with no brightness of dawn; let him trust in the name of Yahweh, and lean upon his God" (50 : 10). Faith must issue in service, but not the formal service of the ritualist. The fast that Yahweh chooses is not a matter of external observance: "Is not this the fast that I have chosen, says Yahweh: To loose the fetters of injustice; to untie the bands of violence; to set at liberty those that are crushed; to break asunder every yoke? Is it not to break thy bread to the hungry, and to bring the homeless to thy house? When thou seest the naked to cover him, and not to hide thyself from thine own flesh? Then thy light shall break forth as the dawn; thy wounds will quickly heal over;

thy righteousness will go before thee, and Yahweh's glory will be thy rearward" (58 : 5–8).

Apparently there were few who were prepared to appreciate this message. The little community had its full share of unbelievers and scoffers. Some seek satisfaction in outworn superstitions: "They sit among the graves and lodge in vaults; they eat swine's flesh and the broth of abominable things is in their vessels; they say: Stand by thyself; come not near me lest I consecrate thee [by my touch]."[1] No wonder that the prophet cries out: "The hand of Yahweh is not too short to deliver, nor his ear too heavy to hear; but your iniquities have become a barrier between you and your God, and your sins have hidden his face from you, so that he hears not. For your hands are defiled with blood, and your fingers with iniquity; your lips speak lies and your tongue utters depravity; none sues in truthfulness, and none pleads with honesty; men trust in pretence and speak falsehood; they conceive trouble and bring forth mischief. Therefore has our right been far from us, and redress does not overtake us; we wait for light but behold darkness; for bright beams but we walk in gloom" (59 : 1–4, 9). The contrast between the lofty ideal cherished by the writer and the reality by which he found himself confronted expresses itself not only in this rebuke but also in the almost agonising prayer which follows. In prayer the believer finds his comfort, and faith reasserts itself after the struggle with depression.

This contrast between the expectation of a divine intervention and the actual condition of the chosen people is characteristic of Judaism, and the frequent confession of sinfulness which we find in later documents only echoes this prayer. Yet, since we are saved by hope, the postexilic community continued to cherish the vision of a new heaven and a new earth. One of the best expressions of this hope is

[1] Incubation at the shrines of dead heroes is alluded to, 65 : 4, and the abominable things that are eaten at these mysteries include mice as well as swine, 66 : 17.

in a little paragraph which has been preserved for us both in the book of Isaiah and in the book of Micah. Its post-exilic origin needs no demonstration. It tells how in the good time to come "the mountain of Yahweh's house will be established as highest of the mountains, and will be exalted above the hills; and all nations will stream unto it, and many peoples will set forth and say: Come let us go up to the mountain of Yahweh, to the house of the God of Jacob; that he may instruct us out of his precepts, and that we may walk in his paths; for from Zion goes forth instruction and the word of Yahweh from Jerusalem. Then will he judge between the nations, and give decision to many peoples; and they will beat their swords into mattocks and their spears into pruning hooks; nation will not lift up sword against nation, neither will they learn war any more" (Isaiah 2 : 2–4). Universal peace, Jerusalem the capital of the earth, the law of Yahweh taught to the nations and obeyed by them—such was the Messianic hope in its most spiritual expression. The special relation of Yahweh to Israel is only the first act of a great drama whose dénoûment will be the spread of true religion to all nations. Israel is Yahweh's messenger, destined to overcome the world, not by the sword but by the word.

CHAPTER XVI

THE SCEPTICAL REACTION

THE spiritual thoughts of Deutero-Isaiah were apprehended by few of his countrymen. His universalism was lost sight of in the conflicts between parties within the Jewish community. How bitter these conflicts were is made known by the Samaritan schism and by the opposition to gentile wives. In Jerusalem the stricter party organised themselves in a church state, of which the high priest was head, and the main object of effort was to keep the sacred city from defilement. No doubt the Messianic hope animated those who observed the Law and who excluded the foreigner, but it was the Messianic hope in its most particularistic form—the salvation to come must belong to the seed of Israel, and they alone would share in it who kept themselves from contamination. Everything else was under a taboo; it was, in ecclesiastical language, an abomination.

Fortunately, we are allowed to see that this rigid exclusiveness did not go without protest. Two little books which have found a place in the canon reveal a broader spirit. These are Ruth and Jonah, both of them works of fiction, though possibly both have made use of floating traditions, even mythological in their nature. The heroine of one book is a Moabitess, belonging, therefore, to the race against which the lines were most strictly drawn in the postexilic community. She is pictured as a model woman in her devotion to Israel and also to the God of Israel. She is recognised by the Israelite community of Bethlehem as a devout woman, is taken to wife by one of the leading members of that community, and becomes the ancestress of David. The lesson is so plain that it needs no interpreter. If marriage with gentiles were so contrary to the mind of Yahweh as was held by the exclusive party, he would not have so blessed the marriage of Boaz and Ruth.

In contrast with the mild idyllic tone of Ruth is the satire of Jonah. Here we read of the prophet who is commissioned to preach to Nineveh, the typical heathen city. The task is not to his liking, not because of any danger that he fears, but because the preaching may be followed by repentance and the city may be spared, whereas he longs to see it destroyed. He, therefore, tries to flee to a foreign country where he will be out of the jurisdiction of Yahweh. Miraculously he is brought back and forced to carry out his mission. What he has expected follows—the city repents and is spared. By the gourd over whose loss he grieves he is taught the lesson of compassion. The whole is an object-lesson to the narrow and embittered Jews, who would be willing to see no matter what suffering inflicted on their fellow men if only the hostile powers of the gentiles might be destroyed. The book was admitted to the canon not because of this lesson but because it was read as a wonder book, one of the crowning evidences of the power of Yahweh.

The Messianic glory was delayed, and, while every hope of its immediate coming met with disappointment, a painful question arose in the minds of believers. Even supposing that perfect righteousness will rule when the good time comes, what is the *ad interim* principle of the divine government? Ezekiel, as we know, had defended the theory of eudemonism; the man who does right will be rewarded by prosperity; the man who sins will be taken out of the world by an early death. The theory was stated so uncompromisingly that it seemed to challenge investigation into the facts. In the face of facts could this theory maintain itself? The Chronicler was able to rewrite history so as to show that sin had always been followed by misfortune, not only for the nation but also for individuals. In his narrative he records that Asa died of gout because he sought not to

Yahweh but to the physicians, and the ships of Jehoshaphat were wrecked on account of the king's alliance with the ungodly Ahab. On the other hand, Manasseh's long reign was his reward for repentance. But it is easier to write history to fit the theory than it is to discover the theory in actual operation in the world around us. The Jews could not claim that piety and good fortune always go hand in hand. The righteous servants of Yahweh were too often poor and persecuted, while the heathen, who forgot God, were often the ones blessed with riches, children, and long life—the three best gifts. Something of the complaint that the arrogant worldlings are happy, and that, therefore, it is vain to serve God, we have met in Malachi. The longer the Messianic time was delayed, the more acute the problem became.

The perplexity of the pious is revealed to us by the little book which bears the name of Habakkuk. The author witnessed the remorseless advance of a conquering army, perhaps that of Alexander, and questioned whether the great overturning was, in fact, working out the purposes of Yahweh. To all appearance the cruel invader was following his own lust for blood and plunder. So far from recognising any God, he sacrifices to his weapons as though they were the source of his power; his strength is his god (Hab. 1 : 15*f.*). So the prophet cries out against injustice: "How can Yahweh who cannot look upon iniquity be silent when the wicked swallows up the righteous?" To these questionings the author has no answer except that Yahweh must be just in spite of all appearances to the contrary: "Yahweh is in his holy temple and all the earth will at length be silent before him" (2 : 20). The heathen have no God to compare with him, and the prophet's faith takes hold of this fact and will wait for the time of revealing, even though the fig-tree should fail and the vine refuse its fruit (3 : 17–19). The attitude of waiting upon God for the fuller revelation is often urged upon the believer in this period (*cf.* Micah 7 : 7 *ff.*).

This is rational enough, so far as the fate of nations is concerned, for it may well be that the time of a nation's probation is extended through centuries. But the lot of the individual is still a problem. If this lot is apportioned according to justice we ought to discover the fact in the men whom we meet day by day. That we do not so discover it is the conviction of the author who wrote the book of Job. In this book we find various elements combined, but all bear on this one problem. The example which the author brings before us is that of a righteous man greatly afflicted. According to the prologue and epilogue, which are in prose, this man Job suffered the extremes of fortune, but after a time of probation was restored to health and happiness. The story thus briefly told furnishes the framework within which the author of the poem discusses his problem. The problem is: Why should the righteous man suffer? One answer is given by the prologue itself where Satan instigates the affliction. His theory is that virtue is mere self-interest, and that if Job is put to the test his alleged righteousness will be discovered to be no more than this. When the man is tried by loss of fortune and of family, and stands the test, the accuser still holds to his theory; if Job was upright in the first instance because he was rewarded for it, his present steadfastness is due to nothing but fear. If he is attacked by a disease which shall take away his hope of life, and which will, therefore, remove the fear of death, then he will appear in his true colours. This second test is therefore applied without shaking the sufferer's integrity. His devotion to Yahweh is seen to be sincere.

The book might have ended here with the triumph of disinterested virtue. Possibly a version of the story was in circulation in which this was brought out. But in our form of the book the heavenly wager, if we may call it so, has no clear result—Satan does not confess that he is defeated, nor does Yahweh point out the reality of virtue. The author of the poem is too much interested in the experiences of his hero to dwell upon this point. What he brings out is the human document, the action of the soul of a man thus put to the test. Job has no knowledge of the heavenly wager, and the motive of the divine dealing with him is wholly concealed. The perplexity into which he is thrown by his accumulated misfortunes is increased by the conduct of his friends, who claim that they can speak for God and justify his ways, and who do this in terms which both injure and insult the sufferer. The object of the book, then, is not to set forth a theory, but to present a living picture of human experience. And this is broad human experience, not that of the Jew alone. Job is, in fact, not presented as a Jew, and the author has purposely left distinctly Jewish observances out of view.

What we find in the book, then, is a human soul under severe trial, wrestling with its doubts, and coming out at last measurably at peace with its God in spite of the mystery which surrounds his dealings. The real trial comes when the sufferer receives the visit of his friends. Terrible privations and more terrible disease have not shaken him; but when his friends come and sit silent before him he knows why they find no word of comfort. Representing the popular theology, they are applying their theory of retribution to him. They can account for so signal an affliction only by supposing that the one who is visited by it has been an aggravated offender—all the more that his former conduct was ostensibly virtuous. Not only a flagrant sinner, but a consummate hypocrite—this is their judgment. This it is which shuts their mouths when they attempt to condole with the sufferer. The sting is felt by Job, because in his days of prosperity he had judged in much the same way. He had accepted his good fortune as evidence that God smiled upon him. But could he now believe that God was justly angry with him? Against such a thought his conscience uttered its most vigorous protest. What confronted him was loss of his faith in God.

From this point of view we understand the violence of his language as he curses the day of his birth. This day he would blot out of the calendar, because it had seen the birth of him, miserable, or because it had not at once put an end to him when he first saw the light. But, since this had not occurred, his only hope is for a speedy ending of this wretched life. The only rest for the troubled is the grave, and this is what he longs for: "Wherefore is light given to him that is in misery, and life to the bitter of soul? To those who long for death but it comes not, and dig for it more than for hid treasures?" The friends find in these wild utterances only the ravings of one who is under the curse of God, and they are confirmed in their condemnation of the speaker. They are so possessed by their theological theory that they cannot do him justice. This is shown distinctly by the speech of Eliphaz, the most moderate of the three. He evidently endeavours to deal gently with his friend. He begins by pointing out how Job has comforted others in their affliction, and how he ought to apply the same method to himself: "Behold thou hast instructed many and hast strengthened the weak hands. Thy words have upholden him that was falling, and thou hast made firm the feeble knees. But now it is come unto thee and thou faintest, it toucheth thee and thou art troubled!" The sufferer is reminded that his own theory had been that the innocent could not perish: "According as I have seen, they that plow iniquity and sow trouble reap the same" (4 : 4*f.*).

Eliphaz is confident that he has received his doctrine from a higher source. A vision of the night had appeared to him and said: "Can a human being be righteous before God, or a man be pure before his maker? Behold he puts no trust in his servants, and his angels he charges with error; how much more the dwellers in clay, whose foundation is in the dust, who are crushed before the moth, are destroyed between morning and evening!" (4 : 17–20.) This revelation, Eliphaz thinks, is confirmed by observation of the facts of life. No doubt the facts of life are easily made to teach what one believes, and the speaker is able to describe in vivid terms how he has seen the wicked take root and then suddenly be destroyed. The practical application is made by an exhortation to Job to repent and pray to God. If he will only do this, all may yet be well: "At destruction and dearth thou shalt laugh; thou shalt be in league with the stones of the field, and the wild beasts shall be at peace with thee; thou shalt know that thy tent is in welfare and shalt visit thy fold and miss nothing. Thou shalt know also that thy seed shall be great and thine offspring like the grass of the earth; thou shalt come to the grave in a full age like as a shock of corn cometh in in its season. Lo, this have we searched and so it is; hear it and know it for thy good" (5 : 17–27).

The well-rounded periods reveal a man with a settled theory of the universe, who will not be disturbed by mere facts. It is clear, however, that he does not and cannot understand Job's state of mind. His sentences uttered with so much unction sound like bitter mockery to the sufferer. How can a man in the power of fatal disease look forward to days of peace and security? How can he whose children have been swept into the grave expect his offspring to be like the grass of the earth? To exhort the man of conscious integrity to seek God in penitence is to urge him to hypocrisy. The common sinfulness of the creatures of God is a mere truism; it does not explain why one of them should be signalled out for exceptional severity. What Job denies is that he has deserved this exceptional treatment. The whole effect of Eliphaz's exhortation is simply to confuse the sufferer. His suffering goes beyond the common experience, for he is made the direct mark of the divine arrows. His strength cannot hold out for the changed fortune to which the friends would have him look forward, even if it were to come. Added bitterness comes from the lack of sympathy on the part of his friends who are like the streams of the hot countries—when there is need of them they are found to have vanished.

In a somewhat calmer state of mind the hero considers the state of man. This is like the lot of the day-labourer, or of the common soldier—unremitting toil, with no hope for the future. For the question of a future life is raised only to be answered in the negative: "As a cloud is consumed and vanishes away, so he that goes down to Sheol comes up no more. He shall return no more to his house, neither shall his place know him any more" (7 : 9*f.*). This being so, there is no reason why Job should not speak out all his thought. Gathering boldness, as if in desperation, he expostulates with God for the way in which he is treated: "Am I a sea or sea-monster that thou settest a watch over me?" (7 : 12.) We remember that the sea was originally a hostile power, a great dragon, whose subjugation was the best evidence of the power of the Almighty (Jer. 5 : 22). Job's thought is that he is too puny a creature to be treated like the rebellious dragon, made the direct object of the divine vengeance: "If I have sinned what do I unto thee, O thou watcher of men? Why hast thou set me as a mark for thee so that I am a burden to myself? Why dost thou not pardon my transgression and take away my guilt so that I might lie down in the dust and thou mightest seek me diligently but I should not be?" (7 : 20*f.*) To make so much of any possible transgression that a man may have committed seems hardly worth while.

Of course this bold protest must arouse the horror of the friends. To them piety means an anxious fear of God, which will, above all things, avoid exciting his displeasure by criticism of his acts. Job, on the other hand, has reached a point where he can affirm the rights of man's moral judgment, even in the face of God himself. Bildad and Zophar, the other two friends, restate the position of their group with more bluntness than Eliphaz. They are sure that they have all tradition on their side as well as common sense. They argue that there must be some cause for the afflictions of men; what can it be except the sins of men? God cannot pervert justice—this is unthinkable. To this Job replies that it depends on what you mean by justice. The accused man, brought before a judge, gets a verdict condemning or acquitting him. The verdict may or may not be justice. If you mean that in the divine court no one can reverse the verdict, that needs no argument—from that court there is no appeal. But it may not follow that a man who is condemned is really guilty. The friends are willing to declare the verdict right just because it has been pronounced by God. In that case might makes right. But Job cannot rest in this thought; he must inquire whether there is a moral standard to which God himself is amenable. The fact that his hardships indicate a judgment of God against him does not prove that he is really guilty, and this he would make plain to God himself if he could only come before him.

It is clear that the sufferer is now possessed by a longing to set himself right with God. His physical pains are lost sight of in the realisation that to all appearance God has misjudged him. To be under that condemnation is torture. Yet even if he were given the opportunity to come before God and plead his cause he would be so overcome with fear that he would not be able to make his argument. The verdict would go against him by default. If only there could be an umpire to hear the two parties (God and Job), there would be more hope; but this again is impossible. Only one conclusion is open: God destroys the righteous and the wicked alike according to the whim of the moment (9 : 22). But in this conclusion the religious soul cannot rest, and there follows another appeal to God: "Thy hands have framed me and fashioned me; wilt thou turn against me and destroy me? Remember how thou didst form me as clay; wilt thou bring me into dust again?" (10 : 8*f.*) The longing appeal for recognition shows that the more the speaker is repulsed by his friends the more he feels that there must be comfort in God if only he can find it.

Feeling around for some ground of hope, the author peers again into the region beyond the grave, fascinated by the mystery that may be concealed there. Yet he can form no clear conception of a life in another world. The realm of the departed is away from the presence of God: "There is hope of a tree, if it be cut down, that it will sprout again and that the tender branch thereof will not cease; though the root thereof wax old in the earth and the stump thereof die in the ground, yet through the scent of water it may bud and put forth boughs like a plant. But man dies and is laid low; man gives up the ghost and where is he? As the waters fail from the lake and the river wastes and dries up so man lies down and rises not; till the heavens be no more they shall not awake nor be roused out of their sleep" (14 : 7–12). In spite of this explicit statement, a lingering hope still asserts itself: "Oh, that thou wouldst hide me in Sheol, that thou wouldst keep me secret until thy wrath were past, that thou wouldst set me a time and remember me!" (14 : 13.) Sheol is evidently a place where a man would be out of sight of the divinity. For this reason the speaker wishes that he might have a temporary sojourn there, that God might have time to bethink himself. His wrath then might cool and he would remember his servant and recall him from the dark world, receiving him into favour again. But even this wish is set aside as something impossible.

It is unnecessary to follow the debate in detail. The friends have said all that they can say, and can only repeat the same thing, but with increasing positiveness. The progress of the discussion confirms them in the opinion that Job is a great sinner. He is charged by the venerable Eliphaz with destroying religion, and the evidence is drawn from his own words. Nothing is left except to warn him of his perilous condition. So a vivid picture is drawn of the reckless sinner who stretches out his hand against God, bidding defiance to the Almighty. All three of the alleged friends unite in applying this description to Job, so that he is more and more convinced that he has nothing to look for from man and turns again to God. His faith reasserts itself in the well-known words: "I know that my avenger lives, and at last he shall stand upon the earth; and after my skin (even this body) is destroyed, yet without my flesh I shall see God; whom I, even I, shall see for myself and my eyes shall behold and not as a stranger" (19 : 25–27). The language must be interpreted in harmony with the explicit rejection of the thought of a future life of blessedness which we have already cited. The declaration is an answer to the question whether God is the friend or the enemy of the sufferer. His faith is that, though the Almighty had momentarily turned away from him, yet he must bethink himself. Then, after the death of his servant, he will stand over his grave and pronounce him innocent. And the spirit of the dead man will have some knowledge of this vindication. Perhaps he may be permitted to revisit the glimpses of the moon and hear the final verdict in his favour. This seems to us a meagre satisfaction, but for the author it is enough. He has shown his hero fighting his doubts and coming into a reasonable confidence.

This individual believer, then, has the confidence that God will deal with him in such a way as to vindicate him from the false suspicions of his friends and of the world. But the larger problem is still to be attacked. The friends have based their accusations on a definite theory of the divine government. They are sure that God rewards the good and punishes the wicked in this world—they, like Job, know nothing of another world. Job reviews the facts of life as he has observed them, and finds that the theory is not borne out. Instead of the case being as the friends affirm, the reverse may easily be discovered: "Why do the wicked live, become old, yes, wax mighty in power? Their seed is established with them in their sight, and their offspring before their eyes. Their houses are safe from fear, neither is the rod of God upon them." Death may indeed come upon them suddenly, but this is a mercy rather than a punishment as the case of Job himself proves. If it be said that his children are punished for his crimes, how can this be made to vindicate justice? "Let his own eyes see his destruction and let himself drink of the wrath of the Almighty, for what cares he for his house when the number of his months is cut off?" (21 : 7–9.) Consideration of this problem threatens to bring back Job's former perplexity, especially as his friends find nothing to say except to renew their old charges of blasphemy against the one who doubts their theology. Their attacks are met by a renewed protest of innocence, accompanied by a detailed statement of the principles on which he has conducted himself throughout his life (31). So far from being without fear of God as they charged, he has always regulated his life by it: "Does he not see my ways and number all my steps? If I have despised the cause of my servant or of my maid when they contended with me, what then shall I do when God rises up? When he visits what shall I answer him? Did not he that made me in the womb make him?" With calm confidence Job would receive the indictment of his prosecutor even if this were God himself. Such is the conscious innocence of the man who fears God and turns aside from evil.

It is evident that the larger problem has not been solved. Nor is it solved by the speeches of Yahweh, which come after Job has affirmed his integrity anew. The divine interlocutor contents himself with pointing out the wonders of creation and asking Job whether he understands them. In successive questions the objects which meet the eye in earth and sky and sea are brought before the listener, in order that he may have a realising sense of the task of governing the universe (chapter 38). When Job confesses his own insignificance he is again addressed with the sarcastic injunction: "Deck thyself now with excellence and dignity and array thyself with honor and majesty! pour forth the overflowings of thine anger and look upon every one that is proud and abase him!" (40 : 10–12.) In reply Job can only confess that he has spoken rashly in what he has brought forward. Yet this is not a confession that Job was in the wrong, for the epilogue expressly acquits him while accusing the friends.

The result of the inquiry, then, is a *non liquet.* So far as the general problem of the government of the world is concerned, the author is no wiser than other men. He sees the world to be so great and wonderful that the principles by which it is governed are above the comprehension of man.

Only he who made it is able to govern it, but he may be trusted to govern it rightly. One thing stands out clearly: Man must not think that the world is governed for his sake, for, after all, man is only one of the creatures for which God cares. This is the mistake of the orthodox, represented by the friends in the dialogue. They supposed themselves to know the ways of God, and on the basis of this supposed knowledge they were willing to do their fellow man a grievous wrong in misjudging him. The result of the inquiry is not pessimism; the author rejoices in the great world in which he lives. It is not irreligion; for those who wait upon God receive a measurable satisfaction in their confidence in him. But to a certain extent it is agnosticism, the agnosticism of one who would not allow a theological theory to shut his eyes to the facts of life. His earnestness and honesty are evident.

The thought of the author was too advanced for his contemporaries, and the book was increased in size by two insertions which were intended to correct its teaching. One of these is the well-known poem in the twenty-eighth chapter. This is a panegyric of wisdom, which is the prerogative of God alone. The author is deprecating such discussion as is carried on by Job and his friends, on the ground that it is intruding into the sphere of divine things. Man should turn to the practical problems of life, fear God and eschew evil, and be content. More significant is the long speech assigned to Elihu. This personage is represented as a young man who has listened to the debate between Job and his friends and is dissatisfied with both parties. What he really does is to set forth anew the arguments (if arguments they may be called) of the friends. He reveals to us the tenacity of the view that misfortune is a punishment for sin. This view maintained itself in Israel, as we see from many of the Psalms, and is not wholly overcome even at the present day.

CHAPTER XVII

LEGALISM AND PRACTICAL PROBLEMS

Speculation on the ways of God is, from the nature of the case, the occupation of only one thinker in ten thousand. The majority of men are confronted by more immediate problems. This was the case with the Jews in the Greek period. This people, as we have seen, had ceased to be a nation, and the majority of them were living outside of what they still regarded as their true home. In the cities founded by Alexander and his successors the Jews were a prominent part of the population. The great port of Egypt which the conqueror called by his own name speedily counted a hundred thousand Jews among its inhabitants. In this and other large cities they were obliged to learn a new mode of life and to adjust themselves to new modes of thought. The nation of agriculturists had become a race of traders. Men who are engaged in commerce must develop a different ethic from that which satisfies a community of peasants.

Two things conspired to make the problem difficult. The Jew, although living among the gentiles, wished to preserve his own religion. To live in the world and yet not conform to its religious and social usages required no small skill. In the second place, knowledge of the Greek language (which was essential to the business man in this period) brought with it some knowledge of Greek culture. But Greek culture was predominantly intellectual. Both metaphysic and ethic had been studied by the ablest minds among the Greeks, and the claim of the philosophers to possess the truth was a challenge to the Jew to make good the claims of his own Law. Adjustment to practical life and to Greek modes of thought was, therefore, forced upon reflecting minds among the Jews. Hence the rise of what we call the Wisdom literature. Although direct evidence is lacking, we may assume that in this period a regular system of instruction was inaugurated in Jerusalem. The teachers were called *sages;* their instruction was given orally, but the maxims in which they embodied the substance of their teachings were written down and have reached us in the books we have now to consider. The point of view is set forth with all desirable distinctness in the opening words of the book of Proverbs: "To know wisdom and discipline; to discern words of understanding; to receive instruction in wise dealing, in righteousness, and equity" (Prov. 1 : 2 *f.*).

The sage claims to have attained this knowledge and he desires to impart the knowledge to others. The art of right living is something that can be learned, and it is because the young man has not studied it that he so often goes astray. The bad man is a fool, either because he has not had the opportunity of learning how to live or because he has flouted the instruction offered him. The sage, therefore, addresses the young man in order to give him knowledge and discretion: "If thou wilt, my son, thou shalt be instructed, and if thou givest thy mind to it thou shalt become wise," says Ben Sira; and the same author admonishes: "Neglect not the speech of the wise, and reflect on their enigmas; by this thou shalt attain education, so that thou canst appear before princes; despise not the tradition of the ancients which they have received from their fathers; for thereby thou shalt attain insight so that thou canst give an answer when there is occasion" (Sirach 8 : 8 *f.*; 6 : 32).

In dating the Wisdom literature in the Greek period, we do not mean to say that something similar had not existed from very early times in Israel. In fact, the wise men are occasionally alluded to in the pre-exilic period, and from the nature of the case apothegms embodying reflections on the problems of life are current among all peoples which have reached anything like civilisation. We have from Egypt the sayings of Ptah-hotep, who is said to have lived two thousand years before Christ and whose point of view is not unlike that of our book of Proverbs. For example, he says: "How beautiful it is when a son receives what his father says; he shall attain long life. Take care what thou sayest! Let it be such that the nobles will say: How fine is the utterance of his mouth! If thou obtainest me (wisdom) thy body will remain sound, and the king will be content with all thy actions." We have also from Egypt a similar collection attributed to one Ani containing warnings against women and exhortations to care for father and mother very similar to what we find in our book of Proverbs, and the maxims of the Babylonian Ahikar were known to the Jews as early as the sixth century B. C. The Wisdom literature, therefore, is not of purely Jewish origin.[1]

Our reason for dating the books now under consideration in this period is easily understood. The books are four in number (the book of Job, though affiliated with them, has been treated separately), namely, Proverbs, Ecclesiastes, the Wisdom of Jesus the son of Sirach, and the Wisdom of Solomon. The similarity of the four is so great that they cannot have originated far apart in time. One of them we can date with almost absolute certainty. This is the book of Ben Sira (Ecclesiasticus), which must have been written about the year 180 B. C. The others must belong in the same general period, Proverbs somewhat earlier, Wisdom certainly later. Two of the four were received into the Hebrew canon. This was probably because they were attributed to Solomon. Wisdom was written in Greek and so did not appeal to the Rabbinical authorities. The ascription of Proverbs to Solomon is only in line with postexilic custom, which published many books under the name of ancient worthies.

The point of view of this whole school is well put before us by Ben Sira, or rather by his grandson, who translated his book into Greek, in his preface: "Whereas many and great

[1] The sayings of Ptah-hotep and of Ani are translated in Gressmann, *Altorientalische Texte und Bilder*, I, pp. 201 *f.*

things have been delivered to us by the Law and the prophets and the others who have followed after them, for which things Israel ought to be commended for *culture* and *wisdom,* and since it is becoming not only that the learned should themselves attain insight but also that they should be able to profit the unlearned, therefore my grandfather when he had much given himself to the study of the Law and the prophets and the other books of our fathers and had got therein sufficient skill, felt moved himself to write something pertaining to learning and wisdom, that those who are desirous to learn, being attached to these things, might profit all the more in living according to the Law." The grandson in stating his grandfather's desire formulated his own purpose also, since it was his aim in translating the book into Greek to benefit his fellow Jews in precisely the same way. What impresses us is that the Jew has taken up the Greek challenge which claimed culture and wisdom as Greek possessions. The claim is rejected on the ground that in the Law the Jew has the supreme source of wisdom. The Law is already supplemented by the collection known as the prophets and by some other books, which are not described more particularly. But it is plain that the Hebrew Scriptures already exist in the threefold division which still obtains. In these Scriptures the Jew has the supreme code of ethics, and the object of Ben Sira in publishing his reflections is to enable his fellows to live according to the Law. The author of Proverbs avows the same aim: "He that turns his ear from hearing the Law, even his prayer is an abomination" (Prov. 28 : 9). Both authors, however, claim to speak not only from knowledge of the Law but also from long observation of human life. Ritual, to be sure, which occupies so large a space in the Pentateuch, is not made prominent by them. This is because they could trust the priestly scribes to see that this part of the Law was carefully obeyed. What most interested them was the problem of carrying the ethic of the Jewish code into practical life in foreign and often hostile surroundings.

Since these authors deal with every-day problems, they do not permit themselves to dwell much on the specific Messianic hope. Yet the strong racial feeling comes out now and then. Ben Sira prays that Israel may be saved and that Yahweh will send his terror on the gentiles. This author hopes for the gathering of the tribes and the return of Elijah, and in one passage even alludes to the Messiah (Sirach 48: 9; *cf.* 47: 22). His pride in the history of Israel comes out in his panegyric on the national heroes. He is confident that the God of Israel is the only true God (36 : 22), and genuine Jewish feeling shows itself in his hatred for the schismatic Samaritans, "the foolish people that dwell in Shechem" (50 : 26).

So thoroughly has the belief in one God established itself that the polemic against idols such as we find in Deutero-Isaiah is no longer necessary. The hope of the Jew is that the gentiles may recognise that there is no God besides Yahweh (Sirach 33: 5). There is, however, no speculation on the problems raised by the belief in God—as to his character, his toleration of evil, or his government of the world.[1] Ben Sira deprecates such inquiries: "What is too high for thee search not out, neither inquire into what is beyond thy strength; for men have many vain opinions, and evil speculations lead them astray" (3:21 and 24). At the same time certain things are assumed; for example, that the universe is an ordered universe, a kosmos, as the Greeks would say. The principle of its ordering is wisdom, and the glowing words in which she describes her part in the creation of the world testify to the firmness with which this idea of an ordered universe had rooted itself in the mind of these thinkers (Prov. 8). Ben Sira is moved to praise by his contemplation of the works of God in nature, and utters his thought in one of the most elevated passages which have come to us from a Hebrew source (Sirach 42: 15 to 43: 33). To this exalted mood the problem of evil seems to be no longer a problem, for even the evil spirits and the venomous beasts are subject to the will of the Creator (39 : 28–31).

[1] The exception in the case of Ecclesiastes is discussed below.

Religion is the basis of ethics. The motto of the school is: "The fear of Yahweh is the beginning of wisdom." Although the works of Yahweh are wonderful and his deeds among men inscrutable (Sirach 11 : 4), yet on the whole he is on the side of the righteous. "He sees all that men do, and they who think to escape his notice deceive themselves" (23 : 10*f.*). "The ways of men are before the eyes of Yahweh, and he regards all their paths" (Prov. 5 : 21). The wise man is the one who bears this in mind, while the fool is the one who doubts the providence of God: "Say not in thy heart: 'Who has power over me?' For Yahweh is an avenger; say not: 'I have sinned and what happened to me?' for Yahweh is patient. Trust not in forgiveness so as to go on in sin" (Sirach 3 : 3–5). The egoistic nature of this teaching needs no demonstration, but it would be easy to emphasise it unduly. As the man who believes honesty to be the best policy may yet be honest from a higher motive, so with these advocates of wisdom. They believe that godliness is profitable, but the godliness need not, therefore, be mere selfishness. Religion is the fear of Yahweh, but it is also trust in him: "Trust in Yahweh with all thy heart, and lean not on thine own understanding," says the author of Proverbs (3 : 5), and Sirach pronounces a woe on the heart which has not faith, for it shall not be established (2 : 13). Obedience to the will of Yahweh, therefore, was in the last analysis based on the belief that the will of Yahweh is in conformity with righteousness.

This is implied in the treatment of wisdom itself—the most characteristic thing in all this literature. Wisdom is the art of right living, and it has attained consistency in a body of tradition which has come down from former generations. It is not, however, of human origin. It is revealed from above, and its proper home is the bosom of God himself. Wisdom personified declares as much: "Yahweh formed me at the beginning of his way; before his works of old. . . . When he established the heavens I was there, when he set a circle on the face of the deep. . . . Then I was by him as a master workman, and I was daily his delight, sporting before him always, sporting in his habitable earth, and my delight was with the sons of men" (Prov. 8 : 22–31). Sirach, in like manner, says that wisdom dwells in heaven, was created before all things, is the possession of God himself, and has power over the nations (Sirach 1 : 4, 8*f.*, and chapter 24).

The authors of these passages are, in fact, influenced by the speculative tendencies which they have disavowed. There was a theological necessity which compelled men to mediate between God and the world. In early days it had not been difficult to suppose that Yahweh came in person to his people, in theophany and vision. But with the larger view of the universe which came in the Persian and Greek periods, Yahweh in becoming greater had also become more remote. He had need of mediators. The result in the doctrine of angels we have already discovered. The Wisdom literature has little to say of angels, but it finds in the personified wisdom the organ by which the transcendent God reveals himself to men and carries on his work of creation and providence. Doubtless Greek thought influenced the conception, reluctant as the authors themselves would have been to admit such influence.

The mission of wisdom is not only to order the universe; she is the guide and counsellor who invites and warns the sons of men. She is, in fact, the voice of God calling men to right living. By a natural transition (natural to a loyal Jew, that is) she is identified with the revelation of God in Scripture. Ben Sira says that wisdom is given to all flesh, but especially to those who fear Yahweh (1 : 10), and again he makes wisdom declare that she had taken up her residence in Jacob, and he identifies her with the book of the covenant of God, the Law that Moses commanded (24 : 23). In practical life, therefore, wisdom means obedience to the will of God revealed in the Law: "He who fears Yahweh seeks wisdom, and he who keeps the Law attains her," says Ben Sira, and he frequently returns to the theme, exhorting his readers to reflect and to keep the commandments (Sirach 1 : 26; 6 : 37; 15 : 1; 32 : 1–15).

It is evident that legalism has here formulated its simple creed: God has given a law to guide men into right living; this law is to be studied and expounded in the light of tradition and experience; thus studied and obeyed it leads to a really successful life. Wisdom, then, is the most precious possession of man. Gold and jewels are not to be compared to her; those that love her love life; she is a crown of gold to the one who obtains her; all her ways are pleasantness and her paths are peace. Nor is she difficult of attainment. She invites men to her banquet. To the young and uninstructed she says: "Come eat of my bread and drink of the wine which I have mingled; leave off ye simple ones and live, and walk in the ways of understanding" (Prov. 9 : 5*f.*). "She brings her sons to honor and takes the part of those that seek her; he who loves her loves life and those who seek her shall be filled with joy" (Sirach 4 : 11*f.*). Contrasted with her is Madame Folly, who also invites men to her house saying: "Stolen waters are sweet, and bread eaten in secret is pleasant." But those who accept her invitation go to death and her guests are in the depths of Sheol (Prov. 9 : 18).

The reward of obedience is given in this life, and so is the recompense of ill doing. There is no intimation that the future life is a place of recompense. Wisdom "holds long life in her right hand, in her left are riches and honor" (Prov. 3 : 16). "The rebellion of the simple slays them, and the security of fools destroys them, whereas the upright shall dwell in the land and the perfect shall remain in it, while the wicked shall be cut off from the land, and the treacherous shall be rooted out of it" (Prov. 1 : 32; 2 : 21, and often). There is no enjoyment in Sheol, says Ben Sira. After asking: "Who shall praise the Most High in the grave instead of them that live and give thanks?" he answers his own question: "Thanksgiving perishes from the dead as from one that is not; the living and sound alone praise Yahweh" (Sirach 14 : 16; 17 : 27). The righteous man may indeed comfort himself with the hope that after his death his descendants will have part in the Messianic glory, and for the wise man there is always the confidence that his name will be held in honour after he has gone from this life.

So far as these authors are concerned, the book of Job might not have been written. The sufferings of the righteous, so far as they are considered at all, are supposed to be disciplinary: "My son, despise not the chastening of the Almighty, neither be weary of his reproof; for whom Yahweh loves he reproves, even as a father the son in whom he delights" (Prov. 3 : 12). "Gold is tried in the fire, and acceptable men in the furnace of adversity" (Sirach 2:5). He, therefore, who would learn wisdom must make up his mind to be tested by trouble. If his faith stands the test God will at last reward him: "Look at the former generations and see; who ever trusted Yahweh and was put to shame? Who abode in his fear and was forsaken? Who called to him and was despised? For Yahweh is merciful and gracious; he forgives sin and rescues in time of trouble" (Sirach 2 : 10*f.*). The point of view is the one which is represented by the so-called friends of Job.

The existence of evil seems to present no problem to these writers. Each man is endowed with free will and can make or mar his own fate. Nothing is said of a sinful nature, or of inherited tendencies to evil: "God in the beginning made man and left him to his own will; if thou wilt thou shalt keep the commandments, and it is a faithful thing to do what is pleasing to him" (Sirach 15 : 14*f.*). There is no need of expiation, and the sacrificial system, while it is assumed to be divinely ordered, must not be taken to wipe out guilt. The priest is to be honoured, the tithes are to be paid and the sacrifices are to be brought, but one must not think that Yahweh can be bribed by them. "The sacrifice of a wicked man is abomination to Yahweh" (Prov. 15 : 8). The only way of counteracting sin is by right action: "Water quenches fire, and righteousness erases sin" (Sirach 3 : 30).

The system of this school, then, may be called legalism, with the emphasis on the ethical, as distinguished from the ritual, commandments—a common-sense legalism we may say. And there can be no doubt that as a working theory of life it gave satisfaction to its adherents. Ben Sira praises the scribe as the man who has the best of callings, and the general tone of these writers (with the exception to be noted presently) is optimistic. Ben Sira knows that all God's works are good; even man, though so often rebellious, has received eyes and ears to perceive the good, and a mind to understand: "With understanding and insight he filled their heart; good and evil he taught them, to show them his mighty acts, that they might have his fear in their heart, to magnify his wonders always, and to praise his sacred name" (Sirach 17 : 5–10). Therefore the writer is moved to a hymn of thanksgiving for deliverance from danger, and for help vouchsafed in time of peril (Sirach 51). It would be a mistake to think of these men as mere moralists. They had the consciousness of the presence of God, and they appealed to him for blessings not only temporal, but spiritual. Ben Sira invokes God as his father, and prays to be kept from sin, especially from unguarded utterance: "Oh that one would set a watch on my mouth and on my lips a lock of discretion, that I may not fall by them. . . . Let me not have pride of eyes, and keep me from haughtiness of heart; let not the desire of the flesh seize me, nor shameless lust rule over me" (Sirach 22 : 27 to 23 : 6). In similar strain Agur prays: "Two things have I desired of thee; deny me them not before I die: Remove far from me falsehood and lies, and give me neither poverty nor riches; feed me with the portion that belongs to me, lest I be full and deny thee, and say: Who is Yahweh? or lest I be poor and steal and use profanely the name of my God" (Prov. 30 : 7–9).

Two classes of sin seem to tempt the young and inexperienced in the period when these books were written. These are sins of violence and sexual excesses. Proverbs describes the sinners who invite the young man to make common cause with them in robbery: "Let us lurk privily for the innocent; let us swallow them alive as those who go down to Sheol; we shall find all precious substance, shall fill our houses with spoil; cast in thy lot amongst us, and let us all have one purse" (Prov. 1 : 10*f.*). The passage reflects the unsettled state of society during the Greek period. The central government was weak, and the policing of the provinces was neglected. The career of highway robber offered attractions to the adventurous. Moreover, the foreign rule over the Jews gave large opportunities for spies and informers. Blackmail could be collected by the less scrupulous, who were willing to use their advantage. The temptation against which the wise man cautions his pupil must be obvious. From this point of view also we understand Ben Sira's somewhat cold-blooded cautions against easy friendship: "Be at peace with many but let thy friend be one of a thousand; if thou wouldst get a friend, prove him first and be not hasty to credit him; for many an one is a friend for the time, but abides not for the day of need; many a friend becomes an enemy and reveals thy quarrel among the people" (Sirach 6 : 6–9). At the same time it would be a mistake to call this cynicism; the value of a true friend is fully recognised: "Of a faithful friend there is no price, and his worth is incalculable; a faithful friend is a medicine of life; whoso fears God obtains him" (6 : 15*f.*). Proverbs also knows of a friend that sticks closer than a brother.

The state of society is reflected in the warnings against enemies: "An enemy speaks sweetly with his lips but in his heart he is devising to throw thee into a pit; he will weep with his eyes but if he find opportunity he will be insatiate of blood" (Sirach 12 : 16). The prudent man will avoid association with those whom he knows or suspects to be evil. The temptation to court the society of the rich and powerful is to be guarded against (13 : 2–13; *cf.* Prov. 23 : 1–3). The guard which Ben Sira is careful to set on his lips is comprehensible when we consider the way in which this society was honeycombed with espionage: "Even a fool if he holds his peace is accounted wise" (Prov. 17 : 28).

The false friend leads one on to speak perverse things that he may deliver one over to the judge. But the wise man will know how to avoid the trap: "Understanding shall keep thee and deliver thee from every false way, from the man who speaks perverseness" (Prov. 2 : 12 *f.*). Scepticism also was rife, and there were those who were ashamed of the Law, who justified the wicked and condemned the righteous. Such men are an abomination to Yahweh (Prov. 17 : 15). The young man flatters himself that he has sinned once and has not been punished, and so he disbelieves in the divine administration of affairs. In fact, it was a time of intellectual ferment, and many were losing the old faith.

If the young man had cause to avoid the society of sycophants, false friends, and those who would lead him into crime, he had also reason to guard against the seductions of the strange woman. Whether the notorious laxity of Greek custom with reference to the relations of the sexes is in evidence here is doubtful. Ezekiel shows that Hebrew manners down to the time of the fall of Jerusalem left much to be desired. In the Law, indeed, we have strict injunctions against sexual licence, and Jewish writers of this period doubtless felt that their morality was superior to that of the gentiles—this is one of the points emphasised by Philo and the Sibylline books. Our authors show plainly enough how constantly young men were beset by temptations to unchastity. There is in the exhortations of the sages, however, no trace of asceticism, as though marriage were a less perfect state than celibacy. On the contrary, the young man is exhorted to rejoice in the married state, and while many of the references to women in this literature are derogatory to the sex, yet the virtuous woman receives high praise. The classic panegyric of Proverbs is too well known to need citation here (Prov. 31 : 10–31), and Ben Sira says: "A good wife is a good gift, and she is given to the man who fears God" (Sirach 26 : 3).

It is unnecessary to give further details concerning the

teachings of the sages. The line between manners and morals is not easy to draw, and both manners and morals are treated in detail by these writers. As we have seen, a certain type of mind is able to rest in such a practical, common-sense system, and it is clear that the sages thought highly of their own attainments. Ben Sira, after describing the various professions and trades and the advantages of each, comes to that of the scribe, the student of the Law: "But he that gives his mind to the Law of the Most High, and is occupied in the meditation thereof, will seek out the wisdom of all the ancients and be occupied in the prophecies; he will seek out the secrets of grave sentences and be conversant in dark parables; he will serve among great men and appear before princes" (Sirach 39 : 1–4). In fact, if there be an art of right living there can be no nobler calling than that of him who makes this art the object of his study and who imparts the results of his reflections to others. But the limitations of the method of the sages are obvious. They had no profound philosophy of life. They purposely avoided speculation on the nature of things. That more thoughtful inquirers could not rest in the philosophy of common sense is made evident by one book of this group, and to this we now turn.

This book bears, rather unfortunately, the name Ecclesiastes. The Hebrew title Koheleth is not altogether clear in meaning, but probably intends to describe the author as one of the group of teachers who, we have reason to believe, carried on systematic instruction in Jerusalem. That the book gives itself forth as a work of Solomon can cause us no surprise. The tradition of Solomon's wisdom made him the patron saint of all this school, and his reputation for wealth and luxury made him the appropriate character to inculcate the lessons Koheleth had at heart.[1] For Koheleth claims to have found by careful observation of the world that all is vanity—*absolute emptiness and a*

[1] On the date of the book the reader may consult the commentary of Barton (1910), p. 62.

striving after wind is his watchword. His reason is, first, that the course of nature is an eternal grind with no visible progress toward a goal: One generation goes and another comes, the sun travels his daily round, the winds turn from one side to another without being able to find a new quarter of the compass; the rivers run to the sea only to receive their supplies from the same source—"that which has been is that which shall be, that which has been done is that which shall be done, and there is no new thing under the sun" (Eccles. 1 : 9). Human experience is of the same sort. The king with all the resources of wealth and power at his command may experiment with every pleasure, sensual, æsthetic, intellectual, only to find that no one of them gives real satisfaction; each is a striving after wind. Even wisdom, though of a certain practical advantage, makes no real difference among men, for one event happens to all, to the wise man and to the fool. God does not intervene, either to reward the righteous or to punish the wicked, nor yet to regulate the course of the world to any end. He does, indeed, ordain what comes to pass, but this only adds to man's misery, for it shows him that, however he may strive, his fate is not in his own power: "I beheld all the work of God, that man cannot find out the work that is done under the sun; because, however much a man labors to seek it out, yet shall he not find it. . . . All things come alike to all; there is one event to the righteous and to the wicked, to the good and to the bad, to the clean and to the unclean, to him that sacrifices, and to him that sacrifices not; as is the good so is the sinner; he that swears is as he that fears an oath" (8 : 16*f*.; 9 : 2).

Man's freedom is thus an illusion, and the theory of retribution, either in this life or in another, has no foundation. God purposely treats men and animals alike that men may know that they are no better than the brutes (3 : 18*f*.). All go to one place. The theory of a future life is met with the stern, almost angry, question: "Who knows whether the spirit of man goes upward and the spirit of the beast goes downward?" (3 : 21.) Specific denial is made of any work or device or knowledge or wisdom in Sheol to which we go (9 : 10). Even the poor consolation that Ben Sira found in the thought that one's memory will abide through the generations proves illusory, for the memory of the dead perishes like their loves and their hates (9 : 5). If one comforts himself in the thought that his children will give him a sort of immortality, this also proves groundless, for who can tell whether they will be an honour or a disgrace to their parents? It is a bitter thought to the wise man that after labouring to accumulate an estate he may leave it to a stranger, or if he leaves it to a son that son may turn out to be a fool (2 : 19).

The world, then, is an unintelligible world. Worse than this, it is a perverse world; the wicked sit in the place of judgment; the cry of the oppressed finds no response; the righteous perish in their righteousness; slaves ride on horseback while princes go afoot; the race is not to the swift nor the battle to the strong; riches are not apportioned to men of understanding nor favour to men of skill (3 : 16; 4 : 1; 7 : 15; 9 : 11*f.*; 10 : 7). A similar complaint was uttered by the author of Job, but the indictment is here much stronger. The author of Job was able to rest in the faith that the government of the world, though incomprehensible by man, was yet in accordance with true wisdom. Koheleth has lost this faith.[1] It is probably not true that he had ceased to believe in the existence of God. This frame of things cannot be without a mind, he might have said. But his search for a rational order in the conduct of affairs brought no result. It is as if God purposely arranged to confound the pride of men. "One fate comes to man and beast, that man may know that he is no better than the lower animals." There is, therefore, no real good for man. "The dead are better off than the living, better than either is the untimely birth which does not open its eyes to the light" (4 : 2; 6 : 3).

[1] A glimpse of agnosticism in Proverbs (30 : 2–4) shows that he was not alone in his negations.

In the book as we have it there is, indeed, the assertion that a relative good is attainable in the enjoyment of the pleasures of life, but it is a question whether these Epicurean passages are by the original author. Whoever inserted them, however, drew a natural conclusion from the premises of the author.[1] In the book there are, moreover, a number of passages which plainly contradict its main teaching. Where Koheleth saw only perversity in the administration of the world and wickedness in high places, the pious annotator assures us that God will judge the righteous and the wicked (3 : 17). Direct rebuke seems to be administered to the author by the insertion: "Because sentence against an evil work is not executed speedily the heart of the sons of man is fully set in them to do evil; but though a sinner do evil a hundred times and prolong his days yet surely I know that it shall be well with them that fear God; but it shall not be well with the wicked, neither shall he prolong his days which are as a shadow before God" (8 : 11–13). Most instructive of all is the edifying conclusion of the book in which the orthodox defender of the faith shows his assurance that he has silenced his adversary: "The end of the matter when all has been heard is: Fear God and keep his commandments, for this is the whole of man; for God will bring every work into judgment even every hidden thing whether it be good or whether it be evil" (12 : 13).

If it had not been for these edifying insertions it is probable that Ecclesiastes would not have been received into the Jewish canon. And some may even now demur at the inclusion of the original author among the sages of Israel. Yet there is no reason to doubt that he counted himself a loyal Jew, and that he claimed a place among the teachers of Israel. The editor of his book assures us that because Koheleth was wise he still taught the people knowledge. Scattered through the book we find wise saws such as adorn the book of Proverbs: "Better a handful of quiet than two handfuls of toil"; "Two

[1] These Epicurean passages are 3 : 12*f.*, 22; 5 : 17–19; 8 : 15 and 9 : 7–10.

are better than one"; "Better is a poor and wise youth than an old and foolish king"; "Better the rebuke of the wise than the song of fools." Such passages impressed the average reader more distinctly than did the scepticism of the book, and they gave it currency. No doubt, the thought that the riches and wisdom of Solomon convinced him of the vanity of worldly prosperity also attracted many minds. For us who seek to know the actual course of religious thought in Israel the book is significant, as showing the near approach to bankruptcy of faith made by one who sought an explanation of the phenomena of life.

How it escaped bankruptcy in the case of some minds is made evident by the latest book in this group, the Wisdom of Solomon. Since the book was written in Greek and at the very end of the Old Testament period, it might be a question whether it belongs in our discussion. Yet the author is a loyal Jew, and he makes use of Solomon to teach the lessons he has at heart. Far from making the great king the *blasé* and disillusioned pursuer of pleasure, however, it holds him up as an example, a man who has attained the best there is in life. We can hardly avoid seeing in this an intentional confutation of the older book. Ben Sira and Koheleth are apparently opposed to Greek philosophy. The author of Wisdom, on the other hand, finds the solution of the problems of life in the doctrine of immortality, and this not in the Jewish form of a resurrection of the body, but distinctly in the form already wrought out by Greek philosophy, that is, the immortality of the soul set free from the body by death. To him it is the sinner who says that in the death of a man there is no remedy, neither is any known to return from the grave (Wisdom 2 : 1). "In the world to come the righteous shall enjoy eternal felicity in the presence of God and receive a beautiful crown from him" (3 : 8).

CHAPTER XVIII

APOCALYPTIC DEVELOPMENT OF THE MESSIANIC HOPE

ECCLESIASTES shows a rationalising tendency at work on the religion of Israel, and it is a question whether Greek thought was not undermining the distinctive beliefs embodied in the Jewish Scriptures. What might have happened had there been no violent attack on those beliefs (and the practices which went with them) we cannot tell. What actually took place is clear to us. The persecution of Antiochus kindled the zeal, not to say fanaticism, of the observers of the Law and gave to Legalism a new and stronger hold on the affections of the faithful. The conflict with the Syrian monarchy showed that a considerable party in Jerusalem sympathised with the desire of the king to "civilise" his subjects, as he phrased it. These men were not moved altogether by a desire to secure court favour. Some of them were attracted by Greek ideals. They were to be found among the more educated of the nation and were in any case only a minority. Opposed to them were the strict observers of the Law, and the course of the struggle showed that these were divided into two parties. One we may call the Maccabeans, adherents of the heroic family which led the revolt. They were at first moved only by the determination to resist tyranny, but as they achieved success they indulged hopes of restoring the politicial independence of their nation. The other fraction consisted of the Asideans, the Pious, as they called themselves. They would take no part in political affairs, believing that Yahweh would set up his kingdom in his own time by an act of miraculous intervention. Until that time should come, the duty of the loyal Jew, as they believed, was to obey the Law to the letter, and wait upon God. This party did, indeed, make common cause with the Maccabeans when the possibility of keeping the Law was threatened, but as soon as they were again allowed to observe their customs without interference they withdrew from the struggle.

We have seen the importance which the Messianic hope assumed in postexilic Judaism. What now interests us is the intensity with which the hope was held in the time of persecution. It is only in accordance with human nature that the expectation of divine intervention should rise to fevered heat in proportion as persecution becomes more bitter. At such times believers argue that God cannot long leave his people to be a prey to the wicked. In the history of the Christian Church expectation of the Second Coming becomes acute at those times in which the puritan party is oppressed by worldlings. So in the Jewish Church the Messianic hope was kindled into flame when persecution arose. It then took new and fantastic forms, and the more ardent spirits even ventured to calculate the time of the end and to revive the spirits of their coreligionists by specific promises that the day was just at hand. The evidence is found in a group of books to which we give the name apocalypses.

The author of an apocalypse conceives of prophecy as essentially predictive—the miraculous revelation of what is to come to pass. But the older books of prophecy very imperfectly conform to this ideal. The predictions which they contain are much less definite and specific than the believer would like to have them. This defect is remedied in the apocalypse. On the basis of a tradition or of visionary experiences, or of both, the author sets forth the divine plan as he conceives it. And since this plan embraces the past as well as the future, he dates his work in the past, ascribing it to some ancient worthy. This name will carry weight with the reader. The predictions embodied in the work are really history under the guise of prophecy, and they are usually couched in the form of vision, that being the traditional means of revelation. In the theory of the book the ancient seer to whom it is ascribed had the course of human history unrolled to him in trance from his own time until it reached its end with the triumph of the Kingdom of God.

The representative apocalypse in the Hebrew canon is the book of Daniel, in which all these points are fully illustrated. It has, however, precursors in some older fragments. Ezekiel has distinctly apocalyptic features. It was he who first set forth the scheme adopted by later writers, according to which there would be a miraculous annihilation of the heathen world-power, followed by an equally miraculous rebuilding of the temple. In the other prophets we have similar utterances. Thus Habakkuk describes the coming of Yahweh to judgment: "Yahweh comes forth to judge his people; his presence shakes the earth, dries up the streams, causes the sun to forget his rising, and the moon to cease her shining" (Hab. 3). Several passages now included in the book of Jeremiah have the apocalyptic colouring, and with them we may class the little book of Joel. This example is especially instructive, for it shows how any extraordinary event in nature may awaken the expectation of Yahweh's coming. The extraordinary event in this case was a plague of locusts such as often visits the countries bordering the desert. The author describes what seems to him an unprecedented event and the description is in such terms that expositors have been in doubt whether a veritable swarm of locusts is intended or whether the author is picturing the approach of a hostile army: "A people has invaded my land mighty and without number. . . . Like heroes they run, like veteran warriors they climb the wall, they march every one in his way and they do not break their ranks" (Joel 1 : 6 and 2 : 7). The decision, however, cannot be doubtful; the author is describing an invasion of locusts pure and simple. It is significant of his point of view that his chief grief is that the desolating swarm has cut off meat-offering and drink-offering from the house of God (1 : 13).

He is thoroughly priestly in his sentiment, and he shows this further by his view of the efficacy of fasting. It is only necessary that the people fast, the priests setting the example, in order that the grace of Yahweh may be manifested. Yahweh is moved for his people, the oncoming plague is driven back, the rain follows in its season, and the bountiful harvest of the new year more than makes good what has been destroyed by the invaders.

All this is preliminary. The invasion of locusts is immediately followed by the supernatural phenomena of the Messianic age. The day of Yahweh is ushered in by great overturnings in nature and in the world of man. It is a time of clouds and thick darkness, of gloom and terror (2 : 1 *f.*, 10). There are prodigies in heaven above and on earth beneath, blood and fire and pillars of smoke, the sun turned into darkness and the moon into blood. Among mankind, also, there are miracles. The spirit, the organ of revelation, will no longer be restricted to a few chosen members of the race, but will be poured out on all. Even slaves and maid servants will possess it or be possessed by it (3 : 1). This we may suppose will be true of Jews alone, for punishment is to be the lot of the other nations. Yet a chance of salvation is left for those gentiles who become proselytes and call upon the name of Yahweh.

The final scene is the great day of judgment, described in terms that have influenced all subsequent thinking. After the gathering of Israel to its own land Yahweh will summon the nations to the Valley of Jehoshaphat (the Valley of Yahweh's Judgment), which the author doubtless located just under the walls of Jerusalem and in the immediate presence of Yahweh, who dwells in the temple. There the divinity will call them to account for their treatment of the exiled Israelites. The penalty will be their own sale into slavery by the Jews. The sentence will not be put into execution without a conflict, but Yahweh will be victorious: "He will roar from Zion and utter his voice from Jerusalem, so that heaven and earth shake; Yahweh will be a refuge to his people and a stronghold to the children of Israel; so shall you know that I am Yahweh your God, dwelling in Zion, my sacred mountain; then shall Jerusalem be sacred and no foreigner shall pass through her any more" (3 : 16*f.*). The transformation of the land will follow so that the mountains will distil sweet wine, and the hills will flow with milk. Ezekiel's expectation of a fountain flowing from the temple mount and watering the waste places will be fulfilled, and, on the other hand, Egypt will be a desert and Edom will be desolate. The Messiah is nowhere mentioned. The dwelling of Yahweh himself in Jerusalem is supposed to make a human king superfluous.

A very similar composition has found a place in the book of Isaiah (chapters 24–27).[1] The author expects a day of judgment. Yahweh will lay the earth waste for the sinfulness of its inhabitants. The judgment will extend to the host of heaven on high—the first intimation that the angels will be punished for disobedience (Isaiah 24 : 21*f.*). The same idea is apparently expressed in Yahweh's sword piercing Leviathan, the crooked serpent, the dragon (27 : 1). Early mythological ideas seem here to be taken up by the Hebrew writer, for in Babylonian mythology there is a conflict between the chief of the gods and an opposing monster. The struggle with hostile powers will be followed by Yahweh's dwelling in Jerusalem, where he will make for all nations a feast of fat things; he will wipe away tears from all faces, and the reproach of his people he will take away over all the earth (25 : 8). In this document, as in Joel, the human Messiah is not mentioned; he is made superfluous by the thought that Yahweh himself will dwell in the midst of his people. Here we meet for the first time the distinct assurance of a resurrection for Israel, the full significance of which will be seen when we look at the book of Daniel.

Still another passage, which may be called apocalyptic in the larger sense, is now contained in the book of Zechariah

[1] Whether more than one hand is discoverable in the section does not now concern us.

(chapters 9–14). This passage begins with a denunciation of the neighbours of Judah against whom Yahweh is about to assert himself. He will use Judah as his bow, and Ephraim as his arrow against the sons of Greece. This day of Yahweh will be a day of battle in which the nations will gather against Jerusalem, and though at first successful they will finally be conquered by the direct act of God. In this sense Jerusalem will be a goblet of intoxication to all nations (Zech. 12 : 2). The consummation comes when Yahweh himself takes up his abode in Jerusalem and becomes king over all the earth: "And it shall come to pass that every one that is left of the nations shall come up from year to year to worship the king Yahweh of Hosts, and to keep the feast of tabernacles" (14 : 16). The land will be miraculously transformed so that there will be neither heat nor cold, and there will be no night. Ezekiel's fountain will flow as a perpetual stream, and the ritual ideal will be fully realised, so that all the cooking utensils in Jerusalem will be consecrated and the worshippers will be able to use any of them for the sacrificial flesh (14 : 20*f.*). Whatever universalism the author cherished, therefore, had a distinctly Jewish colouring. For this reason we must interpret ritualistically the declaration that Yahweh will open in Jerusalem a fountain for sin and uncleanness (13 : 1). Only ritual offences can be removed by the application of water, and there is no intimation that sinfulness in its darker aspect will be forgiven or purged away. What crime will be repented of by the people, "like the mourning of Hadad-Rimmon" (12 : 11), is entirely obscure.

The apocalyptic nature of these chapters is most clearly manifest in the conviction that the Messiah is about to appear. Jerusalem is exhorted to rejoice because her king is at hand. He is pictured as the meek and lowly one, riding on the peaceful ass instead of the warrior's horse (9 : 9). Since he is the prince of peace he will abolish the implements of war—the chariots from Ephraim, the horses from Jerusalem: To destroy the bow of war and to offer peace to the nations. His dominion will extend from one sea to the other and from the Euphrates to the ends of the land, that is, he is to possess the traditional empire of Solomon (9 : 10). Such fragmentary utterances enable us to understand how constantly certain circles nourished their faith on the thought of a divine intervention that would restore the ancient glories of Israel. It was when the Maccabean revolt was at its height that the hope assumed the definiteness with which it is pictured in the book of Daniel.

In this period the whole power of the Syrian kingdom was brought to bear on the little company of faithful Jews in the endeavour to make them apostatise. The first need was to encourage the faithful to stand fast in the observance of the Law. The author of our book makes use of an ancient tradition which told of Daniel, a righteous man, who stood high in the favour of Yahweh (Ezek. 14 : 14 and 19; 28 : 3). This Daniel he makes the mouthpiece of his own convictions, authenticating the story by the correspondence of the vision with the actual course of history. That the book was completed just after the first successes of Judas Maccabeus is so obvious that we need not stop to argue the question. Whether it does not embody older material is unimportant for our present purpose.[1]

One aim of the writer of the stories in the first half of the book is to show that the wisdom of Israel is superior to that of the gentiles. In this period, as we have seen, Greek philosophy was forced upon the attention of the world, making the claim to possess the truth. At the same time the ancient reputation of the Babylonians as men having superior knowledge was reaffirmed by men like Berossus. Daniel is made the example to prove that the Jews were proficient in the arts which the astrologers of both nations were claiming as their own. Specifically, the wisdom of Daniel was the power of interpreting dreams. In this he shows himself master of the art and brings contempt on the far-famed

[1] Professor Torrey has pleaded for the earlier composition of the first half of the book, not quite convincingly, as it seems to me.

Chaldeans. A heathen king may receive a revelation in a dream, but he is unable to understand it, or even to give an intelligible account of it, without the help of the inspired interpreter.

The God of Israel is thus shown to be the only God, and to be the arbiter of the destinies of mankind. He has a definite plan, according to which the various empires have their day and, by successive stages, lead up to the consummation of all things. The empires of Babylon, Media, Persia, and Greece mark successive stages of decadence, and Antiochus fills the cup of iniquity to overflowing. The downward movement is symbolised by the gold of Babylon, succeeded by the silver of Media, this by the bronze of Persia, the lowest stage being indicated by the mingled iron and clay in Greece. Not only is the divine plan fully determined upon; the deeds of men and the crimes of the nations are written down in a heavenly record. In the judgment which is about to be held these records will testify against the accused (Daniel 7 : 10). All this is made to bear upon the situation of the persecuted Jews by the stories of deliverance in which the divine power comes directly into operation. Daniel and his friends, though living at the court of a heathen king, are model Jews. They will not eat of the king's dainties for fear of being defiled; they will not bow to the image set up by him, though threatened with the most cruel of deaths. The deliverance of the three, the protection of Daniel in the lions' den, impresses even the heathen monarchs with the uniqueness of Israel's God, and they give solemn testimony to this effect. Equally convincing is the anecdote of Nebuchadrezzar's madness, followed by his restoration and a renewed testimony to the God of the Jews. What tradition may have furnished the basis on which these stories are built can no longer be discovered. That neither they nor the story of Belshazzar's feast are history ought to be self-evident. Nebuchadrezzar, or Belshazzar, or Darius, the king who claims divine honours for himself, who insults the God of heaven, or who thinks to impose his religion on the Jews, is in each case only Antiochus Epiphanes wearing a mask.

Our author has no confidence in the help of man, and looks for the setting up of the Kingdom of God by a direct act of God himself. In his sketch of the fortunes of the Syrian and Egyptian kingdoms he unhesitatingly condemns those of his people who attempt to bring in the fulfilment of prophecy by human effort (11 : 14). When he speaks of the Maccabean successes he says only that they are helped with a little help, and he shows his distrust of the movement of Judas and his brothers by saying that many join themselves to them by flatteries (11 : 34). The whole duty of the faithful according to him—and that he represented a considerable party among the Jews must be clear to one who follows the course of history—was to wait in resignation for the divine intervention. But the very point of his writing was to express the conviction that this intervention was just at hand. The kingdoms of the world have had their day; they reached the extremity of guilt when Antiochus erected the altar or statue of a Greek god in the temple. This is the abomination that makes desolate, an insult to the divine majesty so gross that it must bring down the divine vengeance. In various ways the sweeping nature of this vengeance is set forth. In the case of the image which represents the successive world-powers we read that the gold, the silver, the bronze, the iron, and the clay are ground to dust and blown away, and the stone which represents the Kingdom of God becomes a great mountain, filling the whole earth (2 : 35). On the other hand, the parallel vision of the beasts seems to intimate that the nations will continue to exist (though without power), at least for a time (7 : 11 *f.*). The most impressive of the visions shows us the judgment going on: After the blasphemies of the eleventh horn "the thrones were placed and the Ancient of Days did sit; his raiment was white as snow, and the hair of his head like wool; his throne was fiery flames, and the wheels thereof were burning fire; a fiery stream issued and came forth from before him;

thousands of thousands ministered to him, and ten thousand times ten thousand stood before him; the judgment was set and the books were opened. I beheld at that time because of the words which the horn had spoken, even till the beast was slain and its body destroyed, and it was given to be burned with fire. . . . I saw in the night vision and behold there came with the clouds of heaven one like a man, and he came even to the Ancient of Days and they brought him near to him. And there was given him glory and dominion and a kingdom, that all the nations should serve him; his dominion is an everlasting dominion which shall not pass away" (7 : 9–14).

There has been much discussion of the question whether this passage refers to an individual Messiah. The true interpretation seems to be that the one *like a man*[1] is contrasted with the beasts which have appeared in the vision, and as they symbolise kingdoms, so he represents a kingdom. This is demonstrated by the author's own interpretation of the vision, in which he says that the kingdom and greatness of the kingdoms under the whole heaven shall be given (not to the Messiah, the son of David, but) to the *people* of the saints of the Most High: "His kingdom is an everlasting kingdom, and all dominions shall obey and serve him" (7 : 27; note the whole passage, vss. 21–27). The author, we must conclude, had no interest in a personal Messiah. His ideal was that Israel as a sacred people should become the chief nation of the world, to whom all others should be subject. They would dwell at Jerusalem with their God as their ruler, and his high priest as the chief executive. Nowhere in the book of Daniel is there any intimation of a Messianic king, the son of David. The only thing which seems at first sight to militate against the collective interpretation of the phrase "one like a man" is the fact that he is represented as coming on the clouds of heaven. But all that the author intended

[1] As has frequently been pointed out, the Aramaic phrase "like a son of man" means simply *like a man*. Whether Son of Man was later a Messianic title is another question.

to express is that Israel, as the people of Yahweh, had a heavenly origin. It was kept in the special care of God until such time as he should see fit to bring it to its own.

It has already been said that the conception of prophecy held by the apocalyptic writers is that it foretells the course of history. From the books of the prophets it ought to be possible, therefore, to calculate the time of the end. But in the older books there is only one passage which seems to give an exact date. This is Jeremiah's prediction that the captivity would last seventy years. The non-fulfilment was evident to the author of Daniel, because in his view the captivity had lasted until his own time. His conclusion was, not that Jeremiah was mistaken—this would, in fact, be unthinkable—but that the prediction had not been understood. Where the literal sense of a sacred book is unacceptable, recourse is had to allegory. The author, in endeavouring to understand Jeremiah, conceived the theory that the seventy years were not literal years, but mystical years. With a somewhat inexact knowledge of chronology he had no difficulty in making out that about seventy periods of seven years each had elapsed between the fall of Jerusalem and his own time. Jeremiah's seventy years then meant these seventy year-weeks. The importance of the number seven in Hebrew chronology would seem to him to confirm this interpretation.

Our author puts this interpretation into the mouth of the angel who shows Daniel the course of future history. The four hundred and ninety years from 586 B. C. he divides into three periods. First comes a jubilee period of seven times seven years from the fall of Jerusalem to the time of Joshua the high priest, whom he calls characteristically the anointed prince. There follows a period of sixty-two weeks of years during which Jerusalem is inhabited but is of no great importance. Then comes the final period of seven years (one week) which will be a time of trouble—the birth pangs of the kingdom. This begins with the cutting off of the anointed prince, that is, with the deposition of Onias the high priest (9 : 26).[1] This is followed by the desecration of city and temple and this by the crowning calamity, the arrest of the daily offering. The author indicates that this cessation of the offerings will last through one thousand one hundred and fifty days, or about three years and a half (*cf.* 12 : 7). His last eventful week, therefore, is divided into two parts; the first half has passed, the second is still in the future. He anticipates that in this remaining half Antiochus will make a final expedition against the Holy Land and will be cut off by an act of God. In the general overturning of the nations Michael will interfere to protect the faithful Jews. After three years and a half of wars and tumults those martyrs who testified on behalf of the true religion will be raised from the dead, as will the renegades who were not punished for their treason. This is in order that the one group may take part in the Messianic kingdom, while the other will receive just punishment for their deeds (shame and everlasting contempt, 12 : 1 *f.*).

The endeavour to find in this book foreshadowings of the Christ of the Church, or even predictions of the course of events for centuries of Christian history, need not be dwelt upon here. They belong in a history of biblical exposition. All that we need to note is that the author of Daniel was firmly convinced that the great event of the world's history, the termination of the world's history, in fact, and the opening of a new period, was three years and a half away from the date of his writing. In this he was, of course, mistaken, as every one has been mistaken who thought he knew the time of the Messiah's coming or of the Parousia of the Christ. Within the period he had set he must have become convinced of this, unless, indeed, he suffered martyrdom with the little band of faithful observers of the Law for whom he wrote. What concerns us here is the religious faith which found such vivid expression in the book. The book attests first of all the prominence which the angels had taken in the belief of the

[1] The verse does not necessarily mean that Onias was murdered, but that there was no longer a legitimate high priest.

Jews. Angels were not altogether absent from earlier documents; their appearance in Zechariah's visions has already been noticed. But now for the first time we learn their names. Gabriel and Michael appear from now on as friends and defenders of true believers, first among the Jews and then in the Church. It is no longer Yahweh himself who speaks to the prophet—Gabriel brings the word. The defence of Israel against its enemies is committed to Michael. The throne of Yahweh is surrounded by thousands upon thousands of such ministers (7 : 9 *f.*).

In the heavenly hosts some are hostile to Israel. When Gabriel is sent to comfort Daniel by a revelation he is confronted by the guardian angel of the kingdom of Persia who succeeds in detaining him three weeks. The issue would have been doubtful had not Michael come to Gabriel's help (10 : 13). Gabriel expects the battle to be renewed after his errand to Daniel has been accomplished and anticipates that the angel of Greece will reinforce the Persian (vs. 20). The heavenly government, in this conception of it, simply reflects the loose organisation of Asiatic empires, where the satraps are often at war with each other. The theory that each human nationality has its heavenly satrap, who shares the predilections and animosities of his clients, was welcome to the Jews of this age, for it allowed them to account for the evil in the world by laying the blame on seditious angels. These angels are not yet the evil spirits who have rebelled against God and organised a kingdom hostile to his, but they are on the way to it. That, in fact, the old heathen gods survive in these patron angels of the nations seems evident. A poem now incorporated in the book of Deuteronomy asserts that Yahweh himself apportioned the nations to the Sons of God, that is, to the angels, reserving Israel for himself (Deut. 32 : 8, emended text).

In the minor apocalypse which we discussed in the early part of this chapter we noticed a statement that the dead are to be raised. The book of Daniel reveals the way in which this doctrine came to have importance in the thought of the Maccabean sufferers. In earlier times the Hebrews had no definite belief in a future life. Sheol (Hades is the Greek equivalent) was conceived as a place in which there is no joy and no life unless a shadowy existence away from God and the light of day may be called life. It is pictured as an uncanny monster which opens its jaws and swallows men. Sometimes men and tents descend into it by the opening of a chasm in the earth (Num. 16 : 25–34). Isaiah threatens the nations: "Sheol will stretch wide its jaws and open its mouth without measure, and their glory and their multitude and their pomp shall descend into it" (Isaiah 5 : 14). The inhabitants of this region are sometimes thought of as asleep: "Till the heavens are no more they wake not" (Job 14 : 12); but on occasion they may be roused so as to notice what is going on. When the king of Babylon goes to the underworld Sheol itself stirs up the shades to look upon the newcomer, and they feel the shock of surprise that the mighty ruler of an empire is reduced to a mere shadow like themselves (Isaiah 14 : 9*f.*). But this does not imply that these souls, if we may call them by so definite a name, had any real life. Certainly there was no theory of reward and punishment in Sheol. Speculation on this subject was, in fact, discouraged by the Jewish religion because the worship of the manes was felt to be contrary to the will of Yahweh.

Moreover, the early documents—even down to the time when the book of Job was written—denied the possibility of any return from the region of the dead. But the book of Daniel expressly affirms that at the time of the end many of them that sleep in the dust of the earth shall awake, some to everlasting life and some to shame and everlasting contempt (Daniel 12 : 2). This partial resurrection was inferred by a logical necessity from the religious belief of the times. The most painful thought to those who witnessed the persecutions of Antiochus was that the martyrs who were faithful even unto death would not share the glory of the Messianic kingdom. That kingdom was not located in Sheol; it was not located in heaven; it was to be on a renewed and purified earth. If the martyrs were to have their reward they must be raised from the dead and allowed to share in the glories of the kingdom. Conversely, the sinners—especially the renegade Jews who had conformed to the impious command of the persecutor, perhaps had turned informers against their brethren—had not had their punishment, for they had often gone down to the grave full of riches and honours. If justice were to be done, these also must be raised to suffer the shame which was their portion. Their punishment, like the reward of the righteous, is to take place in Jerusalem. At the end of the book of Isaiah we read that the men who come to Jerusalem to worship shall look upon the dead bodies of those who have transgressed: "For their worm shall not die neither shall their fire be quenched, and they shall be an abhorring unto all flesh" (Isaiah 66 : 24). The spot in the vicinity of Jerusalem where the sinners shall thus suffer shame is the notorious Valley of Hinnom the scene of earlier idolatrous rites. Its name (Gehenna) passed over into later Jewish literature as that of the place of torment for evil angels as well as for evil men. The prominence of this belief in Christian and Moslem systems is well known.

The book of Daniel, as has already been intimated, is an example of a kind of literature which flourished in the second and first centuries of our era and even later. It is the product of the puritan party, so often opposed, scorned, and oppressed by the wicked or careless many. Even after the persecution of Antiochus ceased this party remained depressed and pessimistic. The Maccabean princes were far from being the nursing fathers of the Church which they ought to have been according to the ideas of these Chasidim. The conflicts which arose in the time of John Hyrcanus between the Pharisees (as we may now call the puritans) and the Sadducees (adherents of the ruling house) show how impossible it is for a civil administration to live up to the demands of a rigid ritual law. From this time on, therefore, we find a sharp distinction drawn by all Jewish writers between the righteous and the wicked. This distinction is carried back to the beginning of history, and ancient worthies are introduced to us to make clear the eternal conflict between the two parties. Of these the favourite seems to be Enoch. This antediluvian patriarch was the appropriate teacher of religious lessons, for, according to tradition, he had been translated to the presence of God where he had opportunity to learn heavenly wisdom. The body of literature which gathered about his name made him the founder of astronomy and the regulator of the calendar. The author who thus presents him to us has a religious interest in his stringent demand for a Jewish reckoning of the year. The Sabbaths and festivals are celebrated in heaven as well as on earth, and the days should correspond. If, however, a miscalculation be made in the calendar, men will be found observing days which are not truly sacred and desecrating those which God has set apart as holy. Mohammed was moved by a similar belief when he forbade intercalation. This point of view is fully stated in the book of Jubilees (Jubilees 6 : 30–32).[1]

Although the Enoch literature is the most important that has come down to us in this class, we know that books were published under the names of Noah, Moses, Baruch, Ezra, and others. Complete discussion of them would take a volume. Here we can notice only their leading ideas. The one most prominent is the one already indicated in Daniel, that is, the course of history is divinely foreordained so that it is possible to calculate the time of the end. The plan of the ages is set down on heavenly tablets, and chosen men are permitted to see it. Enoch saw all that was on the heavenly tablets, considered and read the book concerning the deeds of men, all the children of flesh down to the latest generation.[2] The numbers which are most prominent in these schemes are seven and four. Seven is distinctively

[1] The obstinacy of the author of Enoch in insisting on a year of 364 days (Enoch 82; *cf.* Secrets of Enoch, 48, and the recently discovered fragments published by Schechter) may be based on the biblical account of the Deluge which makes a solar year ten days longer than twelve lunations.

[2] Enoch 81, *cf.* Jubilees 1 : 29, where the angel of the Presence takes the tables of the divisions of the years and shows them to Moses.

the sacred number of the Hebrews, so its dominance does not surprise us. Four was suggested to the author of Daniel by the four world empires which he found in history, though it is possible that some early mythological scheme of four world periods influenced his thinking. An echo of Daniel's scheme is found in Enoch, where the seventy shepherds of the nations are divided into four groups (Enoch 89 *f.*). In Enoch we find, however, the statement that there will be seven weeks in the history of the world, and that the Messianic time will come at the end of the seventh (Enoch 93). Other documents seem to have computed twelve periods (Ap. Baruch 56 *ff.*).

All this literature is pessimistic, that is, it regards the present age as one of degeneracy, and looks for no relief until God shall violently reverse the present order and bring in a new age. In the more advanced of the documents the degeneracy is traced to the wickedness of the angels. Jubilees tells us that the angelic ministers were created on the first day of the creative week. They were placed in charge of the movements of the planets, the rains, the winds, and the storms. They are now divided into good and bad. They are of different ranks, the highest being the two, or four, or six archangels. Precedents may be found in Persian or Babylonian mythology. The activity of these beneficent angels is for the good of mankind. They appear in battle on the side of the Jews (II Mac. 10 : 29). They teach Enoch astronomy and the art of writing.

On the other hand, the evil angels are active in corrupting mankind. Their fall is traced to their love for mortal women, the account of which is given in the book of Genesis. This is elaborated so that we learn the number of the rebels to be two hundred. Their leader is named Shemaiah. They came down to earth in the days of Jared (Descent), and the place of their conspiracy was Mount Hermon, an ancient heathen sanctuary as the name indicates. The names of the twenty leaders are recited for us, and in some passages their chief is identified with Azazel, the desert demon who plays a part in the ritual of the Day of Atonement (Enoch 9 : 6; 10 : 4). They taught their wives magic and astrology (Enoch 7 *f.*), showed men how to make weapons for each other's destruction, and taught women the use of cosmetics and jewelry. Although some of them are confined under the earth until the day of final judgment, some of them are allowed to roam about and seduce men to idolatry and other sins (Jubilees 10 : 1–12).

Men who are puzzled to account for the existence of moral evil in a world created good find a certain relief in thus laying the blame upon superhuman free agents. The author of Chronicles had not hesitated to make Satan the inciter to sin, where the older writer had attributed the suggestion to Yahweh himself. The literature now before us advances further in the same line. It is the evil one who tries to kill Moses on his return from Midian, and it is he who suggests that Abraham's faith be tried by the command to sacrifice Isaac (Jubilees 48: 2; 17: 16). Ashmodeus (the name is evidently borrowed from Persia) is in love with a Jewish maiden and strangles her successive bridegrooms to the number of seven (Tobit 6 : 14). He is finally driven away by the help of Raphael. It is only a short step to the theory that each pious Jew has a guardian angel in constant attendance upon him (Tobit 5 : 22).

Yet, when all is said, the present government of the world is largely in the hands of the evil powers. The end so ardently longed for by the righteous will be ushered in by a judgment in which these world rulers will be called to account. Enoch assures us that the Almighty will come down upon Mount Sinai with the myriads of his angels and there chastise the wicked for all their ungodly deeds (Enoch 1 : 4–9). Elsewhere the scene is laid in the Holy Land or, specifically, in Jerusalem (47–53). The precedent has been set by Joel, but now it is not the nations of earth only that are called to the bar. The Lord of the sheep (Israel) has the recording angel bring the book in which he has entered the evil deeds of the angel shepherds (90 : 20), or the judgment begins with the angels who sinned in the antediluvian time, then deals with the oppressive shepherds, condemns next the renegade Israelites, and finally justifies those who have observed the Law. After this the old temple is taken away, a new one is brought, and the Messiah is born (90 : 28–38).

The variety of details shows the composite nature of this literature. The general scheme, however, is the same: The end of the present state of things is not far away, and the kingdom of God is about to be set up. But whether it will simply renew the glories of Solomon, whether it will be supersensible, whether it will be located in Palestine or in one of the seven heavens—on these points we find a variety of views. Daniel's hope of a resurrection for the exemplary righteous, especially for those who have been martyred for the faith, is improved upon until we get a general resurrection. The sufferers of the Maccabean age express their confidence that they will be raised (IV Mac. 9 : 8*f.*), and one writer goes so far as to say that Judas Maccabeus was moved by his belief in a resurrection to offer a sin-offering for those who had died in their defilement (II Mac. 12 : 43–45).

The expectation thus set forth in varying forms may be called in the general sense Messianic, but the individual Messiah is not a constant figure in the picture. Where he does appear it is not always clear whether he is thought to be transcendent, a ruler for eternity or for a thousand years, or whether the perpetuity of the dynasty in successive members is intended. To make room for his reign of a thousand years two resurrections are sometimes posited, one at the beginning of the Messianic age, the portion of exemplary Jews, the other at the end of the period, when the whole of mankind will be revived for the final judgment. In one passage Enoch asserts that at the end of the seventh week of the world's history the righteous will rise, and during the eighth week they will execute judgment on the sinners. After this, in the tenth week, will be the general judgment, when: "He will execute judgment on the angels and the first heaven will depart, and a new heaven will appear, and all the powers of heaven will shine sevenfold for evermore, and after that there will be many weeks without number in goodness and righteousness, and sin will be no more mentioned" (Enoch 91 : 10–17; *cf.* Jubilees 21 : 24).

The Son of Man who appears in the book of Daniel is a symbolic figure representative of the people of Israel. The writer thought of the coming commonwealth as a theocracy without human king. A part of the Enoch literature takes the same view. But a part of it looks for a personal Messiah, king of Israel and vicegerent of Yahweh. Enoch borrows from Daniel the figure of the Son of Man and describes him: "With the Ancient of Days was another being whose countenance had the appearance of a man and his face was full of graciousness like one of the holy angels. And I asked the angel who went with me concerning that son of man who he was and why he went with the Ancient of Days; and he answered me and said: This is the Son of Man who has righteousness, with whom dwells righteousness, and who reveals all the treasures of that which is hidden, because the Lord of Spirits has chosen him, and his lot before the Lord of Spirits will surpass everything in uprightness forever." There follows a promise that the Son of Man shall overcome all the kings of the earth who oppose themselves to him (Enoch 46). The language might be construed in consistency with the vision of Daniel, where the Son of Man stands for the people, but when the next chapter goes on to say that the prayer of the righteous ascends before the Lord of Spirits in his days (days of the Son of Man) it seems clear that the Son of Man is not himself the personified righteous. Here, therefore, we have the fully developed personal Messiah, who will come to judge the earth. He is, moreover, a superhuman being, one whose name was named before the Lord of Spirits, before the sun and the constellations and the stars were created: "For this reason was he chosen and hidden before him before the creation of the world, and from eternity" (48 : 1–6). Enoch saw the Elect One of righteousness and faith, and how righteousness shall prevail in his days, and the righteous shall be without number before him forever. "And I saw his dwelling place under the wings of the Lord of Spirits, and all the righteous are before him beautifully resplendent as lights of fire" (39 : 6 *f.*). Elsewhere the Elect One is described sitting on a throne and so dwelling in the midst of the righteous (48 : 3–5). He is said to judge Azazel and the wicked angels (55 : 4), and several passages might be quoted to show his office as judge in heaven.

We have before us, then, the fully developed theory that the Messiah who is to rule the coming kingdom is a superhuman person, pre-existent in heaven and only waiting for the time appointed to come from heaven and take the throne. He was created before the stars, but is kept hidden until the day of judgment. This is not so violent a hypothesis as we are at first inclined to think it. If Enoch, the antediluvian patriarch, sees all these things in vision, they must have some sort of existence in his time before they actually become real in the course of history. It is not probable that the writers asked themselves whether this was a real or an ideal pre-existence. In the later Jewish conception many things existed from eternity, or at least from the creation, which were revealed in time—the Law, for example. The book called the Secrets of Enoch declares that all souls were created in the beginning before the foundation of the world (Secrets of Enoch 23). The hypothesis of pre-existence enables the author of Enoch to explain the vision of Daniel where the Son of Man comes on the clouds of heaven. To the oppressed people of God the thought of an angelic Messiah would be most welcome. His superhuman dignity would be a guarantee of power and permanency for his reign.

While this literature shows that the Messianic hope was cherished by a large section of the Jewish people in this period, it also shows how far the hope was from being consistent. The future glory is to be manifested in Jerusalem, but Jerusalem may be either on earth or in heaven; it may be a new Jerusalem, a new creation, or it may be something already existing in heaven, shown to Adam, to Abraham, or to Moses. The home of the saints may be in the paradise in which Adam first dwelt, and which is either in one of the heavens or on the earth, in the far east or in the far west; or, on the other hand, the tree of life, the central object of that paradise, may be transplanted to Jerusalem (Enoch 24, 25, and 32). The place of punishment is to be below the earth and its entrance is the ill-omened Valley of Hinnom. Located thus, just under the walls of Jerusalem, it will contribute to the pleasures of the righteous, since they will be able to contrast their own happy state with that of the damned (Enoch 27, 62 : 12; *cf.* Isaiah 66 : 24). Yet the underworld is also conceived as a temporary paradise, one division of it being the place where the souls of the righteous are reserved until the resurrection. According to one view, when the righteous are raised the wicked will simply be left in this Hades. More general was the idea of a judgment for all men. The Messianic time is in some cases thought to last only a thousand years, during which the righteous will enjoy material good, will possess land of great fruitfulness, will sow seed that will increase a thousandfold, and will beget a thousand children (Enoch 10 : 17–22). The two monsters, behemoth and leviathan, will be slain and given to the righteous for food, the earth will bring forth a thousandfold, each vine will have a thousand branches, each branch will have a thousand clusters, each cluster a thousand grapes, each grape will yield a cor of wine, and the manna will again fall from heaven so that no one need hunger (Apocalypse of Baruch 29). Similar millennial dreams were cherished in the Church, as we well know. They show the power which the apocalypses exercised over the minds of those who sighed for the redemption of Israel.

CHAPTER XIX

THE TREASURE OF THE HUMBLE

By common consent the book of Psalms represents the culmination of Israelitic religion. This is attested by the New Testament and by the place which the book has taken and still holds in the Christian Church. It is the culmination not only in tone but also in time, being one of the latest, if not the latest, of the Old Testament books. The tradition which ascribes, or which seems to ascribe, a large number of the poems to David as author is now generally given up. It is as certain as anything can be that the collection contains Maccabean compositions,[1] and the final redaction of the book took place not long before the beginning of our era. This being so, it is not probable that any portion of it can be older than the Exile, and for our purpose it is safest to see in it the expression of Jewish piety of the latest period. That the book as we have it is made up from a variety of sources is evident on the surface. Poems similar in tone to the Psalms are found in some of the prophetic books and must be judged to be late insertions in those books.[2]

The Psalter is a book of devotion. It is often called the hymn-book of the second temple, but this is somewhat misleading. Some parts of it seem to have been contributed by the musical guilds (those ascribed to the sons of Korah, to Asaph, or Jeduthun), and the ascriptions of praise which fill the last section of the book are appropriate for the public service. But these make up only a fraction of the

[1] The most convincing example is Psalm 74.

[2] Examples are Isaiah 12 and 25 : 1–5, the psalm of Habakkuk, already discussed, and several passages in Chronicles.

book. Many of the poems are distinctly petitions of the individual, and we must think of the book as one of those compendia of prayers such as our fathers often used for their private devotions. One of the most widely used of the Psalms ends with the petition: "Let the words of my mouth and the meditation of my heart be acceptable in thy sight, Yahweh my Rock and my Redeemer" (19 : 15). The sentence indicates that the preceding verses had been the murmured meditation of the reader in the time set apart for prayer. We see also that the long panegyric of the Law (Psalm 119) can never have been a part of the temple liturgy, and must have been composed as an alphabet of loyalty by a devotee of Israel's legal system. The believer was accustomed to engage in prayer three times a day, as one of the poems tells us (55 : 18), and the use of a written guide to thought by those who felt unable to give extemporary expression to their aspirations cannot surprise us.

Although the collection had no direct connection with the temple service, there is no reason to doubt that it was used in the synagogues. The synagogue was originally the school in which the people were taught the Law. But people who gathered for instruction in religion were led to engage in common prayer, especially at times when the temple was inaccessible. The Psalms being expressions of the desires, beliefs, perplexities, and aspirations of the pious naturally suggested themselves as the appropriate formulæ for such common worship. The much-debated question of the *ego* of the Psalter is answered by this reflection. The most original of the Psalms are the expression of individual experience and individual emotion. But the communion of saints is communion in just these experiences. Hence came the adoption of these compositions for the public service. Then came the time when the more gifted members of the community, conscious of the common faith, ventured to compose psalms which should utter the faith, joy, or contrition which were shared by all. It is this which gives the book its value; it is the expression of a piety which was shared by a considerable number of men whose situation was the same.

The majority of the Psalms are not didactic, though there are a few which may be so classed. The great majority are expressions of the religious feeling. They are "contemplative or intuitive, using the religious imagination or fancy rather than the logical faculty and the reasoning powers."[1] But since the feelings expressed imply certain beliefs we have no difficulty in ascertaining, at least in outline, the theology of the book. First of all, of course, Yahweh God of Israel is the God of the universe and the only God. For the most part this is so thoroughly assumed that the gods of the nations are not alluded to at all. Where reference is made to them it is to emphasise their impotence. It is, indeed, said that all the gods cast themselves down before him (97 : 7), but the reference may be to the angelic satraps of which we had evidence in the book of Daniel. The assurance that the gods of the nations are mere silver and gold, the work of men's hands, reads like an echo of Deutero-Isaiah (115 : 3–7). Yet, that the believer was tempted at times to pay some sort of reverence to these other alleged divinities is indicated by the energetic rejection of such a thought occasionally expressed (16 : 1–4).

It is the believer's comfort that Yahweh is all-powerful: "Our God is in the heavens; he has done whatever he pleased" (115 : 3). A well-known poem emphasises the omnipresence as well as the omnipotence of Yahweh: "If I ascend to heaven thou art there; if I make my bed in Sheol thou art there; if I take the wings of the dawn and alight in the uttermost part of the sea, even there would thy hand lead me and thy right hand hold me" (139 : 7–10). The older theology had not risen to the thought that Yahweh was present in the dark realms of the dead; even some of the Psalmists think that the shades of the departed are no longer before him; but our author reserves nothing from the divine omniscience.

[1] Briggs, *Commentary on the Psalms* (International Critical Commentary), I, p. xcvi.

The thought of the majesty of Yahweh inspires other singers, and the glory of his work in creating and sustaining the world of nature is a frequent topic. I need only allude to the familiar nineteenth and the even more attractive one hundred and fourth. Briefer lyrics call upon all nature to join in praise of the Creator—mountains and all hills, fruit-trees and all cedars, beasts wild and tame, creeping things and winged birds (148). The thunder-storm is special evidence of the divine power, but the ordinary and beneficent processes of the seasons are also ascribed to him: "He crowns the year with his goodness and his paths drop fatness" (65 : 9–12).

Though Yahweh is God of the whole earth, yet he is in special relations with Israel: "Happy the people whose God is Yahweh, the people he has chosen for himself as his heritage" (33 : 12). It is for the sake of Israel that he governs the world. The history of early times is recited to prove the election of this people. And in the favourable events of the present time the believer recognises his merciful intervention: "Thou hast pleaded my right and my cause; hast sat on the throne a righteous judge; thou didst threaten the heathen, destroyedst the wicked, didst blot out their name for ever and ever" (9 : 4 *f.*). In present distress the contrast between the earlier presence of Yahweh with his people and the present apparent desertion is affectingly dwelt upon (44). This contrast was a frequent trial to the believer, but for the most part faith was able to triumph over depression and comfort itself with the thought that Yahweh will yet protect his own. His attributes are, in fact, kindness, fidelity, and justice: "Thy kindness reaches up to the firmament, thy faithfulness to the heavens; thy righteousness is like the mountains of God, thy judgments like the great deep" (36 : 5 *f.*; *cf.* 33 : 1–10). Gratitude for present mercies has furnished the form of thanksgiving for all generations of believers (103). Yahweh is thought to reside in Jerusalem and also in heaven. From his throne above he is able to observe all the actions of men. Here he sits as judge, destroys the sinners, but delivers those who fear him (9 : 8 *f.*;

33 : 13, 52). His judgment is not based on actions alone; he tries heart and reins (7 : 10). He hates the doers of iniquity; the arrogant dare not appear before him; he abhors men of blood and deceit (5 : 4–6).

The religion of these writers, then, may be defined as faith in a faithful God. When faint-hearted friends exhort the believer to flee as a bird to the mountains, he replies that his trust is in Yahweh, who dwells in Jerusalem and who holds the righteous dear (11 : 1, 5). In the midst of foes when many say that there is no help for him in God the believer sleeps peacefully because Yahweh sustains him (3 : 6; 4 : 8*f.*) The fullest expression is in the Christian as well as Jewish classic (91), where the angels guard the righteous so that his foot does not slip. Even those Psalms which were written in deep despondency usually end with an expression of trust. It is the inextinguishable conviction of the authors that Yahweh is the God of the oppressed: "He does not forget the cry of the humble; for the groaning of the poor he will arise and put him out of danger" (12 : 6*f.; cf.* 9 : 10–13). He is father of the fatherless and judge of the widow (68 : 6). He is near the broken-hearted (34 : 19). All conceivable figures of speech are used to express this faith: "Yahweh is a rock, a deliverer, a fortress, a strong tower, a shield, a horn of victory, a stronghold" (18 : 2). He is the light and salvation of the faithful so that they will not fear though the earth be removed. The faithful are those who wait upon Yahweh, who look to him as servants look to the hand of the master (123). On occasion of victory vouchsafed to the Jewish arms this faith rises to joyous triumph (46), and in quiet times it expresses itself in thanksgiving and contentment (103). The believer who is exiled from the temple is consumed by thirst for the presence of Yahweh like the thirst of the hart in times of drought (42). The joy of religion leads men to shout aloud in praise of Yahweh, and even rises to the affirmation that he has not dealt with any nation as he has dealt with Israel. It would be a mistake to interpret all these affirmations as expressions of national feeling.

The personal note comes out very clearly in those Psalms which appeal to Yahweh as shepherd, guide, or host, and which commit the believer's life and lot to him (23, 31, 16).

This joy in the Lord is evidence that legalism is not inconsistent with deep and sincere piety. For it is clear that the Psalmists are wholly devoted to the Mosaic Law as the expressed will of God and the binding rule of life for man. The righteous man is the one who studies day and night in the Law (1 : 2). The perfection of Yahweh's work in nature is parallel to the perfection of his revelation in the Law (19).[1] One writer cannot say enough in praise of the testimonies, statutes, precepts, commandments, and judgments of Yahweh (119). In order to induce the present generation to obey the Tora the story of the wilderness wandering is rehearsed (78 and elsewhere). Prominence is given to the ethical precepts, but the ritual is prized as well. The man who washes his hands in innocency does it that he may go about the altar in the sacrificial procession. The not infrequent exhortation to pay one's vows or to sacrifice sacrifices of righteousness is to be taken literally. Religion includes affection for the temple. The grief of the exile is made poignant by the recollection of the time when he was privileged to take part in the festival procession (42 : 5). Blessed is the man who dwells in the temple (65 : 5) even as a doorkeeper (84 : 11). Jerusalem partakes of this affection because it is the residence of the great king, that is, of Yahweh himself, and the Psalmist is confident that the holy city is established forever (48, also 27 : 4–6, and elsewhere).

This distinctly Jewish colouring is apparently contradicted by some passages which declare that God does not require sacrifice (40), and one writer thinks it necessary to confute the popular notion that Yahweh eats the flesh of bulls and drinks the blood of goats (50). These expressions are in part echoes of the prophetic opposition to the ritual; in part they indicate that religion is more spiritual than in the days

[1] Whether, in fact, the two parts of this Psalm are by the same author does not affect our estimate.

when the ritual was all in all. The believer who is remote from the temple finds in prayer a substitute for sacrifice, and is conscious that his communion with God is real though without the customary ritual accompaniment. The writers, however, do not intend to do away with sacrifice, for almost in the same breath in which they say that sacrifice is not required they pray that the offerings may be regularly brought (50 : 23; 51: 21; 66 : 13–15). The fact is that the worshippers found satisfaction in the forms handed down by tradition, yet have come to the consciousness that sacrifice without obedience is worthless. Obedience to the Law, including its ritual requirements, is to them the whole duty of man.

Yet, undoubtedly, ethical precepts take a large place in the thoughts of these writers. Worship is unacceptable if offered by the unrighteous. He who is to be Yahweh's guest on the temple mount must have clean hands and a pure heart, must walk in uprightness and do righteousness, must speak truth in his heart, not slander nor defraud nor take usury; must honour the pious and take no false oath (15). This decalogue almost deserves a place beside the other one with which we are familiar. The profession of a righteous man is: "I have followed Yahweh's paths and have not wickedly departed from my God; ever present to me are all his decrees, his precepts I keep ever in mind" (18 : 22). The man called to public office resolves not to set any base thing before his eyes, and adds: "Whoso privily slandereth his neighbor him will I destroy; him that has a high look and a proud heart will I not suffer; my eyes shall be upon the faithful of the land that they may dwell with me, he that walks in a perfect way shall minister unto me" (101: 3–6).

The character of the righteous is brought out by its contrast with that of the opposite party, and we are scarcely ever allowed to forget that the wicked were distinctly in evidence in the community in which these poems took shape. The conditions in Jerusalem (for most of the Psalms seem to have been composed in the sacred city) appear, in fact, to have been anything but ideal. The opposition of parties reaches a frightful pitch in some Psalms. The city is described as full of strife, violence, oppression, and guile. This comes not from the heathen, which might be borne; it is from men allied by blood and ostensibly by religion with the complainant: "Smoother than butter is his mouth, but his heart is war; more glib than oil are his words, yet they are drawn swords" (55 : 22). Those imprecations in some of the Psalms, which have given so much trouble to apologetic expositors, are evidence of the same state of feeling.[1] No doubt the writers were confident that their cause was the cause of God and that they were justified in hating them that hate Yahweh. The men so described were, moreover, apparently morally defective. They are accused of deceit; they dig a pit for the righteous or hide a snare to catch him, that they may take the poor in their net; they lurk by the way like a lion (52 : 3–6; 5 : 9–11). The crowning evidence of their depravity is that they do not believe in God (14). This may not mean a theoretical atheism, which was always foreign to the thought of the Jew. It means rather that these evil men did not believe in Yahweh's active government of the world. They do not consider the works of Yahweh; they say: "He does not see, he hides his face" (10 : 4 and 11).

The righteous poor, oppressed by the unscrupulous rich, here make their voice of protest heard. They characterise themselves as the humble, the contrite, the needy, while the opposition is made up of the proud, the arrogant, the scoffers. The comfort of the believer is the thought that Yahweh will judge the wicked: "His eyes behold, his eyelids try, the sons of men; he will recompense the righteous, but on the wicked he will rain coals of fire and brimstone" (11: 4*f.*; *cf.* 92 : 8). The theory of reward is, therefore, the same that we have met elsewhere, and which gave the author of Job such misgivings. He who desires many days should keep his tongue

[1] For example, 69 : 23–29 and 109. False friends are denounced in 35 : 11*f.* and 41 : 6–11.

from evil and his lips from speaking guile; should turn from evil and do good, seek peace and pursue it (34 : 12–14; 37 : 25). The discordance between the theory and the facts of life does not altogether escape observation, however, and in some cases it calls forth earnest, we might say agonised, protests. Scepticism like that of Koheleth threatened some minds. The observer sees, to be sure, that riches and honours do not save their possessor from the common fate: "Man that is in honour abideth not, he is like the beasts that perish" (49 : 21). But this is an unsatisfactory solution, and the problem still rankles: "Surely in vain have I kept my heart pure and washed my hands in innocency; for all the day long am I plagued, and my chastisement starts afresh every morning" (73 : 13*f.*). This is what one of these tempted ones thinks, though he is able to reassure himself, finding, like the friends of Job, that the feet of the wicked are set on slippery ground and that they will be hurled to ruin in a moment. So another expresses the assurance that the transgressors will be extirpated together, and that the future will bring destruction to the wicked (37).

Under a complicated Law the misfortunes of the believer may in part be accounted for by the hypothesis that they are sent in punishment for unwitting sins. And there is also in the Psalms a lively consciousness that afflictions accomplish the purification of those who are tried by them. But many experiences of life are perplexing, even when all allowance is made for this theory. The prosperity of the wicked contrasted with the misfortunes of the righteous causes despondency, and many of the Psalms strike this note. In time of sickness the believer inquires anxiously for the sin which has brought this upon him. The so-called penitential Psalms seem to have been called out by experiences of this kind: "My wounds are noisome and fester because of my folly; I am sore oppressed and cast down, I go in mourning all the day long; for my loins are full of decay, and there is naught of soundness in my flesh; I am wholly benumbed and sore bruised, I groan louder than the roar of the lion"

(38 : 4–9). There is no reason to suppose that this is a description of anything else than a literal sickness. Confession of sin in such a case is not evidence of any deep depravity from which the sufferer has just awakened; it is rather a logical deduction from the belief that Yahweh punishes in this life. The prayer that one may be kept from secret sin—that is, unwitting violation of the Law—shows the anxiety of conscience produced in sensitive souls by a complicated code. At the same time we must remember that the faith of the sufferer was usually able to triumph over his despondency and find peace in the assurance that God forgives. The blessedness of forgiveness is vividly brought before us by the experience of one who had found relief in confession (32). The classic example (51) shows a deep desire for purity, prays for a clean heart and steadfast spirit, and finds in Yahweh the helper who is able and willing to confer this boon.

On the other hand, the danger of self-righteousness is not remote. The observer of the Law in time of prosperity congratulates himself that he is being rewarded for the cleanness of his hands. A clear conscience boldly invites God to judge him, for he has walked in integrity (26 : 1 *f.*). In some cases it is evident that the speaker who uses these Pharisaic expressions is not an individual, but the community of the faithful. Protestations of fidelity on the part of the company of believers who are conscious of their devotion to Yahweh are less objectionable than they would be in the mouth of a single individual. The most conspicuous example of self-righteousness must apparently be judged from this point of view (18 : 21–25). In the mouth of David this paragraph would be evident hypocrisy or else egregious self-deceit. If, however, it be the boast of the righteous remnant which remained faithful to Yahweh when the whole power of the Syrian kingdom was brought to bear upon them to induce apostasy, we can at least understand it and to some extent justify it. Fully intelligible is the protest of the community in the midst of persecution, setting forth that it has not deserved Yahweh's apparent indifference to their sufferings (44 : 18*f*.).

Undoubtedly the temptation of the believer became most acute in times like this, when the nation seemed threatened with extinction. They protest that it is for Yahweh's sake that they are slain, and yet he seems not to take their part: "For thy sake we are killed all the day long, and are accounted as sheep for the slaughter. Wherefore hidest thou thy face, and forgettest our affliction and our oppression?" (44: 23 and 25.) Most agonising of all was the thought that the temple, Yahweh's own house and the centre around which clung the prayers and aspirations of the faithful, was given over to desecration by the heathen (79). The pious were not only precluded from paying their vows at the sanctuary hallowed by tradition, they were compelled to hear the taunt: "Where now is your God?" A partial solution of the problem was found in the old prophetic declaration that the sinful nation was being punished: Yahweh's wrath has flamed out against an unfaithful Israel, and he has, therefore, given them over into the power of the enemy (74), and goes not forth with their armies (60 : 3–6). But how was it consonant with the justice of God to involve the righteous in the punishment of the wicked, and, in fact, to throw the brunt upon them? For it was evident that it was just the pious who suffered most in these calamities. All that we can say is that these believers never came to a complete solution of the difficulty, but that for the most part they were able to hold on to their faith in spite of it. The complaint that Yahweh stands aloof is in itself an expression of the hope that it will not always be thus. When the enemy says of the pious, "There is no help for him in God," or when faint-hearted friends declare, "The foundations are destroyed, what has the righteous accomplished?" (11 : 4) the believer answers: "Yahweh's throne is in heaven; his eyes behold, his eyelids try, the children of men." In the darkest hour, when a conspiracy of the surrounding nations threatens Jerusalem, the Psalmist is able to reassure himself and his fellow believers that Yahweh will shine forth as the God of vengeance and that he has set his king on Zion, the sacred hill (94; *cf.* 2 and 83).

We have seen that in this period the belief in a future life was struggling for recognition. Koheleth's energetic rejection of it shows that some men were insisting on it, probably as affording a solution for these very problems of the divine government. The majority of the Psalmists seem untouched by this innovation. The affirmations are so clear as to admit of no mistake: "In death we no longer remember thee; in Sheol who praises thee?" (6 : 6.) "In the very day in which a man's breath goes forth he returns to the dust and his thoughts perish" (146 : 4). These two statements from the beginning and the end of the book may be taken as typical of the general belief of the Psalmists. And this general belief explains the despair which some of them express in view of the approach of death. Had they supposed that death was entrance upon a larger life, or that it would introduce them into the immediate presence of God, they would have welcomed instead of dreading it. The thought which threw them into despair was that passing out of this life they would be cut off from the presence of Yahweh and the opportunity of worship: "What profit hast thou in my blood, that I should go down to the pit? Shall the dust praise thee; shall it declare thy fidelity?" (30 : 10.) Even more explicitly: "Wilt thou show wonders to the dead? Shall the shades arise and praise thee? Shall thy lovingkindness be declared in the grave, or thy faithfulness in the abyss?" (88 : 11 *f.*) The problem of the afflictions of the righteous is nowhere solved by the intimation that their reward will be given after death, nor do those who complain of the prosperity of the wicked reassure themselves by the thought that punishment will come in another world. Reflection on the brevity of human life, in contrast with God's eternity, is not relieved by any suspicion that man may have another life awaiting him (90).

As to the prevailing theory, then, there can be no doubt.

A few isolated passages seem, however, to show some hope of future blessedness, though even in these there is some question whether in our interpretation we are not influenced by Christian ideas. The religious realisation of the presence of Yahweh would seem to lead to a hope that this presence would not be withdrawn at death. When the believer asserts that Yahweh is his share and his portion, and adds, "Yahweh I keep ever before me; with him on my right hand I shall not be moved" (16 : 9), he may have hoped that even death would not divide him from the object of his affection. Moreover, occasional intimations that Yahweh's power extends even to Sheol point in the same direction. To all appearance a definite hope for the future is expressed by the writer just quoted, who goes on to say: "Therefore glad is my heart and my liver rejoices, my body also shall rest in peace; for thou wilt not commit me to Sheol, nor suffer thy faithful one to see the pit; thou teachest me the path of life; in thy presence is fulness of joy, fair gifts in thy right hand forever" (16 : 9–11). Yet in spite of appearances it is still possible that the author was thinking of a long and happy life which he hoped to enjoy on the earth and in the presence of Yahweh in Jerusalem. More explicit, however, is the following: "Yet do I stay by thee forever; thou holdest my right hand fast; thou leadest me according to thy counsel and wilt afterward take me in glory. Whom have I in heaven but thee; whom besides thee do I care for on earth? My body and my heart may pass away, but the rock of my heart and my portion evermore is God" (73 : 23–26). It seems clear that the poet expects his nearness to God to endure after his heart and his body have passed away. And although the text is not free from difficulty, we may understand the "taking to glory" of a dwelling with God after death. The verb used is the same which describes Enoch's translation, and it was, of course, universally conceded that the patriarch was taken to the presence of God and not relegated to Sheol. Our author can hardly have expected his case to be as exceptional as that of Enoch, but his faith would not allow him to suppose that even death could separate him from his God. The author of Daniel knows of a resurrection for the righteous few, and our author may have had an esoteric doctrine assuring him that special favour would be granted to the faithful in another life.

The hope most widely cherished by the Jews was that Yahweh would intervene in the affairs of men and set up his kingdom in the near future. This was partly a corollary from the belief in the divine justice: "He who planted the ear shall he not hear? He who formed the eye shall he not see? He that instructs the nations shall he not correct, even he who teaches man knowledge?" (94 : 9*f.*) "Yahweh looks from heaven at the children of men to see whether there is any wise, any that seeks after God" (14 : 2). This is, no doubt, in order to reward and punish men according to their deserts in the ordinary course of providence. But, as we have seen, this ordinary course of providence leaves much to be desired. In the near future there will be a judgment in which the apparent wrongs of the present system will be remedied. God will ascend the throne and judge the peoples (7 : 7*f.*). In that judgment sinners shall not abide, nor evil men in the assembly of the righteous (1: 5). The throne of wickedness, that is, evil-minded kings, cannot stand in that presence (94 : 20). The judgment will reach the heavenly powers, that is, the angels who have been appointed to conduct the affairs of men and who have not carried out the will of Yahweh: "Yahweh stands in the heavenly assembly; he judges in the midst of the gods" (82 : 1). Hence the frequent praise of Yahweh because he is coming to judge the earth: "He will judge the world with righteousness and the nations according to his truth" (96 : 13). That the judgment was actually in process was assumed when victory crowned the Jewish arms. Israel congratulates herself that Yahweh has already subjected the nations to her: "Thou didst save me from the strife of peoples, didst set me as chief over the nations; people that I knew not were subject to me" (18 : 44). What seem to us the insignificant successes of the

Maccabean period were taken as earnest of the good time coming, when Israel was to become chief of the nations of the earth.

In the general sense, then, of hoping for the kingdom of God the Psalmists are inspired by the Messianic faith. Did they also look for a personal Messiah, a king of David's line? The Psalm just quoted ends by describing Yahweh as the one who shows favour to his anointed, to David and his seed forever (18 : 51). The rest of the Psalm, as we have seen, expresses the faith of the pious community, and this makes it probable that the mention of David and his seed is to be interpreted in favour of the restoration of the dynasty, but not as laying any emphasis upon an individual as the future king. The covenant with David, which is rehearsed in another Psalm, is introduced simply to give force to the impassioned protest that Yahweh has not favoured his people as they had a right to expect (89). Even here the anointed one is not an individual but the people (89 : 51). In other passages also the anointed (the word is the same that we translate Messiah) designates the people rather than an individual (28 : 8 and probably 84 : 10).

The passages traditionally interpreted as Messianic, therefore, must be viewed with some reserve. But there are allusions to a king which may have been intended to apply to the ideal king, that is, the Messiah. The best known is the prayer for the king (72), the language of which seems to transcend what might be said of an ordinary ruler. The declaration in another Psalm, however, that the king is both king and priest (though not of the order of Aaron) must be interpreted of one of the Maccabean princes (110). The vivid description of the nations plotting against Yahweh and his anointed (2) refers to some actual event, no longer clear to us. But the king whom Yahweh is here affirmed to have set on Zion, his sacred hill, is apparently the people. The conclusion from an examination of these passages is that while the figure of the Davidic king was present to the minds of some of these writers, he was not the most prominent object of their hope. The coming kingdom of God, that is, the personal reign of Yahweh, was the object of their hope. Already to the eye of faith, this kingship is realising itself: "Thy foes, O Yahweh, are perishing, and all evil-doers are scattered" (92 : 10). Yahweh has assumed the sovereignty; he has clothed himself with majesty (93 : 1). God has taken his seat on his holy throne; men of their own free will from among the gentiles have joined the people of Abraham's God; for to God, our shield, belongs the world; he is exalted on high (47 : 9*f.*). If called forth by the Maccabean victories these expressions are nevertheless evidence of a strong religious faith, which looked for the coming of a universal kingdom, in which all nations will recognise the sovereignty of Yahweh, when "All the nations whom thou hast made shall come and fall down before thee, O Lord, and glorify thy name" (86 : 9). How far this means the genuine conversion of the nations to the religion of Israel is not clear, but it doubtless prepared the way for distinct missionary activity. When one writer declares his readiness to teach sinners the way of God (51 : 14), and another affirms that he has not withheld the knowledge of Yahweh's faithfulness from the great congregation (40 : 10), the reference is only to the instruction of careless Israelites.

One subject of subordinate importance may here be touched upon. This is the doctrine of angels. We have seen how prominent in the thought of this age were these mediators between God and man. It is rather surprising, therefore, to find them so rarely mentioned in the Psalter. The explanation is that for the most part the Psalms were not the work of the writers to whom we owe the apocalypses. That the Psalmists are not hostile to the doctrine of angels is proved, however, by a number of references. In one instance the *sons of God* are called upon to praise Yahweh—a reminiscence of the phrase in Genesis which in this period was understood of the angels (29 : 1). Another passage declares that the angel of Yahweh camps round about those who fear Yahweh and rescues them (34 : 8). More explicit is the promise to the one who abides under the shadow of the Almighty: "He shall give his angels charge over thee to keep thee in all thy ways; they shall bear thee up in their hands lest thou dash thy foot against a stone" (91 : 11*f.*). One notable Psalm takes the position of Daniel, that the heavenly powers appointed to administer affairs among men have been unfaithful to their trust and will be brought into judgment: "In the heavenly assembly Yahweh stands forth and the gods there he arraigns: How long will you judge unjustly, and respect the person of the wicked?" (82 : 1*f.*) There is here a dim remembrance that these angelic shepherds (to use Enoch's term) are the old gods of the heathen once intrusted by Yahweh with the administration of affairs over the nations. Now they are to die like men. Their destruction is, in fact, necessary to Yahweh's complete supremacy over the universe.

The significance of the Psalms is certainly not to be found in any doctrine of angels. Their significance is to be found in their clear attestation of the life of faith, lived in unpropitious surroundings and under a rigid legalism such as is often thought to stifle the life of the spirit. The true state of the case seems to be that the loyal soul delights in obedience to a law, however complicated, so long as that soul retains the faith that the law is the will of its God. The prophetic aphorism, "To obey is better than sacrifice, and to hearken than the fat of rams," finds here its living illustration. The Psalmists identify the righteous with those who obey the Law. But these are also the ones who wait in hope for the fuller revelation of Yahweh. Often in suffering, oppressed by the proud who do not fear God or who virtually deny his existence, they yet hold fast to their faith. This is attested by their songs of rejoicing and also by their utterances in time of trouble. Prayer is becoming more important than ritual service, and these believers are unconsciously preparing the way for the time when they that worship the Father shall worship him in spirit and in truth.

CHAPTER XX

THE FINAL STAGE

WE have now traced the religion of Israel to the latest period of the national existence, and we may attempt to picture it in its final stage. We see a community scattered throughout the world, everywhere in contact with foreigners and susceptible of foreign influence, yet retaining its separateness and conscious that the true fatherland is not the one in which its members sojourn. What gave these people unity was not primarily their purity of blood, though this was one of the things on which they prided themselves, but the conviction that they were the people of Yahweh. And the sense of superiority which they undoubtedly felt was based on the conviction that their God was the one true God. Contrasting their comparatively pure idea of him with the crass idolatry which was everywhere in evidence around them, they had a certain right to assume this attitude so galling to their neighbours. More to their prejudice was the tenacity with which they held to the observance of their Law. Separatism was ingrained in the legal system, and such an example of it as their refusal to eat with their gentile neighbours naturally brought upon them the reputation of being unsocial and surly.

Anti-Semitism, therefore, is not a recent development, and it was probably accentuated by the Messianic hope. The Jews did not conceal their expectation that the time would come when Yahweh would put an end to the domination of the heathen and establish the elect people in the place of supremacy. All Jews were united in these, which may be called the common features of Judaism—the belief in Yahweh as the one God, observance of the Mosaic Law, and expectation of the Messianic time. But there is plenty of evidence that with this unity there was also striking diversity of view. The attempt to observe a complicated system of rules is divisive rather than unifying. Casuistry is capable of indefinite development, and the constantly increasing volume of tradition as to what is allowed and what is forbidden gives room for endless debate which culminates in hatred of one party by the others, if not in actual proscription and schism. The New Testament shows with sufficient clearness that the two parties of Sadducees and Pharisees hated each other as bitterly as either one hated the gentiles. Of the two it seems evident that the Pharisees held to the more developed tradition afterward embodied in the Talmud, while the Sadducees, equally strict in observing the letter of the Law, rejected beliefs and practices which were supererogatory. Their political differences do not concern us. But we may notice that both parties, to all appearance, looked down upon the common people (the people of the land) because they did not keep the many precepts contained in the written and oral Law. Moreover, there was a separate sect called the Essenes, the members of which, if we may trust the documents which have come down to us, regarded themselves as the true Israel, and whose observance (apparently influenced by asceticism from the farther east) was more rigorous than that of either of the other sects. Recently discovered documents seem to show that still another sect had settled in the vicinity of Damascus, with the intention of constituting themselves the true kingdom of God by observance of the Law in their own interpretation of it. At an earlier date the community of Samaritans, Jews to all intents and purposes, had been exscinded by the Jerusalem Jews.

All these sects were located in Syria. But, as we have seen, the larger part of the race was settled outside of Palestine, the most flourishing communities being in the great cities of the Greek-speaking world. That these could not escape the influence of Greek culture we have already noticed. They were, in fact, broader than their coreligionists who spoke Aramaic. In some cases they seem to have recognised that the God whom the gentiles worship is the same known to them as Yahweh. The letter of Aristeas declares that the Jews worship the same divinity with the Greeks (Ep. Arist. 16), though this may be a concession made to conciliate the Greek readers, for whom, apparently, the letter was composed. The claim urged by some Jews that all the good found in Plato was borrowed from Moses is a concession to the genuineness of the religion of the great philosopher. But the Jew, conscious of the superiority of his own faith, probably held in reserve the thought that the gentiles had corrupted the original revelation.

Characteristic of the period is the tendency to secure recognition of Judaism as the true religion by alleged concessions from the gentiles themselves. We have seen how the book of Daniel makes Nebuchadrezzar confess the uniqueness of the Most High in terms that only a Jew could use. The author of the book of Ezra makes Cyrus acknowledge Yahweh God of heaven as the one from whom he had received all the kingdoms of the earth (Ezra 1 : 2), and embodies in his book a decree of Artaxerxes which enjoins that the temple worship be worthily sustained in order that wrath from heaven may not break out on the empire (7 : 23). Of a piece with these alleged documents is the letter of Antiochus, the arch-enemy of the Jews, in which he seeks to win their favour and vows to restore and purify the temple (II Mac. 9 : 19–27). The Greek Esther gives us a decree of Artaxerxes in which he calls the Jews Sons of the Most High (Gr. Esth. 5 : 16).

The sufficient explanation for these insertions is the tradition which grew up that gentile kings had been miraculously induced to recognise the one God and to show favour to his servants and to his temple. The Jews, living in the midst of unsympathetic and often hostile neighbours, were dependent on the favour of the civil ruler. It was necessary to assume an attitude of conciliation toward their *de facto* governors. One writer in this age asserts that rebellion against the gentile monarch is disobedience to God (Baruch 2 : 21–24). The supposititious letter of the exiles in Babylon to the high priest in Jerusalem exhorts him to pray and sacrifice on behalf of Nebuchadrezzar: "That we may live under the protection of Nebuchadrezzar and of Belshazzar his son, serve them many days and find grace in their sight" (Baruch 1 : 10–12). Nicanor is shown the burnt offering that is made for the king of Syria (I Mac. 7 : 33), and Eleazar the high priest assures Ptolemy that he offers sacrifices on his behalf and prays for him and the security of his kingdom (Ep. Arist. 45). Similarly, the Jewish high priest and Council assure the Spartans that they remember them in their prayers and offerings (I Mac. 12 : 11). With evident pride the writers of this period recount the presents made to the temple by foreign monarchs as so many tributes to the power of their God (Ep. Arist. 51 *f.*).

Conscious of gentile contempt, and resenting it, the Jews also comforted themselves by stories of wonderful deliverances wrought on their behalf by their God. The one most familiar to us is, of course, the one which has found its way into the canon under the name of the heroine, Esther. The intensity of hatred with which the heathen are regarded does not prevent the author from making the Jewess an inmate of the royal harem. How intense the feeling is is made evident near the end of the book: "The Jews smote all their enemies with the stroke of the sword, and with slaughter and destruction, and did what they would to them that hated them" (Esth. 9 : 5); and we learn that the number of enemies thus destroyed was seventy-five thousand. Justification is found in the unreasonableness of Haman's persecution—because Mordecai would not prostrate himself before him, the prime minister plots the destruction of the whole Jewish people. That there is no historic basis for the story seems evident.

Even more extravagant in its details is the story known as Third Maccabees. According to this, Ptolemy Philopator desecrates the temple by entering the Most Sacred apartment, and for this he is punished by an act of God. Full of wrath, he orders all the Jews in his realm to be gathered in the amphitheatre at Alexandria, there to be trampled to death by the war elephants. On three successive days the threatened fate is averted, and at the final attempt two angels appear and save the Jews. The king is convinced of his error, and not only releases the Jews but issues a decree that those who wish to return to Palestine may do so. As in the book of Esther, the Jews are given permission to slay their enemies, and these are defined as the renegades of their own race. As in the case of Esther, it is vain to search for an actual event underlying this story. And the same must be said of the book of Judith, another monument of Jewish ferocity. What the Jews would have done had they had the power is revealed by these books and by the method of Judas Maccabeus, who slew all the males in the cities he conquered, for which, to be sure, he was able to urge Old Testament precedent (I Mac. 5 : 35), and by Jonathan's burning of the temple at Ashdod with all that had taken refuge there (10 : 83*f.*).

These books are not intended primarily to utter hatred, but to encourage believers by recounting the wonderful intervention of Providence in their behalf. They belong, therefore, with the anecdotes of Daniel and his friends. The appetite for the marvellous is, however, not easily satisfied, as we see when comparing the second book of Maccabees with the first of the same name. The two are concerned with the same period, but the sober narrative of the first book contrasts strangely with the fantasies of the second. In the latter signs and portents abound, angelic warriors strike down intruders into the temple, lead the Jewish armies to battle, or take Judas between them and protect him in the thickest of the fight. The first book knows nothing of these supernatural events, and we are compelled to see in them the product of the religious imagination attempting to edify believers by instances of direct divine intervention on behalf of Israel.

The difficulties of the Jews in the dispersion arose from the fact that they were forced into contact with heathen customs. In Greek and Roman communities the public buildings, the squares, and the markets were under the patronage of heathen divinities, whose very sight was an abomination to the faithful Jew. Hence arose the desire on the part of the Jews that the places of their sojourn might be cleansed from these defilements. Moreover, acquaintance with the more thoughtful of the gentiles led many to desire that these neighbours might come to the knowledge of Israel's God. In contrast with the state of mind which we find at a later date and which discouraged proselytism, we discover in this period a distinct missionary activity. The Gospels intimate that this was not altogether unselfish, and we may readily grant that the conversion of gentile princes, of which we have mention in this period, was not prompted by purely religious zeal. But when the intensely national, not to say fanatical, book of Judith approves the reception of Achior, an Ammonite, into the household of faith (Judith 14:10), we must suppose a genuine interest in the conversion of the gentiles. The reaction first shows itself in the Psalms of Solomon which assert that in the Messianic time there will be no proselyte or stranger in the community (Ps. Sol. 17 : 28).[1]

Only on the theory of a wide-spread desire to interest the gentiles in the Jewish religion and so to secure their respect, if not their adherence, can we account for the considerable body of literature in this period which puts Jewish ideas into the mouth of Greeks. A notable example is the letter of Aristeas already mentioned. The letter purports to be written by a Greek officer at the court of Ptolemy Philadelphus. The alleged author, Aristeas, writes to his brother as one interested in the good morals and temper of those who observe the Jewish Law. Not only are these men rational and cultivated persons, but the Law which they observe is one of the important literary monuments of mankind. This is

[1] On the attitude of the Talmud, see Bousset, *Religion des Judentums*, p. 269.

shown by making Ptolemy (the founder of the great Alexandrian Library) take special pains to secure a copy of it for his collection; not only to secure a copy but to have it translated into Greek. The narrative tells us how the king sends an embassy to Jerusalem (Aristeas represents himself to be a member of this embassy), requesting the high priest to send a copy of the Law and also a band of competent translators. The visit to Jerusalem is described, and the glory of the temple is enlarged upon. Evidently the reader is expected to form a favourable idea both of the religion of the Jews and of the Law which they observe. Ptolemy is made to recognise the Law as something divine, bowing before the parchments as sacred and venerable, containing as they do the oracles of God. In accordance with the excellence of the Law is the virtue of those who obey it. They are moved by a high religious sense of accountability to the one God. And the Law itself is not the irrational thing which some of the Greeks think it to be. Even those commands which seem strange have in them the highest wisdom. Thus the prohibition of birds of prey for food is intended to teach us that we should not oppress our fellow men. Animals which divide the hoof are allowed, in order to show that we should exercise wise discrimination, and these permitted animals are ruminants, to impress upon us the value of reflection. At the court of Ptolemy the Jewish teachers shine as embodiments of the wisdom which must belong to the observers of such a divine Law.

It has long been recognised that this account of the translation of the Pentateuch into Greek has no basis in fact. The existence of the translation, however, at some time before the Christian era is something of prime importance. It testifies to the extent to which the large Jewish community in Alexandria was Hellenised. The translation must have been made for the Jews themselves, and it is doubtful whether the efforts of Aristeas made any impression on gentiles. The Hebraisms of the Greek Bible would repel the foreigner. The continued existence of the Jewish dispersion, however, would be almost unthinkable without this version of the Scriptures, and its importance for the history of the Christian Church is well known. Its origin is wholly obscure, and as to the date at which it was made all that we can say is that it was in existence some time before the translator of Ecclesiasticus came to Egypt in the year 131 B. C.

A more daring attempt to impress the gentile world was made in the so-called Sibylline books. Traditions of divinely inspired prophetesses must have been wide-spread in the Greek and Roman world. Books ascribed to such prophetesses had official recognition at Rome, and when the alleged Tarquinian codices were destroyed in the year 83 B. C. the Senate had no difficulty in gathering other oracles to replace them. This implies that a considerable body of literature circulated under the name of one Sibyl or another. The Jews saw no reason why these venerable characters should not find a place in their own tradition. They therefore made the Sibyl the daughter of Noah, and in the book attributed to her she foresees the whole course of history—a device with which we are already familiar in the apocalypses. The mixture of Hebrew tradition and Greek legend is crassly made—the Greek gods Kronos, Iapetos, and Titanos being identified with the three sons of Noah (Or. Sib. III, 110–116). The date of the composition is indicated by the supposititious prediction of Rome's rule over Egypt (III, 46). The author expects a judgment in the near future, and this is to be followed by the coming of the Messiah: "The sacred ruler who will wield the sceptre over the whole world for all ages" (46–50). The judgment will be one of wrath for Latin men, with fire and brimstone. It will be introduced by Beliar, who will lead men astray by his lying wonders. "Then the God who dwells in the ether will roll up the heavens as a scroll, the vault above will fall to the earth, and a stream of fire will consume earth and sea" (63–85).

The difference between these lucubrations and the apocalypses which we have considered is that the apocalypses are intended to encourage the Jews in time of oppression; the

Sibylline verses are intended to impress gentile readers by denouncing woes upon them, and to convince them of the happier lot of Israel. When the consummation comes the sons of the great God will dwell in peace around the temple, rejoicing in that which the Creator and just Ruler will give them (702 *ff.*): "For he himself will protect them like a wall of fire. Then all the nations will come to the seat of the divine majesty, confessing the error of their idolatry. The king who is to come will appear from heaven (or from the East), will follow the counsels of God, will judge every one with blood and fire, and will adorn the temple, or even rebuild it."

The reason for the happier lot of the Jews is their superior righteousness, and this is set forth at length. These are the worshippers of the one God, who is contrasted with the demons whom the gentiles revere (*cf.* Procemium). They pay no attention to oracles or signs, necromancy or magic: "But they reflect on righteousness and virtue, and there is not among them covetousness which begets a thousand evils among mortals and endless war and famine. They have just measures in country and city; they steal not nor do they drive away flocks and herds; neither does one remove the landmarks of his neighbor, nor does the rich man oppress the poor. He does not oppress the widow, but rather helps her and supports her with corn and wine and oil; he who has possessions sends a part of his harvest to those who live in want, fulfilling the word of the great God" (218–245). Because of this superiority in the moral life, and because of their monotheism, the people of the great God will be the guides to life for all mortals (194). The gentiles are, therefore, exhorted to give up their sins, to bathe in running water, to pray for forgiveness for the sins of the past, atoning with praises for the bitter godlessness. Then will God repent and not destroy them; he will leave off his wrath if they practise honourable piety in spirit. Otherwise the judgment must come and annihilate the whole race of men (IV, 161–190).

Such works as these may have had some influence upon Greek readers, but their chief power was shown later when they had considerable vogue in the Christian Church. Of a different stamp is the book called the Wisdom of Solomon, to which we have given some attention in an earlier chapter. It differs from the other Wisdom books by its distinctly Hellenistic tone, having been written in Greek for the benefit of Greek-speaking Jews. Its assertion of the superiority of the religion of the Jews as compared with the idolatry of the other nations is in line with what we have already read. An attempt is made to account for the origin of idolatry by the hypothesis that statues of deceased relatives were the first recipients of this sort of homage (Wisdom 14 : 15*f.*). Where the author differs from his predecessors is in affirming the immortality of the soul apart from the body. This is evidently due to Greek influence. At the same time he is a loyal Jew, and believes in the observance of the Law, as is evident from his treatment of the subject of intermarriage (3 : 13; 4 : 6). In connection with this book we may notice another work which attempts to clothe Hebrew religion in a Greek garb and so commend it to gentile readers. This is the fourth book of Maccabees, a sermon such as may have been delivered in the great synagogue at Alexandria. It takes as its text an anecdote contained in the second book of Maccabees, the martyrdom of a mother and her seven sons in the days of Antiochus IV. The lesson which is taught is that Jewish piety is sufficient to sustain the believer in the face of the greatest danger and in the midst of the most acute suffering. The most interesting thing is that the lesson is put in Greek form, being stated thus: "The reason is ruler of the passions." This is the true wisdom or, as the author states it, the true philosophy. This philosophy he thinks is obtained by the Law. If he had gentile readers it must have seemed a curious *non sequitur* when he goes on to commend the avoidance of forbidden meats as a conspicuous instance of the rule of reason.

The most striking example of Hellenistic Judaism is Philo,

a member of the Jewish community at Alexandria, and a man thoroughly acquainted with Greek thought. That he is a loyal Jew is seen by his attitude toward the Pentateuch, which he regards as the perfect revelation of divine wisdom. Everything in these books is an oracle of God, and no word is without its significance. Moses is the great master from whom the gentile philosophers have learned. To prove that the Law is the law of reason he wrote an extended series of treatises, hoping thus, apparently, to bring reflecting and intelligent gentiles to accept the Law and obey it. As he has left on record evidence of the acute hatred felt by some of the gentiles toward the Jews, it is probable that he desires also to show how baseless are the attacks made upon his people and their religion. This he does by affirming the ethical value of the Law and also by insisting that it is identical with the law of nature: The Law begins with the account of Creation to indicate that the world and the Tora are in harmony and that the observer of the Tora is a citizen of the world, since he regulates his actions by the will of nature by which the whole world is guided.

The difficulties which the expositor must encounter in proving such a thesis are met by the allegorical method already in vogue among Jews and gentiles. The book of Daniel opened the way by treating the seventy years of Jeremiah as something other than seventy literal years. It is probable, however, that Philo was influenced here as elsewhere by Greek precedent, for we know that Homer was already allegorised by some of his commentators. The thoroughness with which Philo has learned his lesson is seen from his treatment of the Pentateuch. To him the history of mankind contained in Genesis is only a picturesque psychology and ethic. It may be too much to say that the history, as history, had no importance to him, but the historical content of the book is wholly subordinate. The patriarchs, for example, symbolise the various states of the soul—Abraham and Lot are the two tendencies of man, one striving after virtue, the other after sensual enjoyment. Abraham sends Lot away; so the soul frees itself from the lower desires and appetites and gives virtue the first place. The word of God to Abraham: "Know that thy seed shall be strangers in a land that is not theirs," means that the love of virtue dwells in the body, not as its home, but that it should regard itself as a stranger in a strange land. The sacrifices commanded by the Law, although obligatory on the believer, are not of value for their own sake; they are symbols of the state of the soul in repentance, when it frees itself from sin and is thus rendered acceptable to God.

In spite of the fact that Philo himself was a loyal and conscientious observer of the Law, it is doubtful whether a history of Jewish religion should take further account of him. His philosophy was not that of the Jewish Scriptures, but was the Platonic dualism, putting soul and body into sharp opposition, positing also a great gulf between God and his creation, a gulf that can be crossed only by the mediating Logos which was already a figure of Greek speculation. Philo, in fact, belongs at the beginning of Christian thought rather than at the end of Jewish, for his influence on Christian theology and on Christian exegesis is marked and may be said to have endured to the present day. We can hardly doubt that his emphasis of the allegorical meaning of the Law helped to undermine its force as law. If, in fact, the important thing was the allegory, why not keep the allegory and let the literal meaning go? Christianity answered by rejecting the Law as a system of rules while retaining it as a divine revelation. And though we cannot say that the allegorical interpretation was rejected by the Jews who retained the Law as a rule of life, no doubt there was a sharp reaction against Hellenism, so sharp that the day when the Greek translation was made was regarded by the Rabbinical authorities as a day of calamity parallel to that which saw the manufacture of the golden calf.

Leaving the Hellenistic Jews and turning to those of Palestine, we note that the most significant feature of society is the sharp opposition between Pharisees and Sadducees. We have already met the Pharisees as the strict observers of the

Law. The conflict between them and their enemies came (according to Josephus) in the time of John Hyrcanus. The Sadducees seem to have been adherents of the Maccabean house, and it is probable that we have an important document from a member of this party in the first book of Maccabees. The object of the author is evidently to set forth the merits of the ruling family, and this he does by a plain, unvarnished narrative of the deeds of the heroic brothers who deserved so well of the nation. His piety is of the good, old-fashioned sort such as we discover in Ben Sira. The miraculous interposition of angels on which other narratives of the period love to dwell are absent from his story, but this is not because he doubts the presence of the God of Israel with his people to deliver them in time of peril. He thinks that Antiochus was brought to a realising sense of his sin against Jerusalem by the illness which befell him (I Mac. 6 : 12), regards the death of Nicanor as an example of the divine retribution (7 : 47), and treats similarly that of Alkimus, the Hellenising high priest who tore down the temple wall (9 : 55). He makes the piety of Judas evident by describing his preparations for battle (3 : 56; 4 : 9 and 30), and justifies his slaughter of his male prisoners by pointing out that it is strictly according to the Law. He shows us that Jonathan's title to the high-priesthood is exactly the same as that of Alkimus, whom the Chasidim were so ready to recognise, the appointment in each case having come from the Syrian monarch (10 : 20). His hatred of renegade Jews is genuine, and he takes pains to show that the woes of Israel were due to them rather than to the gentiles (11 : 21, 25). He rarely blames the stricter party, and then only mildly, as when he condemns them for trusting in Alkimus (7 : 13*f.*).

The emphasis laid on the piety of Simon Maccabeus shows the mind of the author, for he dwells on the fact that it was Simon who expelled the heathen from Gazara, cleansed the city from idols, and settled observers of the Law there, entering the city, moreover, with the singing of Psalms (13 : 47*ff.*). The action of the Jewish Council in making

Simon general and leader of the nation was ratified by the divine blessing which followed, for in the days of Simon "they tilled their ground in peace and the earth gave her increase, and the trees of the field their fruit; the old men sat in the streets communing of good things, and the young men put on glorious and warlike apparel. . . . He made peace in the land and Israel rejoiced with great joy, for every man sat under his vine and his fig-tree and there was none to fray them. . . . Moreover he strengthened all those of the people that were brought low; the Law he searched out and every contemner of the Law and every wicked person he took away; he beautified the sanctuary and multiplied the vessels of the temple" (14:8–15). If this be a fair example of Sadducean opinion, the members of this party were not lacking in devotion to Israel's ideals.

The point made against them in the New Testament is that they did not believe in the resurrection of the dead. This is confirmed by the book before us when compared with the second book of Maccabees, apparently a Pharisaic document. Our book makes no reference to a resurrection or to a life beyond the grave, though the description of the death of Mattathias and of his heroic sons would have given abundant opportunity to allude to such a belief. The second book, on the other hand, not only states that Judas believed in the resurrection, but that he caused sin-offerings to be offered on behalf of the dead just because he expected them to be raised (II Mac. 12 : 44). The reason why the Sadducees refused to adopt this belief was no doubt that they did not find it taught in the Pentateuch. It is probable also that this party was not affected by the extravagant hopes of the apocalypses. Adherents of the Maccabean house, they regarded the Messianic hope as reasonably fulfilled in the elevation of that dynasty to the throne. One of the Psalms, to which allusion has already been made (110), congratulates Simon that the divine decree has made him priest for ever after the order of Melchizedek. In spite of this thoroughly religious tone at the outset, however, the Sadducean party became more and more worldly as the princes became mere temporal rulers. Hence the decline in power of the Sadducees, and their final extinction. The Roman rule disregarded any claims that might be put forward for a native Jewish prince.

The mass of the people sympathised with the Pharisaic point of view. This does not mean that the common people could be counted in the strict sense Pharisees. Punctilious adherence to a complicated law and to the casuistic traditions that gather about such a law is impossible to the man in the street. Knowledge of this tradition requires serious and prolonged study, which comparatively few men are in position to give. Strict avoidance of contact with the gentiles, which was the root principle of Pharisaism, was impracticable for those who engaged in active business in the midst of foreigners. The Pharisees themselves, that is, those who were punctilious in observing the commandments and traditions, drew a sharp line of demarcation between themselves and the mass of their coreligionists, whom they called the people of the land. They said: "This people which knows not the Law is accursed." Yet these same people of the land looked up to the Pharisees as their teachers, and were willing to follow them so far as lay in their power. Their attitude was something like the attitude of lay Christians toward members of the monastic orders, as men who have attained a sanctity to which the ordinary man cannot aspire. That the members of the party often succumbed to the temptation to emphasise ceremonial purity at the expense of ethical sincerity is evident from the New Testament; but that the party contained many serious-minded and devoted adherents to the God of Israel we must believe.

Pharisaic legalism has left its mark on a considerable literature. Hatred of the gentiles we have already seen exemplified in the book of Esther. Opposition to intermarriage with other races goes back to the time of Nehemiah, and it is emphasised in a later ordinance that any Israelite who gives his daughter in marriage to a gentile shall be stoned, and the young woman shall be burned (Jubilees 30 : 7*f*.). The author of Esther, it is true, allowed his heroine to become a member of Xerxes' harem. But the supplementer of the narrative, whose work is preserved in the Greek version of the book, makes her express the utmost horror of such a fate (Gr. Esther 3 : 26*f*.). The crime of such a marriage is sacrilege, defilement of the sacred blood of Israel, and it brings all kinds of plague and curse on the nation (Jubilees 30 : 14–17). Later the prohibition was made even more rigid, forbidding a Pharisee to give his daughter to any but a Pharisee.

The book of Jubilees, from which we have just drawn, shows how the most devoted adherent of the sacred code is obliged to supplement it in accordance with the ideas of his own time. The author rewrites the narrative of Genesis in order to make clear things concerning which the original text is silent. It is his conviction that there is strict correspondence between things heavenly and things earthly. Human chronology must be made to correspond with that used in heaven, else the angels will be observing Sabbath on one day, and men will be observing it on another; and so with the New Moon and other festivals (Jubilees 1:5, 14; 6 : 32*f*.). The feast of Tabernacles is inaugurated by Abraham instead of by Moses (16 : 20–31). The Passover is commended because its observance insures against plagues for the following year (49 : 15). Noah observed the law of first-fruits (7 : 1). The conquest of Canaan is justified on the ground that it had first been assigned by lot to Shem (10 : 28–36). These specimens may show the freedom with which the Law was treated in the interest of the Law itself, or rather of the tradition which had grown up about it.

Pharisaic ideals have also coloured the narratives of Tobit and Judith. Tobit, although represented as living in the northern kingdom, sends tithes and firstlings to Jerusalem, and makes the pilgrimage thither, abstains from the food of the heathen, and shares his goods with his poorer brethren. When in exile he buries the unfortunate Jews who are the victims of persecution, braving even the wrath of the king in order to carry out this religious duty. Judith is more pronounced. It declares specifically that Israel will be protected so long as it keeps the Law, but when it disobeys by trespassing upon the sacred offerings, tithes, or first-fruits, it will be destroyed (Judith 11 : 11–18). The deed of Simeon and Levi, which is condemned by the author of Genesis, is now praised because they slew the Canaanites (9 : 2–4). The heroine, though willing to deceive the heathen general, is careful to eat only clean food, and to bathe every night because of possible defilement contracted in the camp of the enemy (12 : 7). A similar point of view animates the series of poems called the Psalms of Solomon, and they show also the deepening breach between the Pharisees and the Maccabean house. The members of this house are said in so many words to have usurped the throne of David, and the writer regards their deposition by the Roman power as a just punishment. The Roman Pompey, however, is punished in turn, for he had desecrated the temple by entering the Most Sacred chamber (Ps. Sol. 17 : 4–10). The calamities which befell Jerusalem were interpreted as the vengeance of God on the Hellenising party, though it is also intimated that the chastisement is intended to rouse the sinner to a sense of his sin. The righteous man is the one who constantly searches his house to cleanse it, who erases unwitting sins by fasting, and who chastens himself thoroughly (3 : 7 *f.*). The sinners who are said to be members of the supreme council of the nation (and we may now call it the Sanhedrin) are probably the Sadducees, and it is they who are stigmatised as the ungodly (3 and 4). While the ideal of this party was undoubtedly that for the present the government should be in the hands of the Sanhedrin, yet they had a lively expectation of the coming of the Messiah. They looked for the return of the dispersed Jews, and for a true son of David to take the throne. "He will crush the unrighteous, will cleanse Jerusalem from the heathen, will judge the tribe of the sacred people, and keep the gentiles under his yoke" (17 : 21–33).

With the fall of Jerusalem in the year 70 all the Jewish parties came to an end except the Pharisees. The Messianic hope had not realised itself, and the various calculations of the time of the end had proved fallacious. Henceforth, although the hope was held, an anathema was pronounced on any one who should attempt to fix the time of the advent. Until that time should come, all that was left to the faithful Jew was to cleave to the Law, the only sacred thing that remained to him. The Bar Kochba rebellion showed, indeed, that the Messianic hope had vitality enough to rally some desperate adherents, but its disastrous termination emphasised the admonition not to determine the times and seasons, which God had kept in his own power. The remnant that survived resigned themselves to the task of building a hedge about the Law, leaving the time of the kingdom to God.

One monument of the feeling of the Jews after the fall of their city may claim our attention. This is the so-called fourth book of Ezra. The deep pessimism with which the author treats the problem of sin and punishment shows how his faith was tried. To the question whether there are few that be saved he does not hesitate to give an affirmative answer (IV Ezra 7 : 47; 8 : 1–3). The spectacle of the triumph of the hated Roman power and the sufferings of the faithful makes him realise that the ways of God are unsearchable, and we wonder that he can attempt to throw light upon them. But his surcharged feelings must find vent. The fact that the present age is wholly evil is taken to prove that it must be succeeded by another. The fulness of times must be at hand and these overturnings are signs of the end (4 : 40 and chapter 5). The reason for these fearful judgments is found in the universal corruption of mankind, for it is evident that if Israel has sinned the heathen are no better. For the first time we meet the unequivocal declaration that Adam's sin brought all these woes into the world (7 : 11 *f*). Hence came the corruption of the human heart (4 : 12, 22, 30). Yet even in his despair the writer asserts that God is merciful, and he again takes up the Messianic hope. God's Son, the

Messiah, will appear and will rejoice the remnant four hundred years. After this he will die—the only distinct assertion of the death of the Messiah which we have yet found. Then after seven days, during which all men sleep, the resurrection comes, followed immediately by the judgment (7 : 26–43).

At this point we must arrest our discussion of the religion of Israel. The religion of the Talmud which prevailed in the Jewish remnant requires separate treatment. Much of that which the people of Israel had developed became the possession of Christianity, and thus entered into one of the great universal religions. Briefly reviewing the ground that we have gone over, we may recall to mind that when the Israelites first came into the light of history they were a group of nomad clans with a religion like that of other dwellers in the desert. Their God, Yahweh, was apparently the local divinity of Kadesh, who was made party to a coalition of the social groups in that region. The success of the coalition led to the invasion of Canaan and the gradual settlement of that country by the immigrants. In Canaan the God took on the features of an agricultural divinity, receiving the first-fruits and tithes of the soil. The attempt of Ahab to introduce the worship of the Phœnician Baal led to a reaction under the powerful personality of Elijah. The prophetic party thus beginning its career was prompted by a desire for social justice as well as for religious simplicity. In some centuries of conflict this party clarified its aims and at last preached an ethical monotheism for Israel. This monotheism would not have triumphed (humanly speaking) had it not been for the exile. In the exile the people found the bond which held them together to be that of religion. They therefore became a church rather than a nation, conscious of possessing a unique treasure in the traditions of Moses and the Prophets, carefully avoiding amalgamation with those of different faith.

The spread of Greek ideas after the time of Alexander enriched the religion of Israel but also threatened to deprive it of its most characteristic features. This danger was counteracted by the persecution of Antiochus Epiphanes. The two things on which the Jews had laid the most stress—the Law and the temple—were now threatened with destruction. A desperate band of believers rallied to their defence, recovered the temple, and gave the Law a new importance. The same period saw the development of the synagogue, a social centre at which each of the scattered Jewish communities could study the Law and engage in prayer. Behind the devotion to the Law, the temple and the synagogue was the Messianic hope, most highly developed in the time of persecution and enriched by the visions of the apocalyptic writers. The synagogue, the Law, and the Messianic hope prepared the way for Christianity, for a powerful personality like Paul was able to show that the value of the Law as a divine revelation might be unimpaired even if it ceased to be binding as a rule of life. The synagogue showed the possibility of worship without sacrifice and priesthood, and thus became the model on which the local congregations of Christians might organise themselves. That gentile influence was at work here is not to be denied, but it remains true that the early Christians were Jews and carried over into the Church the things which were of so much value to them. The belief that Jesus was the Messiah would not have sustained the faith of the infant Church had it not adopted the Jewish expectation of a speedy advent of the Son of David, or the Son of Man, coming in the clouds of heaven to judge the world and to introduce the kingdom of God. Nourished by this hope, the young Christian community organised itself in independence of the Judaism from which it sprang, and started to conquer the world. Judaism withdrew all the more closely within itself (compelled, no doubt, by persecution from without) and devoted itself to legalism, the results of which are embedded in that gigantic monument of human industry, the Talmud.

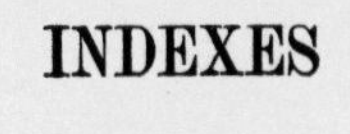

INDEXES

INDEXES

INDEX OF SCRIPTURE PASSAGES

Genesis

Exodus

Joshua

Judges

Psalms

Proverbs

INDEX OF SUBJECTS